PUNISHING JUVENILES

Punishing Juveniles
Principle and Critique

Edited by
IDO WEIJERS
and
ANTONY DUFF

·HART·
PUBLISHING

OXFORD – PORTLAND OREGON
2002

Hart Publishing
Oxford and Portland, Oregon

Published in North America (US and Canada) by
Hart Publishing c/o
International Specialized Book Services
5804 NE Hassalo Street
Portland, Oregon
97213-3644
USA

Distributed in the Netherlands, Belgium and Luxembourg by
Intersentia, Churchillaan 108
B2900 Schoten
Antwerpen
Belgium

Hart Publishing is a specialist legal publisher based in Oxford, England.
To order further copies of this book or to request a list of other
publications please write to:

Hart Publishing, Salter's Boatyard, Folly Bridge,
Abingdon Road, Oxford OX1 4LB
Telephone: +44 (0)1865 245533 or Fax: +44 (0)1865 794882
e-mail: mail@hartpub.co.uk
WEBSITE: http//www.hartpub.co.uk

British Library Cataloguing in Publication Data
Data Available
ISBN 1–84113–284–5 (hardback)

Typeset by Hope Services (Abingdon) Ltd.
Printed and bound in Great Britain on acid-free paper by
T.J. International Ltd, Padstow, Cornwall

Contents

Notes on Contributors

Antony Duff is a Professor of Philosophy at Stirling University, where he has taught since 1970. He publishes widely in philosophy of criminal law, in particular on penal theory (*Punishment, Communication, and Community*, OUP, 2001) and on the normative foundations of criminal liability (*Criminal Attempts*, OUP, 1996); he has recently been working on the relation between restorative justice and punishment.

Loraine Gelsthorpe is a University Senior Lecturer in Criminology at the Institute of Criminology, University of Cambridge. Her research and teaching interests include youth justice, the sentencing of women, race and gender issues in the delivery of community penalties, the detention of asylum seekers, social exclusion, crime and justice and the links between criminal justice and social justice. Her most recent book is *Community Penalties. Change and Challenges* (edited by A E Bottoms, L R Gelsthorpe & S Rex, Willan Publishers, 2001).

Carter Hay is an Assistant Professor in the Department of Sociology at Washington State University. His main research interests involve the conceptualisation and testing of theories of crime and delinquency causation, especially with respect to family- and parenting-related causes of juvenile delinquency. Recent publications include *American Delinquency: Its Meaning and Construction*, 4th edn, with LaMar T Empey and Mark Stafford (Wadsworth, 1999) and articles appearing in *Criminology* and the *Journal of Research in Crime and Delinquency*.

Josine Junger-Tas was Director of the Research and Documentation Centre of the Dutch Ministry of Justice; she is now visiting professor in Criminology at the University of Lausanne and research fellow of the EM Meijersinstitute, University of Leiden. She is a member of the National Council for the Application of Sanctions. Two recent articles in *Crime and Justice* were 'Ethnic Minorities and Criminal Justice in The Netherlands' (1997) and (with Ineke Haen-Marshall), 'The Self-report Methodology in Crime Research—Strengths and Weaknesses' (1999).

Allison Morris was Director and then Professor of Criminology at the Institute of Criminology, at Victoria University of Wellington, Wellington, New Zealand from 1993 to 2001. For 20 years before that, she was a lecturer in criminology at the Institute of Criminology, University of Cambridge. She has carried out research on women's prisons, youth justice systems, violence against women and restorative justice. Her most recent book (an edited collection) is *Restorative Justice for Juveniles: Conferencing, Mediation and Circles* (Hart Publishing, 2001).

Tjeert Olthof is Assistant Professor at the Department of Developmental Psychology of the Vrije Universiteit, Amsterdam, the Netherlands. His research interests focus on children's emotional, moral and social development. He has recently published on children's and adults' implicit conceptions of guilt and shame ('A Developmental Tasks Analysis of Guilt and Shame'), on the nature of moral excellence ('The Morality Paradox: Choosing Not to be Moral as a Component of Moral Excellence') and on the use of computer simulations in studying mother-child interaction.

Mark Stafford is a Professor in the Department of Sociology at the University of Texas at Austin. His research has focused on the relationship between individuals' lifestyles or routine activities and their likelihood of criminal victimisation, the deterrent effects of punishment, and the causes of interpersonal violence. His current research focuses on the development of a control theory of homicide. His recent publications include *American Delinquency* (Wadsworth) and 'Central Analytical Issues in the Generation of Cumulative Sociological Knowledge' (*Sociological Focus*).

Gabriele Taylor studied at Oxford, taught philosophy in Canberra, Australia and was from 1962 to 1995 Lecturer at Oxford University and Fellow and Tutor at St Anne's College, where she is now a Senior Research Fellow. Publications include *Pride, Shame and Guilt: Emotions of Self-Assessment* (OUP, 1985), and articles in various journals on moral philosophy and the philosophy of mind, particularly on the emotions and the vices and virtues, but also on Hume, Kant and Mill.

Lode Walgrave is Professor of Youth Criminology at the Katholieke Universiteit Leuven (Belgium) and director of the Research Group on Youth Criminology; he is also Coordinator of the International Network for Research on Restorative Justice for Juveniles. He has published widely on youth crime, juvenile justice and restorative justice, including recently *Met het Oog op Herstel. Bakens voor een Constructief Jeugdsanctierecht* (2000), and (ed) *Restorative Justice for Juveniles. Potentials, Risks and Problems for Research* (1998) both with Leuven University Press.

Ido Weijers is Associate Professor of education at Utrecht University. He publishes widely on juvenile justice, in particular on its history ('The Double Paradox of Juvenile Justice', 1999) and theory (*Schuld en Schaamte: Een Pedagogisch Perspectief op het Jeugdstrafrecht*, BSL, 2000). He has been working on the issue of punishment and education ('Punishment and Upbringing', 2000); his recent research interests include juvenile court traditions and restorative justice for juveniles.

1

Introduction: Themes in Juvenile Justice

IDO WEIJERS & ANTONY DUFF

THE PASSING OF the Illinois Juvenile Court Act in 1899 is usually taken to have marked the creation of the juvenile justice system: juvenile offenders came to be seen as 'children in trouble' who should be 'saved' rather than punished; and it came to be seen as the state's responsibility to provide appropriate treatment for troublesome young people. The last few decades, however, have witnessed remarkable changes in views both of juvenile offenders and of the proper role of the state. The conception of the young offender as a 'child in trouble' has been challenged, whilst alternative notions of guilt, personal responsibility and 'just deserts' have gained popularity. Meanwhile, the erosion of faith in the efficacy of state-organised rehabilitation has undermined the belief that it should be the state's responsibility to save young offenders, or that the state's institutions can be trusted with the extensive and intrusive powers that their (re)-education would require. A century after its foundation, the future of the juvenile justice system is very much in doubt.

This volume, the result of a seminar held in June 2000 at the University of Utrecht, brings together a variety of responses to these recent changes in conceptions of juvenile justice, from experts in a range of relevant disciplines—criminology, sociology, philosophy, education and psychology. It offers reflections on the foundations of juvenile justice, critical analyses of its central concepts, and explorations of new directions and perspectives. It shows the value of a critical, interdisciplinary debate about the central ideas on which our juvenile justice systems are, purport to be, and should be based—ideas which, after a century of juvenile justice and in the light of recent uncertainties about its justification, need the kind of critical re-examination that this volume offers.

Part I presents three answers to the questions with which any serious study in this field must start: how should we interpret the vicissitudes of juvenile justice in the past century, and understand the recent changes? It begins with Josine Junger-Tas's broad overview of past and present trends in juvenile justice policy. Loraine Gelsthorpe examines post-war developments in juvenile justice policy in England and Wales, while Carter Hay and Mark Stafford focus on the development of the concept of rehabilitation in twentieth century America. All three chapters also offer perspectives on the future of juvenile justice. One thing that emerges clearly from these chapters is the need to rethink some of the foundational concepts of juvenile justice.

Part II offers three perspectives on some of these foundational concepts—punishment, restoration and (re-)education. Despite fundamental divergences of view, all three chapters in this part concentrate on the role of moral communication in juvenile justice. Lode Walgrave argues that we should not punish juvenile offenders, but should 'commit them to restore'. Antony Duff argues that whilst restoration should be a central aim in relation to juvenile offenders, it must be achieved through a punitive response. Ido Weijers focuses on the dialogue in court, arguing, from an educational perspective, that it should function as a moral reference point for the young offender.

Such a focus on moral communication raises a crucial question about the role of moral emotions in juvenile justice. How should we understand the role of feelings like shame, guilt, remorse and repentance in punishing juveniles, in either restorative or court proceedings? Part III brings together a criminological, a philosophical and a psychological view on this topic. A joint reference point is the notion of 'reintegrative shaming' as defended by John Braithwaite. Allison Morris critically investigates the relevance of this notion to the practice of restorative justice, and concludes that restorative justice should appeal to remorse rather than shaming. Gabriele Taylor analyses the emotions of shame, guilt and remorse, and again concludes that remorse seems to offer the most promising clue for restoration. Finally, Tjeert Olthof presents an overview of recent psychological research and theorising on the nature of guilt and shame and their relationship with social and antisocial behaviour, and points out several difficulties in any attempt to ground juvenile justice in either shame or guilt.

In the remainder of this Introduction, we fill in some of the historical, philosophical and empirical background against which these papers are set. But we must first face the question of what is meant by 'juvenile': what age group are we discussing?

Different jurisdictions set very different upper and lower limits to their juvenile justice systems. At the lower end, in Ireland children of seven could (in principle, although only exceptionally in practice) be held criminally responsible. In Scotland young delinquents can be prosecuted from the age of eight, and in England from the age of 10, whilst in the Netherlands the minimum age is 12, in France 13, in Italy and Denmark 14 and in Belgium 16. Likewise, there always has been some variation in the maximum age of eligibility for juvenile justice procedures, between 16 and 20 (see Mehlbye & Walgrave, 1998: 24–27).

This variety has been further complicated by recent developments. As we will see in this Introduction and in the chapters in Part I, a significant shift occurred in the 1990s, particularly in the United States, where many thousands of young offenders who would previously have been dealt with within the juvenile justice system were tried in adult criminal courts and given sentences formerly reserved for adults. Indeed, in some states the maximum age of juvenile court jurisdiction has been formally lowered—for instance from 18 to 17 in Wyoming, and from 17 to 16 in New Hampshire and Wisconsin.

However, we can ground a more principled answer to the question 'Who should count as juveniles?' in psychology: roughly, those between the ages of 12 and 17. As Laurence Steinberg and Robert Schwartz say:

> Although delinquent and criminal acts are also committed by preadolescent children (those under twelve) and by young adults (those eighteen and older), the focus of the contemporary debate over how youthful offenders should be viewed and treated has been, and will continue to be, mainly on individuals between the ages of twelve and seventeen (quoted in Grisso & Schwartz, 2000: 22).

In this volume we will therefore take juveniles, for the purposes of juvenile criminal justice, to be adolescents roughly between the ages 12 and 17.

1. A CENTURY OF JUVENILE JUSTICE: COMMON THEMES AND NATIONAL DIFFERENCES

1.1. Precursors to the Juvenile Court System

The three chapters in Part I concentrate on recent shifts in juvenile justice systems. But to understand these changes, the authors go back further in history; they analyse the historical foundations and development of our institutional responses to young offenders.

As Junger-Tas shows in her survey of past and present trends of juvenile justice systems in Western society (ch 2), it was not until the sixteenth and seventeenth centuries that something like a modern consciousness concerning the protection of dangerous children and children in danger began to emerge. Since then there has been a rise in various modes of institutional care, which set the stage for the juvenile justice systems of the last hundred years. The establishment of special juvenile courts, sanctions and procedures at the beginning of the twentieth century is often taken to have marked the victory of a new 'welfare approach' over the traditional punitive philosophy of criminal justice, and a victory for the champions of a more active role for the state in education and upbringing when 'the interests of the child' seemed to be in danger. However, as Junger-Tas points out, many of the founding principles of the welfare approach had already gained strong support during the nineteenth century (see Radzinowicz & Hood, 1986; also Mennel, 1973; Schlossman, 1977; Platt, 1977; Dekker, 1985; Christiaens, 1999).

Until the early 1800s, families rather than institutions had been the principal instrument through which communities disciplined children (Schlossman, 1995); although children could formally be imprisoned under the stringent laws which existed, judges and juries seem often to have decided that neither the interests of justice nor the child's well-being would be served by imprisoning young offenders, and that it would be better to exonerate and release the child. In the early nineteenth century, however, concerns about this practice of absolving children from punishment, and about the damaging effects of imprisoning them, led to the foundation of special youth prisons and penitentiaries, reform schools and industrial schools, penal and agricultural colonies and houses of refuge all over the western world.

Although the regimes of these juvenile institutions initially hardly differed from those in adult institutions, their goals gradually shifted: education, reform and discipline came to be emphasised over punishment. As the most famous reformer, Mary Carpenter, argued 'Love must lead the way; faith and obedience will follow' (Carpenter, 1851: 325). The discourse of retribution, the concern to inflict punishments whose severity would be proportionate to the seriousness of the offence, was gradually abandoned in favour of a utilitarian discourse that looked to 'the interests of the child', the child's supposed 'need' of moral treatment and re-education, and the prevention of future offences. As the Second International Penitentiary Congress in Stockholm in 1878 resolved, delinquent children should not be punished, but should be educated to enable them to 'gain an honest livelihood and to become of use to society instead of an injury to it' (quoted in Platt, 1977: 50).

The establishment of these special institutions contributed significantly to the creation of a special status for minors within (and in the margins of) criminal law (see Trépanier, 1999b). Seen against this background, the introduction of the juvenile court is less revolutionary than is sometimes thought.

1.2. Turning points

The nineteenth century creation of a special set of institutions for juvenile offenders, and the emerging construction of a new welfare discourse oriented at the young offender and the child in danger, marked the first of three turning points in the history of the juvenile justice system. The focus of this volume is on the most recent turning point, but the interpretation of the origins, character and effects of the second turning point—the establishment of a special juvenile justice system with the foundation of the juvenile court—is crucial to an understanding of these recent changes.

All three contributors to Part I offer brief historical sketches of the twentieth century's development of a special juvenile justice system. There are three striking features of this establishment of a special system for young offenders: first, the increasingly insistent demand that the state take responsibility for these problematic youth; second, a growing belief in the availability of special expertise to help the problematic child; third, a purely consequentialist ethical foundation, in place of an orientation towards retribution, personal responsibility and proportionality.

The Illinois Juvenile Court Act 1899 declared that 'the care, custody and discipline of a child shall approximate as nearly as may be that which should be given by its parents'. The state was to take responsibility both for protecting the 'child in danger' against the harm that might be caused by bad families and neighbourhoods, and for protecting society against the 'dangerous child'—thus blurring the distinction between offending and neglect. New scientific claims, from rising disciplines like criminology, paediatry and psychiatry, strengthened this belief in state intervention (Bailey, 1987; Sutton, 1988, 1996; Weijers, 1999a). Prevention, rehabilitation and the notion of 'the best interests of the child' justified the efforts of the child savers movement, both at the end of the nineteenth century and for more than six decades in the twentieth century. As Junger-Tas argues, the characteristics of the juvenile jurisdiction were essentially the same everywhere, whether it involved a separate juvenile court, a juvenile judge, or a welfare board, as in Scandinavia.

The third turning point started in the mid-1960s, with the beginning of the collapse of the discourse of welfare, accompanied by a crumbling of the belief in state responsibility for re-education and rehabilitation, as well as an erosion of the belief in scientific expertise in this field and a corresponding erosion of the belief in the value of special institutions. Junger-Tas interprets this shift as a result both of a social reaction against the paternalism and the pure consequentialism that characterised the juvenile justice system, and of frustration about the lack of success of its efforts.

Hay and Stafford (ch 4) present a detailed analysis of the far-reaching shift in attitudes towards youth in trouble with the law in the United States, the country that 'invented' the special juvenile justice system. They focus on the vicissitudes of the idea of rehabilitation. They show that an ongoing lack of resources resulted for decades in badly-paid and badly-qualified personnel, and custodial institutions in which children were warehoused and isolated and received little or no guidance, education or training. It is against this background that new scientific findings in the 1960s could have a devastating impact in the United States, casting doubt on whether rehabilitation could have any positive effects at all. Hay and Stafford argue that the obituaries of the philosophy of rehabilitation which have appeared since the late 1960s, declaring that 'nothing works', have been premature: there is growing evidence that, although many programmes admittedly do not reduce recidivism, some successful programmes have been shown to secure considerable reductions.

When one tries to understand the general shift that took place in the United States in the 1960s, of which the 'nothing works' critique of rehabilitation formed an essential part, at least two trends seem important. On the one hand, as Hay and Stafford point out, as a result of decades of frustration with the results of rehabilitation programmes and of perceived failures of crime prevention, American citizens were becoming less willing to treat kindly 'the poor child who has been through so much', when that child was an offender. (Shireman & Reamer, 1986: 10). As the President's Commission on Law Enforcement and Administration of Justice put it in 1967,

[t]he juvenile court is a court of law, charged like other agencies of criminal justice with protecting the community against threatening conduct. Rehabilitating offenders through individualized handling is one way of providing protection and appropriately the primary way of dealing with children. But the guiding consideration for a court of law that deals with threatening conduct is nonetheless protection of the community. The juvenile court, like other courts, is therefore obliged to employ all the means at hand, not excluding incapacitation, for achieving that protection (quoted in Shireman & Reamer, 1986: 12).

On the other hand, an equally important trend that contributed to the shift in the American juvenile justice system can be found in the rapidly rising criticism of the lack of due process in juvenile justice procedures and the heritage of paternalism in this area, as Junger-Tas points out. The lack of procedural rights for young offenders was successfully challenged in such famous Supreme Court cases as *In re Kent* (1966) and *In re Gault* (1967). In *Kent*, the Supreme Court came to the much quoted conclusion that

There is evidence, in fact, that there may be grounds for concern that the child receives the worst of both worlds: that he gets neither the protections accorded to adults nor the solicitous care and regenerative treatment postulated for children (383 US 541, 556 [1966]).

In *Gault*, the Court held that Arizona's code and practices deprived children of procedural safeguards guaranteed by the Fourteenth Amendment: 'Under our constitution, the condition of being a boy does not justify a kangaroo court' (387 US 1, 29 [1967]). The Supreme Court's criticisms prompted reforms in other states to grant children due process rights. By contrast, in England in the 1960s, as Gelsthorpe makes clear in ch 3, a broad consensus on a welfare oriented system of juvenile justice had been achieved. From this perspective, the 1969 Children and Young Persons Act can be interpreted as a radical piece of legislation, portraying offending as a symptom of an underlying pathology and taking rehabilitation as its central aim. However, there was also a rising current of strong conservative opposition to this development, which combined with a justice-based critique. The momentum in England was thus clearly different from the trends in the United States. Whereas Hay and Stafford make clear that in the United States a rising dismay over the system eventually resulted in a radical shift from the 1960s onwards, in England this period can be seen as a crucially ambiguous one, in which the radical belief in rehabilitation that had been slowly strengthening during the previous decades clashed with a complex amalgam of hostile reactions. The net result, Gelsthorpe shows, was 'bifurcation': stronger repression for serious and persistent young offenders, but more leniency towards those guilty of more trivial offences.

Similar trends could be observed in continental Europe from the late 1960s: a new concern for the rights (including process rights) of juveniles, and new demands that they be held accountable as well as being protected; a strong discourse of rights and of just deserts; and bifurcation. However, the welfare approach, which emphasised the idea of children in danger over that of dangerous children, and focused on need rather than on crime and on rehabilitation rather than retribution, seems to have retained much of its influence throughout Western Europe—especially in Scandinavia, and in Scotland with the creation of the Children's Hearing system in 1968 (see Martin & Murray, 1976), but also in France, Belgium and Germany. (For other interpretations of these developments, see Schultz, 1973; Klein, 1984; Shireman & Reamer, 1986; Ferdinand, 1989; Bernard, 1992; Krisberg & Austin, 1993; Howell, 1997; Dünkel *et al*, 1997; Mehlbye & Walgrave, 1998; Trépanier, 1999b; Weijers, 1999b; Schüler-Springorum, 1999.)

The contributions to Part I of this volume offer both a general overview (ch 2) and analyses of national developments (chs 3 and 4). Our understanding of the problems and the prospects of juvenile justice would also be enhanced by comparative studies of differences in the context and development of juvenile justice provisions in different jurisdictions. Some such differences concern deeper political structures and ideologies—for instance about the nature and role of the welfare state (see Esping-Andersen, 1990; Gittens, 1994; Sutton, 1996; Golden, 1997; Weijers, 1999a). Others concern differences in conceptions of the proper institutional relationship between justice and welfare, in particular as to whether there should be a unitary, welfare-based system that would deal with both children in danger and dangerous children—with *any* child in need of special state intervention; or a bipartite system which involves a juvenile court for young offenders, and a separate welfare process for dealing with other children in need (see Dünkel & Meyer, 1985; Shoemaker, 1996; Mehlbye & Walgrave, 1998). Others again concern differences in criminal justice procedures, especially those that reflect the differences between civil law and common law traditions: differences in, for instance, the judge's role in inquisitorial and in adversarial trials, or in the extent to which the criminal process allows any room for a moral dialogue between court and offender (see Weijers, ch 7 in this volume; Adler, Müller & Laufer, 1994; Fairchild & Dammer, 2001). We cannot pursue these matters here, but comparative investigations of these differences might provide new insights, both into the recent history of our juvenile justice systems and into the directions in which we want our systems to converge, or diverge. We hope that Part I of this volume will offer encouragement to further systematic comparative research in this field.

2. HOLDING YOUNG OFFENDERS RESPONSIBLE

Part II of this volume moves from historical interpretation to normative theorising. The three contributors to this Part agree that juvenile offenders should be held responsible for the crimes they commit; that this requires a process of moral communication; and that considerations of welfare are crucial—in holding juvenile offenders responsible we must also seek their good. They disagree about whether this requires, or precludes, a system of *punishment* for juvenile offenders, and about where and how that essential communication should take place. In this section, we sketch some of the background to that disagreement, and some of the features of juvenile offenders which any normative theorising must take into account.

2.1. Punishment, Restoration and Moral Communication

The question of whether we can justifiably punish juvenile offenders is of course inseparable from the question of whether, and how, we can justifiably punish *anyone*; and that perennial, complex and morally troubling question is not one to which we can do justice in this volume. It is perhaps a reflection of the success of the retributivist, or anti-consequentialist, revival in penal theory since the 1970s (see Tonry & Morris, 1978; Allen, 1981) that all the contributors to Part II agree in rejecting any purely consequentialist answer to the question of punishment: if we are to justify the infliction of painful burdens that punishment necessarily involves, we cannot do so *merely* by showing that this is likely to achieve some consequential good. (On the central objections to consequentialist theories, and some consequentialist responses, see Duff, 2001: ch 1.) Beyond that agreement, they differ radically.

Walgrave (ch 5) rejects criminal punishment altogether, since it involves the deliberate infliction of pain. Whilst we must communicate appropriate disapproval to the offender, and ensure that he makes suitable reparation to restore the harm that he caused (a process which might in fact be burdensome or painful), criminal punishment cannot serve these aims: what we should seek, for juvenile offenders as for adults (Walgrave does not differentiate between them), is restorative rather than retributive justice. Walgrave thus associates himself with a movement which has been growing in prominence and influence in the last two decades (and which he himself has done much to promote), and which has been particularly influential in the context of juvenile crime (see Morris, ch 8 in this volume, on Family Group Conferences; and, more generally, Morris & Maxwell, 2001).

This is not the place for an analysis of the many different forms that the restorative justice movement has taken (for two useful surveys see Braithwaite, 1999; Kurki, 2000). The central slogan is that what is required in the wake of a crime (or, as some prefer to call it, a 'conflict' or 'trouble'; see Christie, 1977; Hulsman, 1986) is a process of reparation and reconciliation—of 'restoration'; and that such restoration cannot be achieved through the traditional criminal process of trial and punishment. If we ask *what* is to be restored or repaired, the answer will usually refer to the harm caused by the crime, and to the relationships (between the offender and the victim, between the offender and those wider communities in which he and the victim live, and perhaps also between the victim and those wider communities) that it affects. If we ask how such restoration is to be achieved, the answer will usually refer to the importance of dialogue or conversation, both between offender and victim, and amongst all those affected by or with an interest in the crime: this is how the offender is to be brought to confront the implications of what she has done; how those involved are to come to a better understanding of each other, of the crime and its implications, of their relationships and how they can be repaired; and how they are to come to agree on a suitable reparative measure for the offender to undertake.

Three salient themes for our present purposes are, first, a rejection of the formal criminal trial, as a professionalised and oppressive process which allows no room for the kind of equal, respectful conversation that restoration requires; second, a rejection of criminal punishment as a species of deliberate 'pain delivery' (Christie, 1981) which can only hinder rather than help the restorative process; and third, an insistence that the reparation must be agreed, and must be undertaken voluntarily by the offender, if it is to have restorative value. Walgrave takes up the first two of these themes, but not the third: a distinctive feature of his restorative account is that he would have courts impose 'restorative sanctions' on those who will not undertake them voluntarily.

Duff (ch 6) agrees with restorative theorists that our responses to crime should aim for restoration, reparation and reconciliation, but argues that we should reject the sharp contrast between 'retributive' and 'restorative' justice that both restorative theorists and their critics draw. Developing the familiar idea that a central purpose of punishment is the communication of the censure that the offender deserves (see Feinberg, 1970; von Hirsch, 1993; Duff, 2001: ch 3), he argues that what should be salient in our responses to crime is not just the harm caused, but the wrong that was done: whether our response involves some restorative process, such as victim-offender mediation, or criminal punishment as more orthodoxly conceived, it must aim to communicate to the offender the censure he deserves, to persuade him to repent his crime, and to bring him to make apologetic reparation to his victim and his fellow citizens. The kind of mediation process which restorative theorists favour should be punitive, and retributive, in that it seeks to impose on or to induce in the offender the suffering (of remorse, of necessarily burdensome moral reparation) he deserves; whilst both mediation and orthodox punishment should have the forward-looking aims of bringing offenders to a repentant concern to avoid re-offending, and of reconciling them with those they have wronged, they are also essentially retributive, in that those aims are properly achieved *through* bringing offenders to suffer as they deserve to suffer.

Punishment as thus understood is appropriate for juvenile as for adult offenders, although the sanctions applied must be adapted to the particular characteristics of the offender. We can indeed properly talk here of punishment as a kind of moral education. Some theorists (see eg Morris, 1981; Hampton, 1984) have portrayed punishment in general in these terms; and whilst we should have doubts about whether it is appropriate to treat adult offenders as being in need of such (re-)education (see Duff, 2001: 89–92), that perspective can seem more appropriate for juvenile offenders (this is central to Weijers' argument).

Duff's communicative theory is thus extremely ambitious. Other communicative theorists argue that the 'hard treatment' dimension of punishment, the imposition of some burdensome deprivation (imprisonment, fines, compulsory community service . . .), cannot be justified as a part of the process of moral communication, but must be given some other, perhaps deterrent, rationale; but Duff argues that the hard treatment itself, imposed as punishment, must serve as a penance that furthers the aims of moral communication and restoration. Weijers (ch 7) finds this argument implausible: hard treatment punishment is utterly ill-suited to those aims. Moral communication is, he agrees, crucial: but it should take place in the courtroom, during a trial, rather than through the punishment that follows the trial.

Weijers looks for a juvenile criminal process that will be appropriate to the characteristics and capacities of juvenile offenders (see s 2.2 below): this will be, he argues, a process that is morally communicative and educative, and that addresses the young offender as someone who is becoming, but has not yet fully become, a responsible member of the civic community (and that helps him towards achieving that mature responsibility). Drawing on the idea of an ethics of care, he argues that it should be the judge's task to engage the offender in a moral dialogue: this will involve not only trying to bring him to face up to and reflect upon the wrong that he committed, but also engaging him in a self-reflective discussion of the motives that led to his crime, and of his own identity and values.

Central to Weijers' argument is the claim that we do need a distinctive system of *juvenile* justice, of courts that will be suitable for juvenile offenders; this reflects his emphasis on the ways in which juveniles have not yet achieved the maturity which would make it legitimate to hold them unqualifiedly responsible or culpable for their crimes, or competent to stand trial in an ordinary court.

2.2. Maturity and Responsibility

Zimring (2000: 285) suggests that an important test of the moral quality of any penal policy is whether its treatment of those who are still growing up is consistent with other ways in which the law deals with those who are advancing towards adulthood—for instance with age-related legal rules concerning drinking, driving, marriage, voting, military service and so on. He also argues that we, and the law, should recognise adolescence as a period of life that is 'mistake-prone by design' (2000: 283): as a period of radical 'learning by doing' in which competence in decision-making can be achieved only by making decisions and making mistakes. Once we recognise this, and also recognise the diminished responsibility which is an implication of the juvenile offender's immaturity, we will recognise that whatever procedures we implement for juvenile offenders must give them the chance to reform during their adolescent years (the vast majority of juvenile offenders do not grow into a life of crime: see Farrington, 1986; Hirschi & Gottfredson, 1983; Moffit, 1993).

If we recognise that juvenile offenders are in the process of becoming, but have not yet become, fully responsible members of the civic community, we must ask how far they can be held to be culpable for their crimes, and how far they can be held to be competent to be tried in a criminal court.

Their culpability depends crucially on their powers of moral reasoning and judgement, and of self-control: how far are they capable of grasping the wrongfulness of the conduct in question, and of controlling their own conduct in the light of their moral understanding? Their intellectual capacities may be well developed, but they lack much of the experience on which the exercise of those capacities depends; they have not yet fully developed that practical grasp of the longer term future, and the ability to control their actions in the light of future concerns, which practical rationality requires; and they are more susceptible to the influence of others, especially their peers, and less secure in their own identity than we can hope they will become (see Scott *et al*, 1995; Elliot & Menard, 1996; Steinberg & Cauffman, 1996; Howell & Hawkins, 1998). Whilst none of these considerations suggest that juvenile offenders are simply non-culpable, they do suggest reasons for regarding youth as a normally mitigating factor when culpability is to be assessed (see further von Hirsch, 2001).

A juvenile offender's eligibility for criminal trial and punishment depends, however, not only on her responsibility or culpability at the time of the (alleged) crime, but also on whether she is competent to stand trial. It is a standard requirement of any civilised legal system that a defendant should be brought to trial only if she is competent to be tried; and this requirement becomes even more important if the trial is conceived as both Weijers and Duff conceive it, as a communicative process in which an alleged offender is called to answer the charges against her (see Duff, 1986: ch 4). The defendant's competence is a matter of her ability to grasp the meaning of the legal procedure as one which calls her to answer a charge of wrongdoing, and to play her part in that procedure; this must involve the capacity to understand and answer the questions put to her and to grasp the significance of what is said and done. Although there has been little systematic research in this area, the evidence suggests—very plausibly— that young adolescents are not always fully capable of understanding the process or of playing their part in it (see generally Scott *et al*, 1995; Steinberg & Cauffman, 1996; Masten & Coatworth, 1998; Grisso, 2000).

It is thus plausible that juvenile offenders are often less culpable for the crimes that they commit than are normal adult offenders, and less competent to understand and participate in their trials than adults are supposed to be. Does this show that we need a separate system of juvenile courts and juvenile criminal justice, one specially designed for juveniles rather than for adults? Weijers is clear that this is the conclusion we should draw: we need both trials and sanctions that are apt to the moral educational task that the immaturity of juvenile offenders makes necessary. But others deny this. Some argue that the diminished culpability of juvenile offenders can be accommodated at the sentencing stage in the ordinary criminal courts (Feld, 1997), and it could likewise be argued that any limitations on their understanding of, or ability to participate in, the criminal process could be accommodated by suitable adaptations to the procedures of ordinary courts. One might also suggest, as Duff does, that we must first decide what criminal procedures are appropriate for adult offenders (since it is far from clear that our existing procedures are), and only then ask whether they can also be appropriate for juvenile offenders. (Walgrave does not face this precise question, since he thinks that no one should be subjected to the criminal process of trial and sentence; but he argues for a restorative process which will be apt for both adult and juvenile offenders.)

3. MORAL EMOTIONS

Neither an adequate understanding of adolescent behaviour, nor an attempt to communicate with juvenile offenders about their crimes, can be set in purely cognitive or intellectual terms (see Harris, 1989): we must grasp the emotional dimensions and springs of their conduct, and appeal to their emotional capacities, if we are either to understand their actions or bring them to grasp and be moved by the wrongfulness of what they have done.

Such 'moral emotions' as guilt, shame and remorse have become central to the debate about how juvenile offenders can be brought to face up to and to deal with their wrongdoing. Psychological research on the development of such emotions was given new impetus by the seminal work of Lewis (1971), and flourished during the 1990s; meanwhile, discussion of the role of such emotions in juvenile justice had been stimulated by Braithwaite's work (1989) on 'reintegrative shaming'. Part III brings together authors from different disciplines to reflect on the moral emotions, and particularly on Braithwaite's account of shaming. They reflect on the ideas of shame, guilt and remorse from the perspectives of practical experience with restorative justice (Morris), of philosophical inquiry into the emotions and their significance (Taylor), and of recent empirical research in psychology (Olthof).

In this section we will briefly sketch some trends in recent thought about the moral emotions, especially in relation to child development, and highlight two issues that seem to be crucial for any appeal to the emotions in the context of criminal law in general and of juvenile law in particular. The first issue concerns the interpersonal character of these emotions, and its implications for the ways in which and the contexts in which they can develop and can be properly aroused. The second concerns the far-reaching ethical implications of appeals to such emotions as guilt and shame in the context of law: how far is it likely to be either appropriate or productive to focus our responses to wrongdoing on the elicitation of such emotions?

3.1. Shame, Guilt and the Role of Others

Both scientists and lay people have often drawn no clear distinction between shame and guilt; in everyday discourse, 'guilt' is often used as a catch-all term to refer to both guilt and shame (Tangney, 1998: 2). However, theorists in various disciplines have developed accounts of these emotions and of the distinction between them (eg Benedict, 1946 in anthropology; Erikson, 1950 in the psycho-analytical tradition; Lewis, 1971, Fischer & Tangney, 1995 in psychology; Morris, 1976, Taylor, 1985 in philosophy). The emergent consensus is that whilst guilt is focused on some particular wrong that was done, shame bears on the whole person and her identity: in guilt, an action is found and felt to be wanting—to be wrong, to be condemned; in shame, the whole person is found and felt to be wanting. Both Taylor (ch 9) and Olthof (ch 10) take up and develop this theme. (Remorse has received less attention from theorists: but see Dilman, 1999; Taylor, ch 9 s 4 in this volume; and below, s 3.3).

A further feature of both shame and guilt, again discussed by both Taylor and Olthof, is that other people play important roles in their emergence, though those roles differ as between the two emotions. Shame depends on an actual or imagined negative judgement by others on the person himself—that he is not what he wants to be or ought to be: not just (as Morris thought) that he is failing to live up to some ideal of perfection (see Morris, 1976: 61), but that he is not even living up to those more minimal standards to which his self-image and identity (as he conceives them) are linked (see Ferguson *et al*, 1991; Gilbert, 1998). Guilt, by contrast, focuses on an action that was inconsistent with some authoritative moral law or demand, and involves the condemnation (by the agent but also, in fact or in her imagination, by others) of that action—but not necessarily of the whole person. It might thus be, in principle, easier to deal with a sense of guilt than with a sense of shame, since one can do something to make amends for that wrongful action—paying compensation, offering an apology (see Taylor, 1996, and ch 9, ss 3, 5 in this volume).

Research has shown that the capacity to experience shame and guilt as distinct emotions develops only gradually in young people. Children focus primarily on the valence of the outcomes of events and actions, rather than on the actions themselves or what motivated them; and only from about the age of eight do most children begin to distinguish enduring characteristics of the self from more transient kinds of behaviour (Harris, 1989; Ferguson *et al*, 1991; Tangney, 1995). The character of shame and guilt also changes substantially through the course of juvenile development. They changes with the development of those cognitive and imaginative capacities on which they depend: the capacity to recognise another's pain, for instance, and one's own causality in relation to one's actions and their effects; the capacity to develop a conception of—and a concern for—one's own identity and one's relations to others; the capacity to understand the continued identity of others, the character and depth of their feelings, and the consequences of hurting them (see Damon, 1988: 24–26).

The role played by other people in the development and arousal of these emotions, and their typically interpersonal character, have significant implications for attempts to induce either shame or guilt in the context of the criminal law. Although shame can of course be induced by the imagined gaze of a purely imaginary other, and although guilt can be aroused by the solitary contemplation of one's wrongdoing, both involve judging ourselves or our conduct by standards that we share (or suppose ourselves to share) with significant others in our social milieu—with parents, or teachers, or siblings, or friends and peers, or others whom we respect and with whom we seek to identify ourselves (see Tangney, 1995: 114). When the attempt is made to induce shame or guilt in an offender, it can therefore matter crucially who makes that attempt, and what their relationships are with the offender. Morris's discussion of Family Group Conferencing (ch 8) is of particular interest in this connection: the offender has to deal not with a judge or other kinds of professional, but with the victim, and her own and the victim's families and friends; this makes a significant difference to the kinds of emotion that might properly be aroused. If our responses to crime are to involve the attempt to induce either shame or guilt, we must ask who has the right or standing to try to bring the offender to feel such emotions, and by whom they can be appropriately and properly aroused.

3.2. Shame, Guilt and Remorse as Responses to Crime

Shame, or shaming, has been central to one strand of the 'restorative justice' movement, in particular through Braithwaite's influential account of 'reintegrative shaming' (Braithwaite, 1989, 1993; Braithwaite & Mugford, 1994). Despite some stringent criticism (see eg Blagg, 1997; Vagg, 1998; Yoshida, 2000), the idea of reintegrative shaming is now widely accepted in criminology, and especially in the field of juvenile justice (see Morris, ch. 8 in this volume; also Walgrave & Aertsen, 1996; Retzinger & Sheff, 1996; Garvey, 1998; Whitman, 1998; Book, 1999; Freiberg, 2000; Johnstone, 2001). The three authors in Part III all raise further doubts about the propriety or utility of shame, and of guilt, in this context.

One such doubt concerns the psychological effects of shame, and of guilt. We can reject the crude view that shame and guilt are intrinsically destructive emotions which can have no positive role in human life. We can recognise that—quite apart from the question of whether such emotions might be intrinsically appropriate as responses to one's past wrongdoing—they can serve an adaptive role (see eg Ferguson *et al*, 1991 on shame): that they can strengthen an appropriate awareness of our own failings, and motivate attempts at self-improvement. We can try to distinguish rational, adaptive or appropriate forms of these emotions from neurotic, maladaptive or inappropriate forms (see eg Bybee & Quiles, 1998, on 'predispositional' as against 'chronic' guilt). But we must also recognise the point that Olthof emphasises (ch 10 in this volume): that these emotions *can* be very destructive, and that attempts to arouse them can have effects quite different from those that may be intended. There are obvious and serious risks in unleashing such powerful emotions; we must ask whether they are risks that we should run in our responses to crime.

Another kind of doubt concerns the appropriateness, rather than the efficacy or utility, of shaming in response to a crime. Guilt, we noted above, focuses on the wrongful act that was done, or on the violation of a rule that that action involved; such an emotion seems at least prima facie an appropriate response to the commission of a crime, which is typically defined as consisting in some legally wrongful action. But shame focuses on the person as a whole, and on the unwanted or condemned identity that she is now seen to have: if shaming someone necessarily has this kind of moral implication for her identity, we must surely ask whether our legally sanctioned responses to crime should involve attempting to shame the wrongdoer. By what right could we not merely condemn their wrongdoing, and try to bring them to share that condemnation in guilt, but question their very identity by trying to induce shame in them? Is this really something that should be officially sanctioned or encouraged by the criminal law of a liberal polity? This question becomes especially acute for offenders whose own sense of their identity is uncertain or vulnerable—something that is typically true of juvenile offenders.

Surely, however, it is, in principle, appropriate to try to induce some appropriate emotion in criminal wrongdoers, both adult and juvenile. If the law defines as criminal only conduct that is indeed wrongful (as it should), offenders have done wrong. It is appropriate that they should come to recognise that wrong as a wrong that they should not have committed; as something for which—as advocates both of restorative justice and of some versions of retributivism urge—they need now to make amends; as something that—as consequentialists urge—they should avoid in the future. Such a recognition cannot, if it is authentic, be wholly unemotional. It is not a matter of noting some matter of fact, but involves a recognition that I have wronged others for whom I care, or should care, and flouted values to which I am or should be committed; and that kind of recognition has an emotional dimension commensurate with the concerns—for those I have wronged, for the values I have flouted—it expresses. If we are to bring wrongdoers to such a recognition, we thus cannot avoid the attempt to induce appropriate emotions in them.

Perhaps, then, the question should be not whether in our responses to crime we should seek to induce some appropriate emotion in the offender, but just what emotion we should seek to induce; and perhaps the answer will refer not to shame or guilt, but (as both Morris and Taylor suggest) to remorse. The distinction between remorse and guilt is admittedly not a sharp one: but one could suggest (see Taylor, ch 9 s 4) that remorse is more closely tied to and focused on the action for which it is felt, as a wrong for which I am fully responsible; and that an understanding of that wrong as a wrong done to its victim is intrinsic to remorse in a way that it is not to guilt. Much more would of course need to be said about the nature of remorse (see Gaita, 1991: ch 4), and about the legitimacy of attempts to induce remorse in offenders. Much more would need to be said about the kinds of context within which, and the kinds of procedure through which, such attempts could properly be made—whether the criminal trial could be such a procedure, or whether such attempts require the less formal procedures of Family Group Conferences or of other restorative justice practices. It should at least be clear, however, that this is a path which merits further and serious exploration.

REFERENCES

Adler, F, Müller, G O W & Laufer, W S (1994) *Criminal Justice* (McGraw-Hill, New York).
Allen, F A (1981) *The Decline of the Rehabilitative Ideal* (Yale University Press, New Haven).
Bailey, V (1987) *Delinquency and Citizenship. Reclaiming the Young Offender 1914–1948* (Clarendon Press, Oxford).
Benedict, R (1946) *The Chrysanthemum and the Sword* (Houghton, Boston).
Bernard, T J (1992) *The Cycle of Juvenile Justice* (Oxford University Press, Oxford).
Blagg, H (1997) 'A Just Measure of Shame? Aboriginal Youth and Conferencing in Australia' 37 *British Journal of Criminology* 481–501.
Book, A (1999) 'Shame on You: An Analysis of Modern Shame Punishment as an Alternative to Incarceration' 40 *William and Mary Law Review* 653–686.
Braithwaite, J (1989) *Crime, Shame and Reintegration* (Cambridge University Press, Cambridge).
—— (1993) 'Shame and Modernity' 33 *British Journal of Criminology* 1–18.
—— (1999) 'Restorative Justice: Assessing Optimistic and Pessimistic Accounts' in M Tonry (ed) *Crime and Justice: A Review of Research*, vol 25 (University of Chicago Press, Chicago) 1–127.
Braithwaite, J & Mugford, S (1994) 'Conditions of Successful Reintegration Ceremonies. Dealing with Juvenile Offenders' 34 *British Journal of Criminology* 139–71.
Bybee, J & Quiles, Z N (1998) 'Guilt and Mental Health' in J Bybee (ed) *Guilt and Children* (Academic Press, San Diego) 269–91.
Carpenter, M (1851/1970) *Reformatory Schools for the Children of the Perishing and Dangerous Classes and for Juvenile Offenders* (Patterson Smith, Montclair).
Christiaens, J (1999) 'A History of Belgium's Child Protection Act of 1912: The Redefinition of the Juvenile Offender and his Punishment' 7 *European Journal of Crime, Criminal Law and Criminal Justice* 5–21.
Christie, N (1977) 'Conflicts as Property' 17 *British Journal of Criminology* 1–15.
—— (1981) *Limits to Pain* (Martin Robertson, London).
Damon, W (1988), *The Moral Child. Nurturing Children's Natural Moral Growth* (The Free Press, New York).
Dekker, J J H (1985) *Straffen, Redden en Opvoeden: het Ontstaan en de Ontwikkeling van de Residentiële Heropvoeding in West-Europa, 1814–1914, met Bijzondere Aandacht voor Nederlandsch Mettray* (Van Gorcum, Assen/Maastricht).

Dilman, I (1999) 'Shame, Guilt and Remorse' 22 *Philosophical Investigations* 312–29.

Duff, R A (1986), *Trials and Punishments* (Cambridge University Press, Cambridge).

—— (2001) *Punishment, Communication and Community* (Oxford University Press, New York).

Dünkel, F & Meyer, K (eds) (1985) *Jugendstrafe und Jugendstrafvollzug. Stationäre Massnamen der Jugendkriminalrechtspflege im internationalen Vergleich* I (Max Planck Institut, Freiburg).

Dünkel, F, Kalmthout, A van & Schüler-Springorum, H (eds) (1997) *Entwicklungstenzen und Reformstrategien im Jugendstrafrecht im Europäischen Vergleich* (Forum, Bad Godesberg).

Elliott, D & Menard, S (1996) 'Delinquent Friends and Delinquent Behavior. Temporal and Developmental Patterns' in J D Hawkins (ed) *Delinquency and Crime. Current Theories* (Cambridge University Press, New York).

Erikson, E H (1950) *Childhood and Society* (W W Norton, New York).

Esping-Andersen, G (1990) *The Three Worlds of Welfare Capitalism* (Polity Press, Cambridge).

Fagan, F & Zimring, F E (eds.) (2000) *The Changing Borders of Juvenile Justice: Transfer of Adolescents to the Criminal Court* (Chicago University Press, Chicago).

Fairchild, E & Dammer, H R (2001) *Comparative Criminal Justice Systems* (Wadsworth, Belmont CA).

Farrington, D P (1986) 'Age and Crime' in M Tonry & N Morris (eds) *Crime and Justice. An Annual Review of Research* (Chicago University Press, Chicago).

Feinberg, J (1970) 'The Expressive Function of Punishment' in his *Doing and Deserving* (Princeton University Press, Princeton, NJ) 95–118.

Feld, B (1997) 'Abolish the Juvenile Court: Criminal Responsibility and Sentencing Policy' 88 *Journal of Criminal Law and Criminology* 68–136.

Ferdinand, T N (1989) 'Juvenile Delinquency or Juvenile Justice, Which Came First' 27 *Criminology* 79–106.

Ferguson, T J, Stegge, S & Damhuis, I (1991) 'Children's Understanding of Guilt and Shame' 62 *Child Development* 827–839.

Fischer, K W & Tangney, J P (eds) (1995) *Self-conscious Emotions: Shame, Guilt, Embarrassment and Pride* (Guilford Press, New York).

Freiberg, A (2000) 'Affective versus Effective Justice: Instrumentalism and Emotionalism in Criminal Justice' 2 *Punishment and Society* 365–78.

Gaita, R (1991) *Good and Evil: An Absolute Conception* (Macmillan, London).

Garvey, S (1998) 'Can Shaming Punishments Educate?' 65 *University of Chicago Law Review* 733–94.

Gilbert, P (1998) 'What is Shame? Some Core Issues and Controversies' in P Gilbert & B Andrews (eds) *Shame. Interpersonal Behavior, Psychopathology and Culture* (Oxford University Press, New York/Oxford) 3–38.

Gittens, J (1994) *Poor Relations: The Children of the State of Illinois 1818–1990* (University of Illinois Press, Urbana).

Golden, R (1997) *Disposable Children: America's Child Welfare System* (Wadsworth, Belmont CA).

Grisso, T (2000) 'What We Know about Youth's Capacities as Trial Defendants' in Grisso & Schwartz 2000, 139–71.

Grisso, T & Schwartz, R G (eds) (2000) *Youth on Trial. A Developmental Perspective on Juvenile Justice* (University of Chicago Press, Chicago).

Hampton, J (1984) 'The Moral Education Theory of Punishment' 13 *Philosophy and Public Affairs* 208–38.

Harris, P L (1989), *Children and Emotion. The Development of Psychological Understanding* (Basil Blackwell, New York).

Hirschi, T & Gottfredson, M (1983) 'Age and the Explanation of Crime' 89 *American Journal of Scociology* 552–84.

Howell, J C (1997) *Juvenile Justice and Youth Violence* (Sage, London).

Howell, J C & Hawkins, D (1998) 'Prevention of Youth Violence' in M Tonry & M Morris (eds) *Crime and Justice. An Annual Review of Research* (University of Chicago Press, Chicago).

Hulsman, L (1986) 'Critical Criminology and the Concept of Crime' 10 *Contemporary Crises* 63–80.

Johnstone, G (2001) *Restorative Justice: Ideas, Values, Debates* (Willan, Cullompton).

Klein, M W (ed) (1984) *Western Systems of Juvenile Justice* (Sage, London).

Krisberg, B, & Austin, J F (1993) *Reinventing Juvenile Justice* (Sage, London).

Kurki, I (2000) 'Restorative and Community Justice in the United States' in M Tonry (ed.), *Crime and Justice: A Review of Research*, vol 26 (University of Chicago Press, Chicago).

Lewis, H B (1971) *Shame and Guilt in Neurosis* (International Universities Press, New York).

Martin, F M & Murray, K (1976) *Children's Hearings* (Scottish Academic Press, Edinburgh).

Masten, A & Coatsworth, J (1998) 'The Development of Competence in Favorable and Unfavorable Environments' 53 *American Psychologist* 205–20.

Mehlbye, J & Walgrave, L (eds) (1998) *Confronting Youth in Europe Juvenile Crime and Juvenile Justice* (AKF Forlaget, Copenhagen).

Mennel, R M (1973) *Thorns and Thistles. Juvenile Delinquents in the United States 1825–1940* (University Press of New England, Hanover).

Moffit, T (1993) 'Adolescent-limited and Life Course Persistent Antisocial Behavior: A Developmental Taxonomy' 100 *Psychological Bulletin* 674–700.

Morris, A & Maxwell, G (eds) (2001) *Restorative Justice for Juveniles: Conferencing, Mediation and Circles* (Hart Publishing, Oxford).

Morris, H (1976) *On Guilt and Innocence. Essays in Legal Philosophy and Moral Psychology* (University of California Press, Berkeley).

—— (1981) 'A Paternalistic Theory of Punishment' 18 *American Philosophical Quarterly* 263–71.

Platt, T (1977) *The Child Savers. The Invention of Delinquency* (University of Chicago Press, Chicago).

Radzinowicz L, & Hood, R (1986) *A History of English Criminal Law and its Administration from 1750, Vol 5, The Emergence of Penal Policy* (Stevens, London).

Retzinger, S & Sheff, T (1996) 'Strategy for Community Conferences: Emotions and Social Bonds' in B Galaway & J Hudson (eds) *Restorative Justice: International Perspectives* (Criminal Justice Press, Monsey, NY) 315–36.

Schlossman, S L (1977) *Love and the American Delinquent. The Theory and Practice of 'Progressive' Juvenile Justice, 1825–1920* (University of Chicago Press, Chicago).

—— (1995) 'Delinquent Children: The Juvenile Reform School' in N Morris & D J Rothman (eds) *The Oxford History of the Prison: The Practice of Punishment in Western Society* (Oxford University Press, Oxford) 325–50.

Schüler-Springorum, H (1999) 'Juvenile Justice and the "Shift to the Left"' 7 *European Journal on Criminal Policy and Research* 353–62.

Schultz, J L (1973) 'The Cycle of Juvenile Court' 19 *History Crime and Delinquency* 457–76.

Scott, E , Reppucci, N & Woolard, J (1995) 'Evaluating Adolescent Decision-making in Legal Contexts' 19 *Law and Human Behavior* 221–44.

Shireman, C H & Reamer, F G (1986) *Rehabilitating Juvenile Justice* (Columbia University Press, New York).

Shoemaker, D J (ed) (1996) *International Handbook on Juvenile Justice* (Greenwood Press, London).

Steinberg, L & Cauffman, E (1996) 'Maturity of Judgment in Adolescence: Psychosocial Factors in Adolescent Decision-making' 20 *Law and Human Behavior* 249–72.

Sutton, J R (1988) *Stubborn Children. Controlling Delinquency in the United States 1640–1981* (University of California Press, Berkeley).

—— (1996) 'Social Knowledge and the Generation of Child Welfare Policy in the United States and Canada' in D Rueschemeyer & T Skocpol (eds) *States, Social Knowledge, and the Origins of Modern Social Policies* (Princeton University Press, Princeton) 201–30.

Tangney, J P (1995) 'Shame and guilt in interpersonal relationships' in K W Fischer & J P Tangney (eds) *Self-conscious Emotions: Shame, Guilt, Embarrassment and Pride* (Guilford Press, New York) 114–39.

—— (1998) 'How does Guilt Differ from Shame?' in J Bybee (ed) *Guilt and Children* (Academic Press, San Diego) 1–17.

Taylor, G (1985) *Pride, Shame and Guilt. Emotions of Self-Assessment* (Oxford University Press, Oxford).

—— (1996) 'Guilt and Remorse' in R Harré & W G Parrott (eds) *The Emotions. Social, Cultural and Biological Dimensions* (Sage, London) 57–73.

Tonry, M & Morris, N (1978) 'Sentencing Reform in America' in P R Glazebrook (ed) *Reshaping the Criminal Law* (Stevens, London) 434–48.

Trépanier, J (1999b) 'Juvenile Courts after 100 Years: Past and Present Orientations' 7 *European Journal on Criminal Policy and Research* 303–27.

Vagg, J (1998) 'Delinquency and Shame. Data from Hong Kong' 38 *British Journal of Criminology* 247–63.

von Hirsch, A (1993) *Censure and Sanctions* (Oxford University Press, Oxford).

—— (2001) 'Proportionate Sentences for Juveniles—How Different than for Adults?' 3 *Punishment & Society* 221–36.

Walgrave, L & Aertsen, I (1996) 'Reintegrative Shaming and Restorative Justice: Interchangeable, Complementary or Different?' 4 *European Journal of Crime, Criminal Law and Criminal Justice* 67–84.

Weijers, I (1999a) 'The Debate on Juvenile Justice in the Netherlands, 1891–1901' 7 *European Journal of Crime, Criminal Law and Criminal Justice* 63–78.

—— (1999b) 'The Double Paradox of Juvenile Justice' 7 *European Journal on Criminal Policy and Research* 329–51.

Whitman, J (1998) 'What is Wrong with Inflicting Shame Sanctions?' 107 *Yale Law Journal* 1055–92.

Yoshida, T (2000) 'Confession, Apology, Repentance and Settlement Out-of-Court in the Japanese Criminal Justice System: Is Japan a Model of "Restorative Justice"?' paper presented at the 4th International Conference on Restorative Justice in Tübingen, September 2000.

Zimring, F E (2000) 'Penal proportionality for the Young Offender: Notes on Immaturity, Capacity, and Diminished Responsibility' in Grisso & Schwartz 2000, 271–89

Part I

Past and Present

2

The Juvenile Justice System: Past and Present Trends in Western Society

JOSINE JUNGER-TAS

THE WAY IN which children who are victims of the conditions in which they are living and children who have violated the law are approached, treated, rehabilitated, disciplined and punished, is essentially a reflection of that society's culture and value system, as expressed in its conception of children and youth and its views on how to socialise and educate them. For example, well into the nineteenth century people hardly differentiated between children in need of protection and delinquent children. They were convinced that such need led to delinquency, and the reaction to both need and delinquency was therefore essentially similar.

In this respect western history tells us a sad story indeed. For centuries it was considered normal to flog children with a lash, stick, or other instruments. Children were shackled, chained, gagged and put in the stocks on the assumption that this would have a dissuasive and educative effect. There were hardly any limits, although a Dutch legal text dating from the thirteenth century states 'if one beats a child until he is bleeding he will remember the punishment, but if the child is beaten to death the law will come in action' (Sanders, 1970). Not until the Renaissance do we see more warnings against beating children to death, and we have to wait until the eighteenth century before there is a real decline in the use of violence against children as an educative measure. This change is related to improved living conditions, progress in medical knowledge and increased care for children by mothers. Despite these changes, disciplining children with a lash or reed remains normal punishment for a long time, in some western countries even well into the twentieth century. For example, in England and Wales corporal punishment as a sentence of the court was only abolished in 1948 (Rutherford, 1999).

In this paper I look first at the past, raising questions such as: how did the care of children develop, what prompted people to take initiatives in this respect (section 1), and how did the juvenile justice system come into being (section 2)? In section 3 I consider the present condition of the juvenile justice system and the most recent law reforms in some countries in our part of the world. An important and puzzling question in this respect concerns the likely causes of these reforms (section 4). Finally, in section 3 I consider possible future trends in juvenile justice, in the light of long term processes of change in western societies.

It is not until the sixteenth and seventeenth centuries that one notices an increasing consciousness that the community is to some degree responsible for orphans, foundlings, and abandoned children—that is for children who, according to our standards, are in need of protection. One of the first measures in this respect was taken in London in 1552, when Christ's Hospital was established with a capacity of 400 children (Sommerville, 1982: 21). The reputation of this institution was so good, in terms of care and education, that dozens of foundlings were placed on its doorstep every day, so that finally the institution could no longer cope. At that point the state interfered. Benefits were given to poor parents so that they would not be forced to get rid of their children, and the authorities also tried to find foster parents. However, the level of child-care was subject to considerable fluctuations. When in the seventeenth century England's financial situation was less favourable, thousands of orphans were shipped to America as indentured servants. For example, in 1619 the Virginia Colony made a contract for the shipment of orphans and destitute children from England (Howell, 1997: 5).

In The Netherlands the situation in the sixteenth and seventeenth centuries was fairly similar to that in England. Thousands of begging children roamed all over the country, many from neighbouring countries from which they had been driven out by wars, plague and famines. Because many of these children joined groups of adult beggars, vagrants and thieves for protection, they tended to adopt their lifestyle. As is the case to-day, the problem of beggars, pauperism and juvenile delinquency was mainly a big city problem. As a consequence, numerous hospices and almshouses were created in the cities. They were administered by rich merchants who performed this duty without being paid, but who had no understanding or sympathy for the children who were entrusted to their care. The almshouses were run by a warden or master and his wife, very simple people who worked for a low salary. Although the quality of the care provided was low, the orphanages were flooded with children: the Amsterdam Almoners orphanage started in 1666 with 800 children, but in 1800 there were 2,500! The youngest were placed with wet nurses and the oldest with farmers or manufacturers who had to provide food, clothing and training, requirements that were rarely met. Forced apprenticeships were everywhere considered to be an effective measure of social control for troublesome youths (Howell, 1997: 5).

Another rather popular solution was to send young boys to sea (there was a similar practice in England). When companies faced a shortage of men on their ships, pressure was put on the expensive orphanages to provide boys for the merchant navy. At specific times the older boys were gathered together and their eventual entry into service with the companies was discussed. We can safely assume that some force was used to convince the boys, because many of them did not want to go to sea; the conditions were such that only 50 per cent of them survived (ter Schegget, 1976: 89, 95).

However, all in all there was some improvement in the care given to children in the sixteenth and seventeenth centuries. It was a time of fundamental social change and the emergence of the central state. State intervention was gaining in importance, which was reflected in, among other things, the approach to social problems and to ways of raising children (Ariès, 1973). This was not always based on altruistic motives. It was partly the result of self-interest because the mass of abandoned children roaming over the country caused a lot of trouble to citizens. On the whole, however, attempts were being made to develop sounder policies in this respect and the level of child-care in general and child protection in particular was slowly raised.

Similar considerations apply with respect to juvenile delinquency. On the one hand juveniles were punished in ways we consider barbaric today; but on the other hand some documents show that the courts, when dealing with children, did take their age into account. In the sixteenth century corporal punishment was normal for adults and children alike, including flogging, cutting a thumb in the case of pickpockets, branding and pillorying. However, an interesting study of penal practice in Utrecht in the sixteenth century shows that the court documents do not mention any children below the age of 12 (Penders, 1980: 87). The author concludes that children of this age either did not appear in court, or received such light punishment that it was not worth registering. This practice suggests that, even in the sixteenth century, children below the age of 12 were not considered as criminally responsible; in fact, they appeared in court exclusively as witnesses or as victims. Children between age 12 and 15 received milder punishments than adults. For example, they were mainly sentenced to floggings 'in the presence of the court', which means that they were punished behind closed doors and not in public. In the case of recidivism, punishment was more severe and might include the pillory or banishment in addition to flogging. From age 15 there was no more distinction between young people and adults, and both could be convicted and sentenced to the death penalty.

The growing interest in socialisation processes in the seventeenth century was reflected in a flow of pedagogical literature, mainly addressed to aristocratic and rich parents. At the same time the school system gained in importance and included a growing number of children. Children came to be viewed as individuals, and parents were expected to exercise proper supervision and discipline and to instil in them respect and obedience to authorities. However, real change did not come until the eighteenth century when the ideas of the enlightenment, based on humanity and the use of reason, and culminating in the French revolution, spread all over Europe and the United States. One of its consequences, in terms of reactions to crime, was a growing opposition to corporal punishment, which was rejected not only because of its cruelty but also because the spectacle of such public punishments was distasteful to many and increasingly intolerable. The first element to disappear was the pillory, followed by forced labour in public view. Next, the gallows were displaced from the city centre to the outskirts of the city. Finally, executions were no longer carried out in public. In addition it was felt that behavioural change could not be realised by harsh coercive measures, but had to be achieved by the force of internal norms of behaviour. Corporal punishment was considered not only to be barbaric but also to be ineffective. New ideas of resocialisation and rehabilitation were developed and psychological interventions came to be preferred to physical punishment. The new rationalism looked for interventions that would have a more profound effect on the behaviour of children as well as being more humane. It was essentially based on two notions or beliefs.

The first was that deviance and delinquency are caused not so much by the child's innate wickedness, as by its environment. Poverty, neglect and abandonment would lead to vagrancy, deviancy and finally to delinquency. The second was the optimistic illusion that anti-social behaviour could be banned from society by taking the correct measures.

In England, the London Philanthropic Society was founded in 1788:

> for the Prevention of Crimes, and for a Reform among the Poor, by training up to Virtue and Industry the Children of Vagrants and Criminals, and such who are in the Paths of Vice and Infamy.

Its institution accepted without distinction juvenile delinquents as well as poor and abandoned children (Schlossman, 1995).

The juvenile institution,[1] which seemed indeed the ideal solution to the reformers, was developed in the western world in the eighteenth century and flowered in the nineteenth century (see also Hay & Stafford, ch 4 in this volume). Views on the importance of a structured and orderly upbringing (Ariès, 1973) found their counterpart in the isolation of an orderly institution with iron discipline. The child would be successfully re-educated through education and labour. The institution would offer security and form an ideal environment for training and moral development, both for children in need of protection and for delinquent children. On the basis of these ideas large institutions were founded, first for orphans and later for neglected, vagrant and delinquent children. The philosophy underpinning this reform can be summarised as follows (Platt, 1969: 54):

—The children had to be separated from alcoholic, wayward and corrupting parents or adults.
—They were to be taken away and placed in institutions which combined guidance and affection with firmness and restraint.
—There was no need for legal rights because they were not punished, but re-educated in their 'best interests'.
—The children should be placed in the institution for an indeterminate period (often until their majority), until they were reformed.
—Reform did not mean sentimentality: the child should if necessary be punished.
—The children had to be protected from idleness, indulgence and extravagance by physical exercise, constant supervision and discipline.

---

[1] Different names were used for these institutions, such as youth penitentiaries, reform schools, industrial schools, houses of refuge, penal colonies, etc.

—Institutions had to be built in the countryside, far from the corrupting city.
—Labour, education and religion should be essential elements of the re-education process.
—The values of austerity, thrift, industry, prudence, realistic ambitions and adaptability were to be taught.

As far as The Netherlands is concerned the trends were similar. At the beginning of the nineteenth century the country suffered an economic depression which caused great poverty among the lower classes and increased child protection problems. In response to this a later governor-general of the Dutch Indies, Van den Bosch, decided in 1818 to force vagrants, paupers and beggars to develop uncultivated regions in the north of The Netherlands. In 1822 King William I issued a Royal decree stating that all children aged 7 and over who were in the charge of the authorities should be brought to Veenhuizen, an agricultural colony in the north. In 1824 the first shipload of orphans and foundlings were transported to Meppel. However, the living conditions in the labour camps were such that the children, who were weak and in bad health, contracted all kinds of illnesses and handicaps. A growing movement of protest and opposition finally put an end to the situation. One of the Dutch reformers, the orthodox Protestant pastor Otto Heldring, was one of the founders of several religiously inspired institutions in 1848 and 1851, whose mission was 'to save abandoned and neglected youths'. Again, as in other western countries, no differentiation was made between residential child care and punishment of delinquent children (Dekker 1985: 13–96).

There was, however, some improvement in the care of children. State authorities began to feel concerned and several state institutions were created in the second half of the nineteenth century, although the Society for the Benefit of the Community (Maatschappij tot Nut van 't Algemeen) complained in 1898 that neglected, criminal and abandoned children continued to be locked up with adult criminals (Roeland, 1975). The Netherlands, like other western countries, considered the institution as the best solution to the problem of children in need of care as well as to that of delinquent children; this is reflected in the growth of the number of institutions from 11 in 1850 to 106 in the period 1874–1914.

Period	1800–1830	1830–1850	1850–1874	1874–1896	1896–1905	1905–1915
Protestant	4	7	16	20	25	39
Roman Catholic	2	4	19	41	47	54
State	0	0	3	2	3	7
Other	0	0	3	2	3	7
Capacity	465	876	4,067	7,504	8,857	11,998

Table 1. Number of youth institutions according to denomination and capacity
1800–1915

Source: Leonard, 1995: 52

As Table 1 shows, the number of available places increased from 465 in 1800 to about 12,000 in 1914, the increase being essentially accounted for by private institutions. Bearing in mind that in 1869 the Dutch population amounted to only 3,500,000, compared to about 16,000,000 now, the increase in the number of institutional places is indeed considerable (Van der Woude, 1985).

Several conclusions may be drawn from this history. First, it is clear that from the sixteenth century onwards, the conviction grew that besides the family, the community had a responsibility for deprived children, which it could not dismiss. Second, people slowly came to recognise the importance of environmental factors and thus the conditions in which children are raised. Third, authorities came to realise that a situation in which children continued to be victims of society's social organisation was altogether unacceptable. Fourth, corporal punishment was increasingly seen as morally wrong and ineffective as a preventive measure. Finally, high expectations were placed on the institution, where children would be taught Christian values and norms and useful labour. Unfortunately, the practice of the reformatories, all over the western world, hardly met these expectations (Rothman, 1971; Leonard, 1995). A consequence of the enormous size of the institutions, the emphasis on discipline, the many punishments involving violence and isolation, was that the central rehabilitative aim disappeared in favour of another dominant goal: the preservation of law and order within the institution. Despite the undoubtedly good intentions of reformers, the institutions degenerated into youth prisons, characterised by constant overcrowding, large dormitories, strict work schedules, rigid discipline and punishment, and very, very little real education.

2. THE JUVENILE COURT

Different reform movements were active in the second half of the nineteenth century. In the United States one group of progressive reformers were called 'charity workers' and later called themselves 'social workers'. Their approach was individualistic in that they wanted to extract the child early from the harmful effects of the city. One of their leaders, Charles Loring Brace, who was a critic of the large institutions and founded the New York Children's Aid Society, removed homeless children from the city slums and placed them with foster families. He wanted to prove the effectiveness of foster placements as an alternative to the institution. The children had to work in exchange for board, religious training and education. A regular control system was created to prevent abuse (Howell, 1997: 9).

A second group, the Chicago progressive reformers, considered that to combat deprivation and delinquency one had to take into account the urban environment and the community setting. They campaigned for compulsory schooling and for the abolition of child labour.

The reform movement which spread in the United States, but also in Canada and Europe, was essentially the outcome of two important developments. First, the urge to rescue children from *damaging* living conditions in an increasingly urbanised and industrialised environment. And second, a change in the conception of childhood, which is related to social and economic change.

In the pre-modern world communities were highly structured and regulated. The social status of families and their members was determined by their position in the social network, and the family had an authoritarian structure. Group values controlled the individual. One of the major consequences of the Industrial Revolution and the change to a capitalistic market economy was the decline of this family structure and a growing emphasis on individual values (Stearns, 1975; Shorter, 1975). The family was no longer an economic production unit. The father's absolute authority and control over his children declined, since he could no longer provide for professional training and direct supervision (Smelser, 1959). According to Shorter, the market economy stimulated individualism: the struggle for life meant that one could no longer take into account the interests of the local community, the norms of group loyalty and obligations towards the extended family. In the family economy of pre-modern society cruelty and abuse of children were private matters and of no concern to authorities. When children started to work in factories, however, the conditions of child labour were a public matter and were perceived as a problem. Many parliamentary and other surveys were conducted into the working conditions of children, finally leading to protective legislation both for children and women.

One of the consequences of the decline of the economic role of children, as well as new professional requirements for the labour market, was the creation of a compulsory school system. This meant that children came into a world which was separated from that of adults, and which helped to emphasise the importance of the individual child or young person and his right to protection and education. In addition, it was felt that the state should intervene and take over the parental role (*parens patriae*), when parents abused their power or neglected their children. A firm belief in education and rehabilitation, and the growing role of the state, between them set the stage for legislation to provide separate legal procedures and disposals for children, including children in need of protection and juvenile delinquents.

One of the first countries to create a modern child protection system was Norway, with its law on the treatment of neglected children, enacted in 1896. The first juvenile court was established in Chicago in 1899 by the Juvenile Court Act. The first juvenile justice legislation in Canada was the Juvenile Delinquents Act of 1908. Belgium, France and Switzerland enacted new legislation in 1912. Not all countries adopted the American juvenile court model. Although the first Dutch children's laws, specifying the conditions which would justify state intervention by limiting parental authority, date from 1901, the institution of the juvenile judge and the supervision order as a civil protection measure were not established until 1922. In France specialised juvenile court magistrates were only established after World War II (Trépanier, 1999).

However, the characteristics of the juvenile jurisdiction as it spread over the western world are essentially the same, whether it involves a separate juvenile court, a juvenile judge or a welfare board, as in Scandinavian countries.

—Large discretionary powers, based on the notion of *parens patriae*. All agents of the system, including the juvenile judge, the juvenile police and the public prosecutor, are supposed to act 'in the best interests of the child'.
—The principle that punishment should be proportional to the offence is rejected.
—The interests of the individual child predominate, which makes it possible to impose a civil measure, such as a supervision order, in penal cases. In this way the juvenile judge helps to put into one category juvenile delinquents and children 'threatened by physical or moral danger'.
—A heavy emphasis on treatment instead of punishment. Later on this led to broadly supported extra-judicial practices to avoid court proceedings, on the part of both the police and the public prosecutor.
—Considerable efforts are made to reduce the formal character of court procedures.
—Hearings are not public, procedures have an informal and confidential character, the privacy of the juvenile is protected.
—In view of the principles of treatment, rehabilitation and protection in the child's best interests, no need was felt for legal procedural rights of the kind that existed for adults.

The ideal was that of a juvenile judge who—like a medical doctor or a psychologist—would make a diagnosis of the child's problems and needs, and then take whatever measures or impose whatever treatment would be suitable to those needs.

The separate juvenile justice system was certainly based on humanitarian concerns. It displays increased consideration for the well-being of children as well as more respect for their individual personality. It had its heyday in the twentieth century, and its philosophy remained practically unchanged in most of the western world until the 1970s.

The establishment of the juvenile court did not mean that juvenile institutions were abolished. Juvenile reform schools were created all over the United States, and increasing numbers of children were sent to them (Howell, 1997: 14). This movement was encouraged by the fact that, within 10 years of the Juvenile Court Act, new legislation was enacted defining incorrigibility, growing up in idleness, gambling, loitering, begging and running away as so-called 'status offences', which allowed the intervention of the juvenile court. As a consequence many children continued to be placed in large institutions for indeterminate periods during the first half of the twentieth century. Although similar behaviours could be observed in Europe, two important differences with the American system made continental juvenile justice somewhat more benign. First, such behaviours were not defined as offences in Europe; and second, most continental countries did not have indeterminate sentences.[2] However, in Europe as in the United States, the child remained a powerless object in the hands of a paternalistic and patronising judge. It was the landmark US Supreme Court's ruling in *in Re Gault* in 1967 that triggered a reform in this respect, prompting other western legislation to grant children due process rights (*in re Gault* 387 US 1967). Moreover, the growing youth emancipation in the second half of the twentieth century led to a drastic reduction in court interventions and institutionalisation. Police dismissals and extra-judicial diversion programmes were encouraged, reducing the number of children appearing in court. In addition, the disappointing results of institutional treatment and the depressing outcomes of placement in large institutions in terms of reconviction and mental health, affected the confidence people had placed in the institutional ideal. As a consequence, in order to avoid court proceedings and institutionalisation, possibilities of diversion at the police and prosecutor level were enlarged, and many new welfare agencies provided for non-institutional treatment and alternative solutions to court appearance.

3. CHANGES IN THE UNDERLYING PHILOSOPHY

This system—called the welfare system—persisted until about the 1970s. By then, however, the system had become obsolete as a consequence of significant social changes in western society since the 1950s, such as increasing prosperity, higher levels of education, technological change, and emancipation movements touching women and youth, but also homosexuals, (mental) patients and prison inmates. People no longer accepted the absolute authority of a paternalistic judge over the lives of their children, nor did the adolescents themselves. The first country to change was the United States through the famous ruling *in Re Gault* (1967) granting juveniles due process rights, such as notice of the charges, right to counsel, right to confrontation and cross-examination, and the privilege against self-incrimination. Although the Supreme Court in the Gault case did not challenge the separateness of the juvenile court, this ruling was the starting point for a gradual blurring of the distinctions between criminal court and juvenile court. It also meant the disintegration of the essentially protective system, based on the principle that the delinquent was primarily a victim of circumstances and environment. Since relative independence and more rights usually go together with more obligations and accountability, the juvenile justice system rediscovered free will and reaffirmed young people's responsibility for their actions. Disappointment with treatment results in general and with institutional treatment in particular (Martinson, 1974) affected confidence in therapeutic interventions and prepared the minds for a renewed emphasis on retribution and punishment.

---

[2] Indeterminate sentences did and do exist for mentally disturbed offenders. Such sentences are now regularly reviewed by the director of the psychiatric penitentiary and by a court of law.

Two American theorists should be mentioned in this context: Van den Haag (1975) and Von Hirsch (1976). Van den Haag defends two ideas. First, despite a lack of empirical evidence, he maintains that punishment deters people from committing crimes. Second, he claims that retributive punishment is indispensable for maintaining the social order. Thus our efforts should concentrate not on rehabilitating offenders but on punishing them.

However, the neo-classical retributive principles are best expressed by von Hirsch (1976) in *Doing Justice: The Choice of Punishments*, the report of a Commission set up to reform the American system of indeterminate sentences. The commission designed a system based on three related principles. First, the principle of *'just deserts'*, meaning that the convicted person should receive the punishment he deserves, based on the seriousness of the committed offence and his criminal record. Second, the principle of *proportionality*, which is to say that the punishment should be directly proportional to the seriousness of the crime. Third, the principle of *equality*, stating that like cases should be treated alike. Although the aim of Von Hirsch and his colleagues was to achieve a fairer, more just and more lenient sentencing system, politicians and justice officials used the theory to justify harsher sentencing policies.

Summarising the main characteristics of the juvenile justice system as it was changed in the last decades of last century, the following elements are of central importance:

— The offender is (again) viewed as a rational being with a free will. Consequently he is seen as fully and individually responsible for his actions.
— This goes together with more severe penal interventions, at the expense of protection and treatment.
— The victim has become a central figure in legal procedures, leading to an emphasis on restitution and reparation for the harm done.
— Due process rights for juveniles have led to considerably more formal justice proceedings than was the case before.
— Although there is an increase in transfers from juvenile to adult court, differences between the criminal justice system and the juvenile justice system have been greatly reduced.
— Because of the increasing use of incarceration for more serious offenders, extra-judicial procedures and community sanctions are limited to non-serious offenders.

A retributive criminal and juvenile justice system was developed in the 1980s and the 1990s, with a heavy emphasis on punishment, and a secondary role for rehabilitation. This happened first in the United States and Canada and then spread to Europe.

In the United States important revisions of juvenile justice legislation took place in more than 90 per cent of the states between 1992 and 1995 (Snyder & Sickmund, 1999). These involved the increased use of transfers to adult criminal courts and a greater use of adult sentences, including imprisonment. Accountability was increasingly translated into punishment and (long term) incarceration. Between 1992 and 1997 all but three states changed their laws, making transfers of juvenile offenders to adult criminal court easier, giving courts more (adult) sentencing options and making records and proceedings more open to the public. Offenders charged with specific offences face automatic transfer to criminal court and in 20 states transfer is possible for any offence. Some states have adopted mandatory sentences for juvenile offenders. In 19 of 47 states the minimum age of transfer to criminal court is 14, in six it is 13, in two 12 and in Kansas and Vermont it is as low as 10. Offence-based dispositions and mandatory sentences result in long-term incapacitation. Confidentiality of procedures and dispositions is no longer guaranteed, the aim being to heighten pressure on offenders by increasing public awareness of juvenile criminal behaviour. There has been an unprecedented growth, unparalleled in any other western country, in incarceration and the building of secure facilities.

If we compare Canada to the United States, some differences in juvenile justice philosophy and practice do appear. Canada was facing two major problems: the over-use of juvenile court for minor offences and the over-use of custody for youths (Doob & Sprott, 1999). Despite variations between provinces, Canada had high rates of youth incarceration, mainly due to a lack of other options for young offenders. In 1998 the federal government decided to introduce a new law to replace the Youth Offenders Act of 1982, which had been denounced as being too soft. The Youth Criminal Justice Act was enacted in 1999, making accountability one of the leading themes and placing more emphasis on the offence than on the offender (Trépanier, 1999). However, contrary to some expectations, the age of criminal responsibility (12) was not lowered. Children below the age of 12 continue to be dealt with by child welfare agencies. Sentencing guidelines for juvenile judges were not introduced, since these had been rejected for adults (Roberts, 1999). Transfer to adult court had to follow elaborate procedures and was limited to a small group of serious violent and sexual offenders. Since almost all juveniles could be dealt with under the new Act, Doob and Sprott (1999) expect that not many more juveniles than are currently transferred to adult court (about 100) will be given adult sentences. Moreover, the new Act introduces more possibilities for dealing informally with cases out of court, such as alternative community-based approaches.

In addition, the new law allows for variable implementation of several provisions and has allocated funds to provincial authorities to promote juvenile justice initiatives, encouraging the development of alternative dispositions.

Legislative reviews are also taking place in Europe. The French and Belgian governments are expected to introduce new legislation. England has already done so. The Crime and Disorder Act 1998 abolished the common-law assumption that children under 14 were 'incapable of doing evil', the *doli incapax* principle, introducing the notion that children can be held accountable for their actions from the age of 10. New 'prevention' orders for young children are the Child Safety Order, Child Curfews and the Parenting Order. Reprimands and

Final Warnings will replace the cautioning scheme, which was considered too soft. By eliminating police discretion, these might lead to substantial increases in the number of prosecutions (Rutherford, 1999). In addition, in many cases the courts have no longer the option of a conditional discharge—used in about a third of all cases—thereby seriously limiting their discretion. Children between 10 and 16 may be detained on remand and a new Detention and Training Order can be imposed on 10 and 11-year old persistent offenders and on all 15–17 year old offenders. However, although the sentencing framework for juveniles is similar to that for adults, guideline judgments developed by the Court of Appeal do not apply to young offenders, nor do mandatory minimum sentences ('two strikes and you're out'). Much is expected from the multi-agency 'Youth Offending Teams' which will prepare pre-sentence reports and intervene at every stage of the process. An additional innovation is that young first offenders are referred to 'Youth Panels', which may place requirements on the offender and his parents in the form of a 'contract'. The English approach, whilst more punitive than in most other European countries, seems to be more pragmatic than the American one, and clear efforts are being made to develop a consistent and graduated approach to juvenile crime. In addition, the English government is investing considerable resources in prevention policies.

In The Netherlands, new juvenile justice legislation was enacted in 1995. Out of court disposals and community sanctions were introduced, and the powers of the police and the prosecutor in these procedures were carefully spelled out. At the same time more punitive interventions have been made available for serious delinquents. The maximum length of detention, which was six months, has been doubled for juveniles aged 12–16 (to 12 months) and quadrupled for those aged 16–18 (to 24 months). By far the most important change concerns the possibility of transfer to adult court. Under the old law three conditions had to be met: the offence committed had to be serious, there had to be aggravating circumstances, such as the commission of the offence with adults, and the offender had to have an adult or mature personality. Under the new law one of these conditions is sufficient for transfer to adult court. Penal treatment measures in special institutions, which may extend to a maximum of six years, are introduced for very serious, violent and sexual offenders needing treatment. The new law led to an increase in the number of 16 to 18 year olds held in adult prisons, longer average detention periods in juvenile institutions and a building programme for more secure places. There are more worrying trends. There is a new focus on children below the age of 12, on the grounds that there is supposedly an increase in delinquency in that age group. In a special project, called STOP, police officers can arrest the children, then invite parents to a meeting and propose to them some intervention by social workers on their behalf. At present the intervention requires the parent's voluntary acceptance, but we don't know what the future will bring. Both the increased transfer of juveniles to the adult court and STOP suggest a lowering of penal responsibility from age 12 to age 10, as well as a lowering of penal majority from age 18 to age 16. Moreover, two

laws on *Penitentiary principles* have recently been enacted, which hardly differentiate between adults and minors, suggesting the redundancy of the juvenile
justice system in this respect.

4. SOME CAUSES OF CHANGES IN THE JUVENILE JUSTICE SYSTEM

One of the main manifestations of increased severity of punishment is the number of adults and juveniles incarcerated. Table 2 shows the trend in custody in
eight European countries between 1980 and 1997, including adults, juveniles
and mentally disturbed offenders.

	1980	1985	1990	1995	1996	1997
Netherlands	23	33	44	67	75	87
Belgium	56	64	66	76	76	82
Germany*	91	95	82	81	83	90
France	66	78	82	89	90	90
England and Wales	86	93	90	99	107	120
Denmark	63	65	63	66	61	62
Sweden	55	52	8	66	65	59
Italy	56	73	57	87	85	86

*from 1995 including the former East Germany

Table 2. Detention rates per 100,000 population, including juveniles and the
mentally disturbed

Source: Ministry of Justice 2000: 11

Some countries do show considerable stability, such as Denmark and Sweden,
demonstrating the Scandinavian humanitarian tradition. This is also true in
Germany, albeit at a higher level. The Netherlands and England and Wales dramatically increased their institutionalised population, with England having by far
the highest rate of detention. The huge increase in The Netherlands is partly
explained by the low incarceration level that had been maintained for a long time.

The question is: why did this happen? What rationale could justify the drastic change from a welfare model, via a justice model towards a pure criminal
justice model in so many western countries. In this respect the following
hypotheses have been advanced (see also Tonry, 1999).

Many think that the increasingly harsher system is a consequence of the rise
in juvenile crime. Although juvenile crime did substantially increase between
1950 and 1980 in most western countries, the bulk of it was property and petty
crime. Furthermore there is no evidence that there has been a similar rise in the
1980s and 1990s. Victimisation studies in the United States show quite stable
rates of violent crimes committed by juveniles between 1980 and 1996. Police
arrest data for the period 1993–1997 indicate an increase in arrests for drug use,

but a decline for property offences and serious violent crime (Snyder & Sickmund, 1999). As far as The Netherlands is concerned, police figures show considerable stability between 1982 and 1990, and some increase in property crime, vandalism and violence between 1994 and 1998. Although theft with violence seems to have declined by about 20 per cent, violence against persons has increased by 60 per cent. Self-report figures also indicate some increase in violence against persons, although mainly with respect to less serious offences (Schreuders, Huls *et al*, 1999). A recent study of trends in violent crime in The Netherlands compared police statistics and victimisation data, finding very different trends in the two sets of data (Wittebrood & Junger, 1999). Whilst according to police data violent crime is increasing, victimisation surveys do not corroborate this finding and even show a decrease since the 1990s. Taking into account other sources, such as hospital records, the authors conclude that the increase in violent crime as shown in police figures is partly due to more efficient registration of crimes by the police, increased computerisation and greater willingness in the population to report these crimes to the police. They argue that the registered increase in violent crimes is real, but not nearly as high as suggested by police figures. A similar conclusion was reached in an analysis of violent juvenile delinquency in a number of European countries (Junger-Tas, 1996).

Another hypothesis is that the general stability in juvenile (and adult) crime rates is the consequence of more severe sanctioning policies. Proponents of this theory believe that deterrence and incapacitation do reduce crime. In fact between 1985 and 1995 data based on police statistics as well as on victimisation surveys in The Netherlands show an annual increase in crime of about 1 per cent per year. Taking into account population increase, registration effects and a greater tendency to report offences to the police, the increase amounts to only 0.5 per cent (Kester & Junger-Tas, 1994). The considerable expansion of prisons and youth institutions started in the 1980s, when crime rates were in fact stabilising. In addition, the need for cell capacity undergoes considerable fluctuations. For example, in 1999 the Dutch Minister of Justice had to admit in parliament that 1,200 cells were unoccupied. As a result, part of that prison capacity has now been converted into youth accommodation. In fact American research has since long established that the manipulation of penalties has little or no effect on crime rates (President's Commission of Law Enforcement and Administration of Justice, 1976; Tonry, 1994: 163–80; Howell, 1997: 193–9). On the basis of the empirical evidence, we can conclude that the two factors vary independently of each other: increases or decreases in crime have very little to do with criminal justice policies.

A different explanation is that the new faith in harsh punishments is a consequence of increased mass media attention to serious, rare and heavily dramatised crimes. As Tonry notes:

> We know that ordinary citizens base their opinions on what they know about crime from the mass media and as a result that they regard heinous crimes and bizarre sen-

tences as the norms, they believe sentences are much softer than they are, and they believe crime rates are rising when they are falling. As a result majorities nearly always report that judges sentences are too lenient (Tonry 1999: 10).

The mass media not only report immediately every spectacular—violent or sexual—crime, but focus on its exceptional character and overstate the frequency of its occurrence, thereby grossly distorting people's views on crime in general. In addition, they only rarely try to explain in a non-sensational way some of the reasons behind, for example, violent crime. In this way the media contribute to the creation of a climate of fear of crime, where people believe that crime is fast increasing and that deterrence and retribution are needed to maintain an acceptable level of social peace.

An additional problem in this respect is that even politicians are frequently led by the media. They feel that the media represent the public's feelings, and base their political actions on the issues figuring in the media headlines. They contribute to the shaping of public opinion and put pressure on prosecutors and judges to be firm and pronounce more severe sentences. The latter are not insensitive to the pressure of public opinion and also tend to support more repressive sentencing policies.

Finally, some explain criminal justice trends by referring to specific cycles in history, in which tolerant and repressive periods alternate. On this account criminal justice policies follow a 'pendulum' movement: repressive philosophies and severe punishment will pass and will be followed by more enlightened and progressive policies as well as the reverse.

Although all these explanations add to our understanding of the present situation in the field of justice, they cannot completely explain what is happening. There are additional and more fundamental movements that must be taken into consideration.

For example, examining trends in the twentieth century, it appears that practically throughout that century crime rates as well as imprisonment and institutionalisation were steadily declining in most western countries. This has been calculated for The Netherlands by van Ruller and Beijers (1995): see Figure 1. It is not until the 1980s that the rate of imprisonment starts to increase.

Van Ruller and Beijers (1995) argue that the main reason for the decline in imprisonment was a slow shift in people's perception of what is sufficiently harsh punishment for a crime, in the same way as people's sensitivity to pain and suffering has been increasing. For example, while in The Netherlands in the 1850s prison terms of five years were seen as long, in the 1970s and 1980s prison terms of six months and more were seen as long. Heightened sensitivity to the degree of suffering that had to be imposed in order to satisfy the need for retribution led to a systematic reduction in the length of prison terms by several means, such as early release (for good behaviour), suspended sentences and the power given to the prosecutor to deal with growing numbers of cases out of court. As recently as 1988, 87 per cent of all minor infractions and 64 per cent of

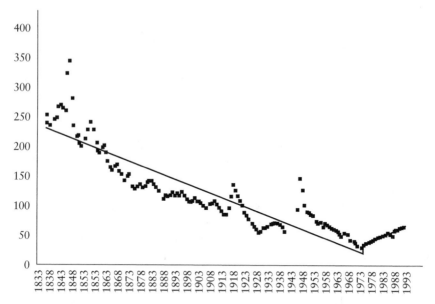

Figure 1. Average daily population in all types of institutions per year and per 100,000 population aged 15–64, including prisons, jails (since 1846), state institutions for juveniles (since 1883) and mental institutions (since 1929)
Source: van Ruller & Beijers, 1995: 38

all crimes were dealt with by the police and the prosecutor, without any court appearance. However, according to Gurr (1981, 1989) the double decline in crime and imprisonment is due to the industrial revolution and the development of an industrial economy. This implied the creation of institutions such as schools, factories and the military, socialising children and adults into essential values of conformity, discipline and obedience and preparing them to perform their role in the modern economy and state. These two explanations are in fact not mutually exclusive and may be related.

Returning now to the present trend of meting out more severe punishments both to adults and to juveniles, my hypothesis is that this trend must be related to some profound changes in the economic, technological and social make up of western societies. In this context I will note three important phenomena which may be distinguished but are in fact related. These are the penetration and pervasive influence of the market economy, changes in the labour market due to the technological (IT) revolution, and mass immigration.

Of course western society has long been based on a market economy. However, after the Second World War and until the end of the 1970s the market's negative effects on people's well-being were dampened by an elaborate welfare system which gave a significant interventionist but generally benevolent role to the state. When, as a consequence of several recessions, this balanced system was in danger of collapse, drastic measures were taken to dismantle it in many, though not all, western countries. The role of the state declined, the state withdrew (much of) its financial support to welfare organisations, education, health and housing, expecting private enterprise to take over. Without denying the necessity and benefits of this development in terms of economic growth, it also had a number of negative consequences. One is increasing social and economic inequality and a growing class of people living in the margins of society. Another is that the breakdown of the welfare system, including its many social agencies, has created a void which is now increasingly filled by justice initiatives, such as diversion programmes, community sanctions and local justice bureaux, where prosecutors and police do justice at the local neighbourhood level. In this context it is worth noting that the Scandinavian countries, including Finland, which continue to have a strong welfare tradition, still have very low imprisonment rates. In addition, countries which have not as yet developed a fully fledged punitive justice and control model, such as France and Germany, are also the last continental countries to dismantle their welfare system. On the other hand, countries which tend to adopt a more liberal and curtailed welfare system, such as the United Kingdom and also The Netherlands, have seen their detention rates skyrocketing.

A second factor is the gradual disappearance of unskilled labour and the emergence of a strong service sector. Compared to the unskilled labour market the new jobs require considerably more training, flexibility, adaptability to changing circumstances and high verbal, social and communication skills. Increasing interdependence among people and institutions requires a controlled environment, reliable and predictable interactions, and a rejection of the use of violence within society. This is why modern society stresses strong control of emotions, a more deliberate and rational approach to problems and a strong emphasis on internalised moral norms of behaviour. One result is high unemployment rates among those who cannot meet these requirements and increasing marginalisation of specific population groups. Furthermore, to the extent that there is a discrepancy between the behavioural requirements of post-industrial society and individual abilities to meet them, deviant and delinquent behaviour may occur.

Finally, a third important factor is mass immigration, both in North America and in western Europe. The United States and Canada have long been immigration countries. In the nineteenth century most immigrants came from Europe, but since 1950 about 18 million immigrants, most of them of non-European origin, came to the United States. In the same period Europe received 15 million immigrants, most of whom were recruited as unskilled factory workers (Yinger, 1994: 31). In fact immigration has never stopped, and at present there is a continual flow of third world labourers and asylum seekers to the western world. The consequences of these population movements are many. First, it is clear that they will affect the composition of the population. For example, in the United States there are large regions where the majority of the population is of Hispanic origin, where the main language is no longer English but Spanish. In Holland's big cities the majority of children below the age of 15 belong to ethnic minorities. Similar trends are apparent in other big European cities, such as Paris and London. Second, as already mentioned, far-reaching changes in the labour market particularly affect these groups, resulting in very high unemployment rates and a growing number of segregated and deteriorated city areas housing an 'underclass' population (Eisner, 1995).

My hypothesis is that these changes undermine society's stability and social cohesion, producing widespread feelings of insecurity and fear. These feelings are then projected particularly onto two groups: a very loosely defined group of ethnic minorities, including refugees and foreign labourers; and those who clearly destroy social peace and social cohesion to an even greater extent—the deviant and the criminal.

Returning to Gurr's arguments, where can we now find the social institutions that should educate and socialise these non-integrated persons into behavioural conformity, adequate social functioning, and respect for the prevailing value system? The education system, in particular vocational training schools, which should prepare lower class children for the labour market and instil in them the necessary behavioural norms and values, has not been able to shift gear and seems to be incapable of meeting the challenge. Big factories have to a great extent disappeared. National military conscription, which played a useful role in offering additional training to unskilled youths, has been replaced by a professional army. The only norm enforcing system that remains in full force and has the pretension to fill the void is the criminal and juvenile justice system. Indeed we can see that the criminal justice system is increasingly intervening in people's lives, not just by putting them in institutions, but also by extending its operations and control in the community. To the extent that social unrest, feelings of insecurity, fear of the future are still prevalent, people will continue to demand that the criminal justice system fulfil the role of pacifying society and re-establishing social cohesion.

5. FUTURE PERSPECTIVES

So what will happen in the immediate future? That future is not entirely bleak, and I think that as far as Europe is concerned, there are some promising signs.

One hopeful sign is that the extremist position of the United States, including mandatory sentences and 'three strikes and you're out' laws, was never adopted in Europe. England has perhaps come closest to taking over the American model in this respect, but so far this has not been the case in the rest of Europe, in particular in countries such as Belgium, France, Italy and Switzerland. There are several reasons for the difference between Anglo-Saxon countries and the European continent. One is based of course on the difference in legal tradition, the tradition of mainland Europe being essentially based on the *Code Napoléon* and the *Inquisitorial* system, while the Anglo-Saxon tradition is based on the

Adversarial system. In the European legal tradition judges have considerable discretionary power, and normally take into account the personality of the offender and the circumstances of the offence committed. In addition, the philosophy of child protection is deeply rooted in most European societies, which is also reflected in their basic provisions for young mothers and children. One can even notice certain differences in juvenile justice legislation and practice in this respect between the more Southern European countries and the relatively Anglo-Saxon orientation of north-west Europe.

However, although processes of structural change have touched all post-industrialised western countries, there remain some important differences in value system between the United States and Europe, which might be related to the history of the United States as a country of immigrants. In the United States 'the individual person is the basic unit of society' (Klein, 1994: 26). Individual responsibility for all personal actions—either good or bad—as well as individual blame, is heavily emphasised. Since society is not to blame for whatever misfortune befalls the individual, the need to change society's institutions is not felt to the same degree as in Europe. It is not society but the individual who should change, preferably through counselling or treatment, but if this does not help, through punishment.

Although the individual is also important in Europe, much more emphasis has traditionally been placed on the fact that every individual is part of a family and of some specific community—a religious community, a village, a region, a country. Geographical mobility is not as widespread as in the United States; people are attached to their local environment and often do not want to move. In addition, in the second half of the twentieth century Europe has developed an extensive welfare state covering most of life's risks, such as unemployment, poverty, illness, invalidity and old age. It is clear that all this reflects a belief in the responsibility of the community towards the individual rather than individual responsibility. As far as juvenile justice is concerned, this means that to the extent that the individual responsibility of children and adolescents is reduced, protection, education and rehabilitative intervention by authorities will be stressed.

One of the consequences of increasing European unity might be that the differences in culture between the two continents will not diminish but might even grow. This might lessen the punitive tendencies that are now apparent in European juvenile justice. Another hopeful sign is the tendency to deal with as many cases as possible out of court. There are different options here.

One option is diversion: the police or the prosecutor refer juveniles to special rehabilitative programmes. If the offender meets the programme's conditions, no official report will be issued, and the case will be dismissed. In The Netherlands the number of such (police) referrals rose from 6,500 in 1990 to 17,000 in 1995. Many of these programmes include some form of mediation, work on behalf of the victim or the payment of compensation.

Another option is community sanctions. These can be imposed either by the prosecutor or by the juvenile judge. The philosophy is based on what is called 'restorative justice', suggesting that the consequences of the offence, in terms of damage or injuries, must be repaired or compensated by the offender, who can thus restore the disrupted social equilibrium. The essence of such reparation is either restitution or compensation, or non-paid work for the victim or for the benefit of the community. Most dealings with juveniles by the prosecutor or juvenile judge fall in this category. England and The Netherlands have added a variety called 'intermediate treatment' or 'training orders', including social skills training, vocational training, job placements and different kind of thera-peutic interventions. Community sanctions have become one of the major tools of the juvenile justice system. For example, in The Netherlands about 80 per cent of all sentences of the juvenile judge are community service (work projects) and training orders.

In a number of countries reparation is the outcome of mediation pro-grammes, often involving the family. If there are signs of a serious problem situation the juvenile is referred to a welfare agency. In this field a rather new intervention, developed in New Zealand and Australia, is the 'Family Group Conference', which involves the families of both the offender and the victim in a kind of moral reparation or 'reintegrative shaming' process (Braithwaite, 1989; and see Morris's chapter in this volume).

Alternatives to pre-trial detention are tested in practice, combining electronic monitoring with a training programme and/or some form of therapy.

Of course all interventions have one overriding goal, which has always been one of the aims of punishment: to bring the young person into line, to control his behaviour as far as possible, and to make sure that he will become 'a useful member' of society. Two new aspects, however, can explain the growing and pervasive impact of the criminal and juvenile justice system on society. One is that most of the control takes place in the community, thereby invading the lives of many more people than ever before. The second is that much more emphasis is placed on acquiring the professional qualities and social skills that are needed to function well in society. In this respect the juvenile justice system makes con-siderably more efforts than it used to make in educating, training and socialis-ing young people in order to make them participate fully in economic and social life. It is through these efforts that both the criminal and the juvenile justice sys-tems are taking over some of the roles that were previously fulfilled by other social and welfare agencies. This development is not without its risks, but to the extent that criminal and juvenile justice can address the social and economic welfare of those entrusted to their care in addition to conformity to its rules, we may have more to gain than to lose.

REFERENCES

Ariès, Ph (1973), *L'enfant et la Vie Familiale sous l'Ancien Régime* (Editions du Seuil, Paris).

Braithwaite, J (1989) *Crime, Shame and Reintegration* (Cambridge University Press, Cambridge).

Dekker, J J H (1985) *Straffen, Redden en Opvoeden: het Ontstaan en de Ontwikkeling van de Residentiële Heropvoeding in West-Europa, 1814–1914, met Bijzondere Aandacht voor Nederlandsch Mettray* (van Gorcum, Assen/Maastricht).

Doob, A N & Sprott, J B (1999) 'Changes in Youth Sentencing in Canada' 11 *Federal Sentencing Reporter* 262–69.

Eisner, M (1995) 'Les Conséquences sur le Crime des Structures Économiques et de leur Stade de Développement' in Conseil de l'Europe, *Crime et Economie*, 11ème Colloque Criminologique—1994 (Editions du Conseil de l'Europe, Strasbourg).

Grapendaal, M, Groen, P P & van der Heide, W (1997) *Duur en Volume— Ontwikkelingen van de Vrijheidsstraf Tussen 1985 en 1995* (Ministry of Justice, The Hague).

Gurr, T R (1981) 'Historical Trends in Violent Crime: a Critical Review of the Evidence' in M Tonry and N Morris (eds) *Crime and Justice: A Review of Research*, vol 3 (University of Chicago Press, Chicago) 295–353.

——(1989) 'Historical Trends in Violent Crime: England, Western Europe, and the United States' in T R Gurr (ed) *Violence in America: The History of Crime*, vol 1 (Sage, California).

Howell, J C (1997) *Juvenile Justice & Youth Violence* (Sage, Thousand Oaks/London).

Junger-Tas, J (1996) 'Youth and Violence in Europe' 5 *Studies on Crime & Crime Prevention* 31–59.

Kester, J G C & Junger-Tas, J (1994) *Criminaliteit en Strafrechtelijke Reactie— Ontwikkelingen en Samenhangen* (Gouda Quint, Arnhem, CBS/WODC).

Klein, M (1994) 'American Juvenile Justice: Method and Madness' 2 *European Journal on Criminal Policy & Research*.

Leonard, C (1995) *De Ontdekking van het Onschuldige Criminele Kind* (Uitgeverij Verloren, Hilversum).

Martinson, R (1974) 'What Works? Questions and Answers about Prison Reform' 35 *Public Interest* 22–54.

Ministry of Justice (2000) *Sancties in Perspeftief—Beleidsnota inzake de Heroriëntatie op de Toepassing van Vrijheidsstraffen en Vrijheidsbeperkende Straffen bij Volwassenen* (SDU, The Hague).

Penders, J (1980) *Om sijne Jonckheyt* (Rijksuniversiteit, Utrecht).

Platt, A (1969) *The Child Savers* (University of Chicago Press, Chicago).

President's Commission on Law Enforcement and Administration of Justice (1976) *The Challenge of Crime in a Free Society* (Government Printing Office, Washington DC).

Roberts, J V (1999) 'Juvenile Justice Reform in Canada' 11 *Federal Sentencing Reporter* 255–60.

Roeland, D (1975) *Zeventig Jaren Justitiële Kinderbescherming* (Sociale Academie, Afstudeer scriptie, Rotterdam).

Rothman, D J (1971) *The Discovery of the Asylum* (Little, Brown, Boston).

Ruller, S van & Beijers, W M E H (1995) 'Trends in Detentie—Twee eeuwen Gevangenisstatistiek' 21 *Justitiële Verkenningen* 35–53.

Rutherford, A (1999) 'The Sentencing of Young people in England and Wales' 11 *Federal Sentencing Reporter* 269–73.

Sanders, W B (1970) *Juvenile Offenders for a Thousand Years* (University of North Carolina Press, Chapel Hill).

Schegget, H ter (1976) *Het Kind van de Rekening—Schetsen it de Voorgeschiedenis van de Kinderbescherming* (Samson, Alphen a/d Rijn).

Schlossman S (1995) 'Delinquent Children: The Juvenile Reform School' in N Morris & D J Rothman (eds) *The Oxford History of the Prison—The Practice of Punishment in Western Society* (Oxford University Press, New York/Oxford) 325–50.

Schreuders, M M , Huls, F W M, Garnier, W M & Swierstra, K E (1999) *Criminaliteit en Rechtshandhaving 1999* (CBS/WODC, Den Haag).

Shorter, E (1975) *The Making of the Modern Family* (Basic Books, New York).

Smelser, N J (1959) *Social Change in the Industrial Revolution* (Routledge, London)

Snyder, H N & Sickmund, M (1999) *Juvenile Offenders and Victims: 1999 National Report* (Office of Juvenile Justice and Delinquency Prevention, Washington DC).

Sommerville, J (1982) *The Rise and Fall of Childhood* (Sage, Beverly Hills).

Stearns, P (1975) *European Society in Upheaval*, 2nd ed. (Macmillan, New York).

Tonry, M (1994) *Malign Neglect—Race, Crime and Punishment in America* (Oxford University Press, New York).

——(1999) 'Why are US Incarceration Rates So High?' 10(3) *Overcrowded Times* 1, 8–16.

Trépanier, J (1999) 'Juvenile Courts after 100 Years: Past and Present Orientations' 7 *European Journal on Criminal Policy and Research* 303–27.

Van den Haag, E (1975) *Punishing Criminals: Concerning a Very Old and Painful Question* (Basic Books, New York).

Von Hirsch, A (1976) *Doing Justice: the Choice of Punishments* (Hill and Wang, New York).

Wittebrood, K & Junger, M (1999) 'Trends in Geweldscriminaliteit' 41 *Tijdschrift voor Criminologie* 250–68.

Woude, A M van der (1985) 'Bevolking en Gezin in Nederland' in F L van Holthoorn (ed) *De Nederlandse Samenleving sinds 1815* (Van Gorcum, Assen/Maastricht).

Yinger, J M (1994) *Ethnicity—Source of Strength, Source of Conflict?* (State University of New York Press, New York).

3

Recent Changes in Youth Justice Policy in England and Wales

LORAINE GELSTHORPE

1. INTRODUCTION

IN THIS CHAPTER I offer an account of the changes in youth justice in England and Wales since the 1969 Children and Young Persons Act. There are a number of different routes that one could take to try and understand these changes. Many have taken an historical route—Bottoms, 1974; Morris & Giller, 1979, 1987; Bailey, 1987; Pitts, 1988; Radzinowicz & Hood, 1990; Gelsthorpe & Morris, 1994; Newburn, 1997 to name but a few, each starting from the premise that one can only understand contemporary policy developments by reference to previous developments. Implicit in some of these accounts is the idea that juvenile justice policy essentially reflects ideological struggles in penal theory.

Another way of looking at changes in juvenile justice policy and practice is to see them as a reflection of changing perceptions of crime and juvenile offenders. But such an approach provides only a superficial understanding, for conceptions of offenders themselves change in different social and political contexts. More pointedly, conceptions of offenders and changes in legislation reflect social and political debates and struggles and are inextricably bound up with changes occurring in the social and political order, and with political debates within which that social order (re)produces itself. John Clarke (1975) for instance, has argued that 'youth' is a social category which has the power to carry a deeper message about the state of society, about social and political changes, without actually employing or engaging in an overtly political discourse. Thus debates about 'youth crime' or juvenile justice' are rooted in what Antonio Gramsci would call 'civil society' (Gramsci, 1971) rather than in the political realm, but the underlying message undoubtedly remains political. In this chapter I suggest that ideological struggles on the penal front are relevant, as are struggles relating to moral education and responsibility, but that these dilemmas are shaped or mediated by historical, social and political specificities. My own route therefore is partly historical but mainly political. My argument is that whilst we may be able to understand the shape and direction of juvenile justice by reading political agendas as *reflective* of broad theoretical and moral education dilemmas, it is a social and political back-cloth which best explains choices in the development of policy. (This chapter is concerned only with youth justice in England and Wales although there are two other juvenile justice systems within the United Kingdom in Scotland and Northern Ireland.)

1.1. The Context for Change

In 1999, the total United Kingdom population was 59.5 million, of whom just over a quarter were aged under 20; the largest proportion of the overall population (over 51 million) live in England and Wales (Office for National Statistics 2001). The UK has an ageing population. Projections suggest that by 2016 it is expected that the number of people over 65 will exceed those aged under 16. In 2000, about one person in fifteen was from an ethnic minority group, and, in general, ethnic minority groups have a younger age structure than the white population, reflecting past immigration and fertility patterns.

The age of majority, and minimum voting age, is 18 years. There is compulsory school attendance until 16, but at the end of 1999, around 75 per cent of both young men and women aged 16–18 in England and Wales were in education or training (Office for National Statistics, 2001). There have been particular efforts to increase the number of young people in higher education over the past 20 years, but General Household Survey data show that, measured in relative terms, the proportions of those entering higher education from manual working families has scarcely shifted by comparison with those from professional and managerial classes (Halsey, 2000). The post-war system of Grammar Schools (for the academically able), Technical Schools (for those with more applied skills), and Secondary Modern Schools (for those with practical interests) reflected selection by tests of aptitude and ability at 11 plus. The movement for a common form of secondary schooling (one school rather than different types of schools), which began with doubts about the reliability and fairness of methods of selection, was given impetus by research evidence of links between social background (measured by father's occupation) and educational selection (Halsey *et al*, 1980). Thus throughout the 1960s, 1970s and 1980s 'comprehensive' schools were developed. In 1996–97 over 85 per cent of schools in England and 99 per cent of schools in Wales were 'comprehensive'. Recent legislative provision in England and Wales has introduced the possibility of schools 'opting out' of local authority control, however. A large number of schools have taken up this invitation—both for the increased access to funding and for the possibility of more selective entry. This policy context of a developing 'quasi market' in education arguably contributes to growing social inequalities (Alcock, Payne & Sullivan, 2000: 174–88).

Since the mid-1960s employment rates for men in the UK have gradually fallen to 79 per cent of the working age population in 1999 (27 million people) whereas among women they have risen to 69 per cent.[1] Unemployment rates are

---

[1] The figures involve men aged between 16 and 64 and women aged between 16 and 59; prior to 1972 figures were taken from the age of 15 in each case.

not uniform across the country (many inner city areas and former industrial areas have the highest rates; conversely, the lowest unemployment rates are in the South of England), but there can be as many differences within regions as between them. Nevertheless, all UK regions have employment rates above the European Union average. Younger people are much more likely than older people to be unemployed, and men are more likely to be unemployed than women. In Spring 2000, 20 per cent of economically active 16 to 17 year old males and 12 per cent of 18 to 24 year old males were unemployed (Office for National Statistics, 2001). These points are not insignificant in attempts to understand involvement in crime (Brown, 1998). Finally, I turn to crime rates. It is notoriously difficult to analyse trends in crime because of the vicissitudes of data collection (Coleman & Moynihan, 1996). Changes in the age of criminal responsibility, changes in the law, changes in time series, and changes in crime categories, for instance, all conspire to make counting difficult. This said, between 1927 and 1937, the years of economic recession and depression, the crime rate more than doubled and had nearly doubled again by 1945. In the post-war decade recorded crime per head of the population increased by only five per cent but after 1957 (in the midst of the so-called 'affluent society') there were further increases in recorded crime (Hood & Roddam, 2000). Indeed, there was reported to be an increase of over 120 per cent between 1957 and 1967, and it similarly doubled over the next decade. From the end of the 1970s to the early 1990s, the rate of increase slowed, and since 1992 the number of recorded crimes has fallen each year though it is still higher than a decade ago (Home Office, 2000). Despite this decline, however, it is still the case that offending is particularly prevalent among young people, although often not to the extent that the public think (Mattinson & Mirrlees-Black, 2000). There were about 1.7 million known offenders in 1999; most (82 per cent) were male, of whom 11 per cent were aged 17 or under (Home Office, 2000). The peak age of known offending for males in 1999 was 18 (the same since 1988). The peak age of known offending for females was 15 in 1999, having fluctuated between 14, 15 and 18 over the previous ten years. Whilst official statistics fluctuate, in a self-report survey Graham and Bowling (1995) found that among 14–25 year olds, one in two males and one in three females admitted that they had committed an offence at some time (though these were likely to be minor and property related offences rather than violent offences). It is against this background that we have seen enormous changes in the direction of juvenile justice policy.

1.2. A Brief Historical Sketch

Prior to the nineteenth century, there was relatively little formal differentiation between adult and juvenile offenders (though there is evidence of some diversionary practices in the eighteenth century; King, 1984). However, over the course of the nineteenth century, a number of developments occurred which changed this: firstly, the emergence of a discourse on juvenile delinquency as a distinct social problem; secondly, the expansion of summary jurisdiction (meaning that young offenders no longer had to be detained in adult gaols); and thirdly, the emergence of Reformatory and Industrial schools which arguably had educational principles at their core though in the context of a need for a disciplined, trained, emollient work force (Carlebach, 1970). But it was not until the 1908 Children Act that the principle of dealing with juvenile offenders separately from adult offenders finally took root in England and Wales. This Act dictated that juvenile offenders should be kept separate from adult criminals and should receive treatment differentiated to suit their special needs, that parents should be made more responsible for the wrong-doing of their children, and that the imprisonment of juveniles should be abolished. Close scrutiny of the Act, however, suggests that far from being a simple reflection of humanitarian ideas and welfare principles, it also reflected ideas and principles derived from concerns about criminal justice and crime control as well as broader concerns about the state of the nation following the Boer War.

This shift in thinking about what to do with juvenile offenders was confirmed in the Probation of Offenders Act 1907 which endorsed the principle of supervising (principally juvenile) offenders within the community, thus consolidating and extending arrangements which had already developed informally. But while imprisonment for juveniles under 14 ended in 1908, the Crime Prevention Act of the same year set up specialised institutions in which rigid discipline and training in work was to be provided in a secure environment. The first of these was at Borstal in Kent; it subsequently gave its name to numerous similar establishments.

Some small but significant changes to the provisions of the 1908 Act were made in the 1930s and these changes were of vital importance to the subsequent reforms in the 1960s. The 1933 Children and Young Persons Act enacted a statutory principle which is still in force, namely:

> Every court in dealing with a child or young person who is brought before it, either as an offender or otherwise, shall have regard to the welfare of the child or young person and shall in a proper case take steps for securing that proper provision is made for his education and training (Children and Young Persons Act 1933, s 44(1), as amended in minor particulars by the Children and Young Persons Act 1969).

Combined with a provision that no magistrate could sit in the juvenile court unless they were a member of the 'juvenile panel' (being 'specially qualified to deal with juvenile cases'), this principle fuelled magistrates' belief that they could very effectively juxtapose the principles and protections of a juridical framework with a real commitment to the welfare of juveniles.

Between 1945 and 1979, England experienced both Labour and Conservative administrations for approximately equal amounts of time. This might have been expected to lead to radical shifts from one set of policies to another, but the closing years of the war saw the development of a broad consensus. The consensus went so far as to create a post-war 'welfare state'. A child care service was set up in the Children Act of 1948—to provide Child Guidance Clinics, child psychiatric clinics and hostels. This service played a part in the merging of the neglected child and the juvenile offender. This then was the context for juvenile justice policy; there was a broad consensus, and certainly no great party political conflict. This is not to suggest that there were not at least some clamours for harsher punishment (Taylor, 1981), but gradually the arguments for a more welfare-oriented system of juvenile justice became stronger. A number of committees were set up by the government in the 1960s to think about how the system might be changed. It was as a result of the work of one of these committees that the age of criminal responsibility was changed from eight to ten (in the 1963 Children and Young Persons Act). Further reviews of the juvenile justice system by the Labour Party (which was in power at the time) led to the 1969 Children and Young Persons Act.

2. A WELFARE APPROACH

2.1. The Children and Young Persons Act 1969

The 1969 Children and Young Persons Act was a radical piece of legislation which essentially viewed an offence as a symptom of an underlying disorder or pathology, and individuals as not fully responsible for their actions; the delinquent child was a neglected, abused or deprived child and the aim was to treat or rehabilitate that child. Key features of the Act were that:

—Juveniles under the age of 14 were not to be referred to the juvenile court solely on the grounds that they had committed offences (thus bringing England and Wales into line with some other European countries). Rather, where it could be established that such juveniles were not receiving the care, protection and guidance a good parent might reasonably be expected to give, it was proposed that there should be care and protection proceedings.
—Criminal proceedings *were* to be possible against juveniles aged 14–16 who had committed offences, but *only* after consultation had taken place between the police and social service departments.
—Sentencers' power to make use of custodial sentences and Attendance Centres was to be limited and replaced by Intermediate Treatment (a range of educational and measures).

2.2. Making Sense of Change

How can we understand this transition? There is first of all what we might call the social democratic analysis: the 1960s was a significant landmark in the construction of the twentieth century social democratic settlement. The ideas of Beveridge and Keynes had consolidated and institutionalised the welfare principles initiated by the liberal government at the turn of the century (Marwick, 1982). However, the growth of the welfare state and the general affluence of post-war Britain had not been able to eradicate the pockets of deprivation and poverty which were still evident in society. The dilemma facing the Labour Government which took office in the 1960s was how to account for these problems, without jeopardising the legitimacy of a Fabian philosophy which generally accepted a capitalist economy plus a welfare state as the solution to class inequality (Clarke, 1980; Pitts, 1988).

Essentially, the argument became that the welfare state had all but eliminated primary poverty, but some people, because of individual and family inadequacies, were unable to take advantage of the opportunities offered by the welfare state. Positive discrimination in the fields of education, employment and housing would therefore deal with the last pockets of material inequality, whilst a new family service would be directed at the residuum, helping those individuals and families who had slipped through the welfare net (Clarke, 1980). Central to this social democratic analysis was the connection between delinquency, deprivation and the family. In this way, Fabian philosophy can be seen to have either reshaped or modified perceptions of the young delinquent.

An alternative analysis, of course, is one that draws heavily from revisionist historical perspectives produced by radical academic historians and sociologists who rejected notions of penal progress and unalloyed humanitarianism. The social control analysis is one in which welfare discourses are seen to justify the surveillance and regulation of working class young people by the 'judges of normality' (Foucault, 1977; Donzelot, 1980; Cohen, 1985).

There is an alternative narrative to the social democratic and revisionist perspectives, however. From 1955 onwards, England saw an unprecedented rise in the crime rate. The strengthening of the economy had led to an influx of labour from commonwealth countries—this ultimately led to race relations tensions in some areas. Also, a series of 'youth cultures' (teddy boys, bikers, mods and rockers and so on) demonstrating both the increased economic emancipation of the young and the commercialisation of that market emerged and, on occasions, got into trouble. Though their perceived profiles were far worse that their actual behaviour, there were confrontations with the police and consequently more panics about young people. Thus tension and increases in crime gradually pressed in on previously shared social policy developments.

Some people, at least, wanted tougher penalties, and a key role in preventing and controlling crime was assigned to the family. The Conservative Party and magistrates were thus united in their opposition to the 1969 Children and Young Persons Act. Some academics (Morris *et al*, 1980, for example) were also opposed to the welfare approach on the grounds that it led to far too much intervention in young offenders' lives and the lives of their families. Surprisingly, reactionaries found unlikely allies from among reformist circles in their struggles for a return to punishment within the juvenile justice system. While the 'back to justice' or children's rights movement launched an attack on the neglect of due process and on the controlling aspects of welfare responses (treatment) which they saw as harmful and unjust interference in the civil liberties of delinquents and their families, and as placing too much discretion in the hands of 'experts', reactionaries pressed home the argument that the only way to deter young offenders was to return once again to a neo-classical disciplinary solution. They simply co-opted the justice critique of welfare in many respects, and, as a result of the combined opposition and convenient changes in government, key sections of the 1969 Act were never enacted. In practice, what really emerged was a 'dual system' of 'bifurcation' (Bottoms, 1974). This involved more custody for serious and persistent young offenders and more diversion for those young offenders who had committed relatively trivial offences.

From the mid 1970s, it was argued that a new 'underclass' in British society appeared (often homeless or in poor and unstable housing, and without employment). The welfare state had not fulfilled the expectations held out for it; and the social and economic policies at the centre of the post-war reconstruction were in crisis as world recession and unemployment took root. This paved the way for an explicit revival of traditional criminal justice crime control values which hit at the root of the social welfare perspective underlying the 1969 Children and Young Persons Act.

3. A CRIME CONTROL APPROACH

3.1. The Criminal Justice Act 1982

The 'crime control' approach reflects the idea that young offenders are responsible for their actions; although a dual approach (punishment and welfare) is acceptable to a degree, what is fundamentally important is to punish in order to deter others from engaging in criminal behaviour. It also reflects the belief that strong penalties are a necessity and that some regard should be given to victims. The 1982 Criminal Justice Act was strongly influenced by punitive and bifurcatory sentencing discourses. In brief, although there was some endorsement for the expansion of diversion (cautioning) and a reduction in the minimum period of custody for which a boy could be held in a detention centre, the 1982 Act made strong moves towards the notion of personal responsibility, punishment and parental responsibility. The Act made available to magistrates three new powers of disposal: youth custody, care orders with certain residential requirements, and community service for 16 year olds. It was also to become normal practice to fine parents rather than the juvenile (Gelsthorpe & Morris, 1994).

3.2. Resistance

Interestingly enough, we know from empirical research (Burney, 1982) that magistrates often resisted the pressure to impose custodial penalties. They often dealt with juveniles as individuals with individualised or specially tailored responses and so, whilst the government propounded punishment at all costs, there was resistance on the ground. There was also a growth in intermediate treatment following a 1983 government initiative; an increasing emphasis on interagency approaches to the problem of juvenile crime (police, social services, probation and education); and, significantly, the development of a practitioner led movement (intermediate treatment workers, social workers and others) with support from some academics. This movement drew its inspiration from a variety of theoretical sources including labelling theory, just deserts theory, management or systems theory, and a view of adolescent offending as essentially transient. So the emphasis was very much on managing young people until they grew out of their delinquency, and on managing the system—to divert people from formal intrusive and custodial responses. Such a movement reminds us that theory, policy and practice may be very different and that political intentions can be thwarted to a degree, a point which is relevant to my conclusion about the political dominance of policy.

3.3. Summing-up the 1980s

In making crime a major election issue, the Conservative Party aimed to re-establish 'Victorian values' in opposition to the legacy of the supposed permissiveness of the 1960s and its 'soft' approach to crime. In such a supposedly de-moralising culture, crime and violence were seen as 'out of control'—hence the need for 'law and order' policies to reassert the virtue and necessity of authority, order and discipline and attempts to realign relationships between the state and civil society as a whole (Muncie, 1999a: 135–6). Critics of the crime control approach have focused on suggestions that it ignores social disadvantage and assumes that every juvenile or his/her family is equally responsible for criminal behaviour; the approach has also led to a high rate of custody (re-offending rates are high and there is no attempt to get to the root cause of problematic behaviour).

3.4. Moving into the 1990s

There are four main strands of developments bringing us into the 1990s which I will mention here:

(a) *Care/control*: The implementation of the 1989 Children Act and the introduction of the 1991 Criminal Justice Act had the combined effect of separating the systems for dealing with children perceived to be in need of care (to be dealt with in the family courts) and those charged with criminal offences (to be dealt with in the newly named Youth Court). Significant here was the cessation of the use of the care order as a disposal available to the court in criminal proceedings and the removal of the offence condition in proceedings justifying state intervention in the life of a family (NACRO, 1989). This change at once recognised the enormous decline in the use made of the care order, the inappropriateness of a care order in criminal proceedings, the principle of determinacy in sentencing and the importance of parental responsibility (Harris, 1991). Hence the 1989 Children Act *separated* criminal and 'care' issues in stark contrast to the 1969 Children and Young Persons Act.

(b) *Just deserts*: The 1991 Criminal Justice Act introduced wide ranging changes based on 'just deserts' thinking, whereby the aim was to ensure that the penalty was commensurate with the seriousness of the offence. Significantly, the Act created the new Youth Court with a higher maximum age limit than the previous Juvenile Court (18 instead of 17 years). There was to be no 'softening' in dealing with offenders though—adult penalties were transferred down. What is interesting here is that there is now little distinction between juvenile and young adult offenders; this marks a return to pre-1908 Children Act thinking.

(c) *Moral panic*: Public and political concerns about juvenile crime reached a pitch following highly publicised joy-riding incidents in deprived areas, and the tragic events of 12 February 1993 and their highly publicised aftermath. Two young boys (aged ten) were convicted of the brutal murder on a railway line of two-year old James Bulger. The abduction and murder of such a young child would always have had significant impact. In this case, however, the arrest and charging of the ten year olds inspired 'a kind of national collective agony' (Young, 1996: 113) and provided the strongest possible evidence to an already worried public that something new and particularly malevolent was afoot (Goode & Ben-Yehuda, 1994: chs 2–3).

(d) *Toughening up*: This trial promoted wide debate about rising crime rates, the nature and causes of juvenile crime and the need to 'get tougher'. Almost overnight, what many saw as a 'unique event' was transformed into a broader moral panic about young people. Indeed, in some public/political discourse, this most unusual and horrific of crimes became confused with the whole issue of persistent, yet less serious, offending on the part of young people. In some quarters there was refusal to see or to treat the two boys as 'children' (Warner, 1994).[2] The Conservative Party Conference later that year provided the platform for yet another 'law and order' package. This involved a reassertion of the centrality of custody in a range of measures that the Home Secretary, Michael Howard, described as having deterrence as their primary aim (Ashworth, 1997). Perhaps as a consequence of the moral panic surrounding young people, the Criminal Justice and Public

---

[2] The European Court of Human Rights in Strasbourg has criticised the boys' general treatment (including their trial in an adult court and in public) on the grounds that it breached the European Convention for the Protection of Human Rights and Fundamental Freedoms. It was believed that the boys were too young to understand the nature of the criminal proceedings or to adequately instruct their counsel.

Order Act of 1994 doubled the maximum sentence in a young offenders' institution for 15 to 17 year olds from one year to two. It introduced the possibility that parents of young offenders could be bound over to ensure that their children carried out their community sentences, and it firmly established the new 'secure training orders' involving custody of up to two years for 12 to 14 year olds. Further proposals to institute harsh remedies were announced (or leaked from Home Office sources) in February 1995—with suggestions that the Government wished to introduce American-style 'boot camps' for young offenders (Nathan, 1995). These developments occurred despite widely publicised scepticism as to the efficacy of this strategy from Home Office funded research (Hagell & Newburn, 1994), and criticisms from a number of professionals working in the field and from national voluntary organisations who between them had a wealth of experience of dealing with young offenders. But the Government of the day decided to press ahead—punitive rhetoric was in the ascendancy. At the other end of the scale, diversionary strategies were also coming under attack and in 1994 it was made clear that a 'first chance would normally be a last chance'; there would be one caution and no more. Restrictions on cautioning were subsequently introduced in the 1994 guidelines for the police.

4. MISSPENT YOUTH

A major review of government policy regarding youth justice by the independent Audit Commission[3] resulted in a report which essentially argued that the existing system (with all its emphasis on control, punishment, and law and order) was expensive, inconsistent, and ineffective. The Audit Commission's first report, *Misspent Youth* (Audit Commission, 1996), called for renewed emphasis on 'criminality prevention', and, in particular, for interventions in early life, which research suggests hold out the greatest promise of reducing youth crime. Recommendations included: speeding up the court process for young offenders; the provision of more intensive supervision for persistent offenders within the community; the need to develop diversionary programmes; more involvement for victims; better ways of addressing offending behaviour; and monitoring the impact of different interventions on re-offending. The Commission also gave emphasis to early intervention strategies, on the grounds that 'prevention is better than cure'. Recommendations here included: assistance with parenting skills; structured education for under fives; support for teachers dealing with badly behaved pupils; and positive leisure opportunities.

---

[3] The Audit Commission oversees the external audit of local authorities, probation services, police forces (except the Metropolitan Police Force) and the National Health Service. As part of this function, the Commission undertakes studies to enable it to make recommendations for improving the economy, efficiency and effectiveness of the services provided by these bodies.

It made explicit that all agencies should work together better, and that central government could help by giving local authorities a duty to lead in developing multi-agency work, allowing resources released from court processes to be put to use in local services aimed at reducing offending, and monitoring and evaluating preventive programmes.

This report was welcomed by academics and many policy-makers and practitioners alike, though there have also been trenchant criticisms. Denis Jones (2001), for example, questioned why the response was so uncritical, and argued that the Commission's report displayed a lack of understanding of youth crime and the criminal justice process. He further suggested that the Report was misleading and drew too closely on the political arguments of the day. These are important points, and it is telling that selected recommendations which involved only relatively cheap and superficial changes (for example, the need for 'speeded up justice' and greater supervision and control of young people in the community) have come to assume far more prominence in youth justice policy than the rather more resource intensive recommendations (pre-school interventions and positive leisure opportunities, for example) which would require infra-structural reform.

There are two other significant events which need to be noted in order to understand contemporary developments in youth justice. The first was the publication of a consultative document (Home Office, 1997a) on juvenile offending by the Conservative government of the day. This Green Paper can be seen as an official response to the Audit Commission Report. Whilst nodding sympathetically in the direction of early prevention (without promises of further resources to accomplish this), however, the Paper endorsed the punitive theme that the government had been pushing throughout their office. 'Parental responsibility' was the major headline following publication of the report—with the suggestion of 'Parental Control Orders' to induce parents to exert greater authority and control over their children. The second significant event was the replacement of a Conservative Government with a Labour Government in May 1997 after nearly 18 years of Conservative rule.

5. NEW LABOUR TACKLING YOUTH CRIME

The newly elected government was exceedingly quick off the mark to produce proposals. The appearance of three consultation papers—*Tackling Youth Crime, Reforming Youth Justice* (Home Office, 1997a); *Tackling Youth Crime, Tackling Delays in the Youth Justice System* (Home Office, 1997b); and *New National and Local Focus on Youth Crime* (Home Office, 1997c)—within six months of Labour's election to power came as no great surprise. The Home Secretary also appointed a multi-agency 'Youth Task Force' headed by Lord Norman Warner, senior policy adviser to the Home Secretary, in June 1997, which itself produced a report a year later which reinforced many of the points made in the consultation papers. The general tenor of these documents was to make proposals 'to improve the effectiveness of the Youth Justice system in preventing, deterring and punishing youth crime' (Home Office, 1997d: 2). The White Paper containing the main framework for the legislation was published in November 1997. Its title gives a telling clue to what lay within—*No More Excuses: A New Approach to Tackling Youth Crime in England and Wales* (Home Office, 1997d). The tone of the White Paper was no less dogmatic:

> An excuse culture has developed within the youth justice system. It excuses itself for its inefficiency, and too often excuses the young offenders before it, implying that they cannot help their behaviour because of their social circumstances. Rarely are they confronted with their behaviour and helped to take more responsibility for their actions (*ibid*: 1).

5.1. The Crime and Disorder Act 1998

The Crime and Disorder Act 1998 which resulted from this process was described as a 'comprehensive and wide-ranging reform programme' (Home Office, 1997b: 1); many of its provisions were explicitly aimed not only at young offenders, but at young people more generally. In many ways, the legislation appears to favour punishment to signal society's disapproval of criminal acts and to deter offending, but at the same time the Government remains faithful to its commitment to be 'tough on the causes of crime' by referring at times to social factors which contribute to crime and by proposing orders to prevent re-offending through interventions. The Act also contains provisions which underline support for the Government's belief in restorative justice principles (to address victims' needs). Crucially, there is what David Garland has described as a 'responsibilization strategy' (Garland, 1996: 452): that is, a desire to exercise more control from central Government, whilst passing active responsibility for crime control onto local organisations.

In a way, none of this was unexpected. The shape of the 1998 Act can be discerned in a number of *signal themes* which characterised criminal justice developments in the 1990s (Bottoms, 1995; James & Raine, 1998; Gelsthorpe & Morris, 1999). As I will show, these themes themselves reflect broad social and political ideas:

—*Just deserts*—an approach to sentencing which focuses on proportionality and consistency, but which, in the public mind, is linked to retributivism. Just deserts thinking has been increasingly influential over the last quarter century, and is epitomised in the 1991 Criminal Justice Act.

—*Managerialism*—an ethos which places emphasis on 'the system', inter-agency co-operation, strategic plans, and the delivery of services and which is frequently referred to as underpinning the three 'E's of economy, efficiency and effectiveness.

—*Risk assessment and 'actuarial justice'*—notions which involve an emphasis on the statistical probabilities of future crime (based on offence seriousness, previous offending and offenders' social characteristics) and taking anticipatory action on the basis of these.

—The incorporation of the *'community'*—which means a new focus on community penalties, and more intrusive controls in the community (for example, electronic tagging).

—*Public voice and participation*—that is, participation based on consumerism and rights, especially the notion of victims' rights.

—*Active citizenship*—which means encouragement for the shared responsibility for crime and crime prevention.

—*Restorative justice*—the central tenet of which is that crime should be seen primarily as a matter concerning the offender and victim and their immediate families and thus should be resolved by them through constructive effort (reparative measures) to put right the harm that has been done.

—*'Populist punitiveness'*—an ideology which involves not just a reflection of public opinion, but also politicians tapping into, and using for their own purposes, what they believe to be the public's punitive stance.

The 1998 Crime and Disorder Act, and the concomitant Youth Justice and Criminal Evidence Act 1999 include elements of all these signal themes.

Details of this legislation are described elsewhere (Fionda, 1999; Gelsthorpe & Morris, 1999; Muncie, 1999b; Ball, 2000; Morris & Gelsthorpe, 2000), but it is important to indicate here that there are new measures to ensure the effective functioning of the system through, for example: i) the introduction of a national Youth Justice Board—to give strategic direction, to set standards for, and measure the performance of the youth justice system as a whole; ii) local multi-agency youth offending teams who will assess young offenders' needs and deliver programmes to deal with their offending behaviour; and iii) various measures to speed up the punishment process. Such measures reflect broad *managerial* aspirations.

Under the Crime and Disorder Act, children and young people are themselves held to account: they are deemed capable of criminal liability from the age of ten; section 34 abolishes the rebuttable presumption that 10 to 13 year olds are *doli incapax* (Bandalli, 1998). There are also new measures in the legislation to ensure that offenders address their offending behaviour and reduce the *risk* to the community (through, for example, pre-court warnings which trigger interventions from youth offending teams, action plan orders, and drug treatment and testing orders), and measures to ensure protection of the community (through, for example, anti-social behaviour orders) (see NACRO, 2000). And there are measures to give attention to victims (through, for example, reparation orders) which serve to address *community interests* and *restorative justice* values. The themes of *risk assessment* and *actuarial justice*, with emphasis on the importance of taking anticipatory action on the basis of the probability of offending, are reflected in the 1998 Act's child safety orders which involve

curfews for children under 10 (Goldson, 1999: 14–15). The 1998 Act also provides for local curfew orders which apply to all children under the age of 10 in
a specific area and which prevent them meeting in specified public places
between 9 pm and 6 am unless accompanied by a parent or responsible adult.
Local authorities can impose these curfews on the grounds that such children
are 'at risk' of committing offences. It is arguable that such provisions effectively lower the age of criminal responsibility (Bandalli, 2000).

The theme of *active citizenship* is reflected in a number of ways—notably
through the 1998 Act's parenting orders (which involve guidance or counselling)
which can be imposed on parents whose children are on a child safety order, an
anti-social behaviour order or a sex offender order (see NACRO, 2000), and
which must be imposed where magistrates believe that a child under 16 may
re-offend unless the parents are instructed in how to take greater responsibility
for their offspring's behaviour (Gelsthorpe & Morris, 1999; Drakeford &
McCarthy, 2000). These orders reflect *risk assessment and actuarial justice*.

Some of the signal themes, particularly *active citizenship* and *restorative justice*, are rehearsed in the 1999 Youth Justice and Criminal Evidence Act, which
introduces a new primary sentencing disposal for 10 to 17 year olds pleading
guilty and convicted for the first time—the referral order (Criminal Justice
Consultative Council, 2001). This disposal involves referral of the offender to
the local youth offender panel—a forum seemingly removed from the formality
of the court—where a contract will be arranged with the young person to prevent further offending. Significantly, panel members may include members of
the public as 'community panel members' and contracts will include reparation
to the victim or the wider community as well as a programme of activity
designed to prevent further offending.

As for *populist punitiveness*, the New Labour agenda for criminal justice following their election to power arguably involved a shift to the right in order to
challenge the Conservative Party on its own ideological territory (Downes,
1998). Indeed, in its early election promises, it became clear that New Labour
wanted to establish itself in the public's mind as the party best equipped to introduce tough and effective measures to deal with offenders—whatever their age.
Jack Straw, then Home Secretary, argued that it was important to listen to
ordinary people in ordinary communities. He claimed that for far too long

> the concerns of those who lived in areas undermined by crime and disorder were
> ignored or overlooked by people whose comfortable notions of human behaviour
> were matched only by their comfortable distance from its worst excesses (*The Times*,
> 8 April 1998).

5.2. Explaining Recent Developments

These eight themes in themselves, of course, hold little explanatory power. They
are clearly informed by penological and crime prevention debates (in terms of

what is just and what is thought to reduce crime), but they also alert us to the social and political context in which the 'criminal justice battles' are being fought. The Labour Government's avowed attempt to 'talk tough' about crime and to say 'no more excuses' has clearly served it well in terms of assisting it to claim back 'law and order' issues from the Conservatives (Brownlee, 1998). Indeed, the main tenor of Labour criminal justice legislation between their coming to power in May 1997 and May 2000, revealed less a continuation of Labour's sympathetic thinking of the 1960s about 'children in trouble' and so on, than a 'melting-pot of principles and ideologies' (Fionda, 1999: 46) which may militate against each other rather than serving the notion of clear and consistent sentencing.

There is much evidence of contradictory thoughts regarding strategies to reduce crime and efforts to maintain political dominance through the adoption of 'crime control' and authoritarian strategies which are associated with the New Right within recent legislation. Parenting orders have the potential to be helpful in encouraging greater parental responsibility for children, for example, but effectiveness is questionable in a context where these orders are *imposed* on parents, rather than there being a voluntary educational relationship between counsellors and parents, for instance (Gelsthorpe, 1999; Robson, 2001). Restorative justice principles implicit in certain orders have the potential to be meaningful for offender and victim, but again this is questionable where orders are *imposed* on offenders without their consent, where reparative tasks become routine and where the issue of consultation with victims is sometimes overridden by the need for speedy justice (Holdaway *et al*, 2001). Recent research findings from the pilot studies in this area seem to suggest that practice is at odds with restorative values which see the offender as a key decision-maker in order for the processes to be fully 'restorative' (Dignan, 2000; Holdaway *et al*, 2001).

As Ian Brownlee (1998) has noted in his searching critique of New Labour's 'new penology', political interests (that is, vote-catching interests) are reflected in the legislation in the continuing tendency to locate the causes of crime at the level of individual failure and the continuing punitive discourse, despite rhetoric to the contrary. More significantly, he points to the dominance of managerial interests and to the tendency to 'identify, classify and manage unruly groups sorted by dangerousness' (1998: 323), and then to impose variable detention depending upon 'risk management' rather than engage in the diagnosis and then rehabilitation of individuals.

Despite a change in government, then, there appears to be little difference in the political parties' respective responses to crime and conceptions of justice. The arguments are not about 'welfare' or 'crime control' in a penological or educational sense; moreover, the new philosophies cannot be allied to the political Left or Right as they once were. The development of a new youth justice system has come to play a key part in politics, but this is 'power politics' as opposed to 'ideological politics'. It is arguable that a 'populist punitiveness' reigns (which fosters consensus around issues where dissensus or moral pluralism exists), whilst the key question of whether or not any government will commit itself to long-term strategies which really do involve a shift from repression to prevention and to penological and educational considerations remains unanswered. The prospects for a move to an enlightened approach to juvenile justice perhaps look bleak.

Another key question, of course, is why current policy is heading in a direction guided by the ballot box rather than by principles or theories of crime. It is here that I suggest that we need to turn to the foundational elements in Labour's new political agenda—authoritarianism, communitarianism, responsibilisation and remoralisation—all of which are worked through a burgeoning and incursive new managerialism (Reiner & Cross, 1991; Muncie, 1999b).[4] That is, a political agenda has emerged which recognises the need to create a new moral, social and public order based on restored communities. From this, one can see how Labour's notions of 'stakeholders' and 'individual duties and responsibilities' emerge. In other words, the foundational elements of the new Labour agenda are associated with social democratic renewal and with what Anthony Giddens (1998) has described as 'the Third Way'—a framework of thinking and policy making that seeks to adapt social democracy to a world that has changed fundamentally over the past two or three decades. The rationale for the pursuit of a 'third way' is perhaps simple enough—the dissolution of the 'welfare consensus' that dominated in industrial societies up to the late 1970s, the final discrediting of Marxism, and the deep social, economic and technological changes that helped bring these about. Put simply, it is a way which seeks to retain the benefits of market forces whilst holding on to the notion of community to care for those who fall behind.

The unfurling of Labour's criminal justice policies, then, is at one and the same time the unfurling of new social democratic principles. The idea of 'crime prevention', emphasised in the 1998 Crime and Disorder Act, is an elastic and nebulous one. It is used freely to justify policies which have social and economic as well as criminal justice implications, and to legitimate wide ranging interventions from training, education and work programmes, and drugs education, to containment in a secure environment (Muncie, 1999b). The focus on young people is perhaps as much about creating social order following social and economic transformations which leave many young people adrift, dislocated, aimless, and marginalised, as it is about the need to respond to youth crime. And, as Jack Straw has put it, one of the major planks in New Labour thinking—that of 'welfare to work'—is 'as much an anti-crime as an economic policy' (Straw, 1998: 2). There is a convenient circularity to social policies.

---

[4] There is a fascinating account of Jack Straw, Home Secretary, and the shaping of home affairs policy in Anderson and Mann (1997). It is clear that Tony Blair, now Prime Minister but previously shadow Home Secretary for a brief period, had a strong hand in the shaping of policy and that he has used the ideas of the American Communitarian movement—particularly the ideas of Amitai Etzioni—to provide intellectual credibility.

5.3. The 'Risk Society'

The social and political context described above takes us some way to a deeper understanding of changes in criminal justice policy in general, and in juvenile justice policy in particular. Further elements of this analytical avenue might include reference to the 'risk society' which arose from the huge social and economic transformations that have led to the marginalisation of youth and the creation of an underclass (Brown, 1998). At the risk of over-simplification, the 'risk society' is characterised by life in a world which is rapidly changing. For Beck:

> Risk may be defined as a systematic way of dealing with hazards and insecurities induced and introduced by modernization itself. Risks, as opposed to older dangers, are consequences which relate to the threatening force of modernization and to its globalisation of doubt (1992: 21).

Whilst the focus of key authors in this area lies primarily on 'high consequence risks' of environmental degradation and nuclear proliferation and so on, certain analysts of crime and punishment have been quick to note parallels between general 'risk management' and the translation of crime control into risk management (Feeley & Simon, 1992; Ericson & Haggerty, 1997). The 'risk thesis' as such is that, as society has become more fragmented, the focus of social control agencies (the police and other criminal justice system agencies in particular) has shifted from traditional modes of crime control and order maintenance to the provision of security through surveillance technologies designed to identify, predict and manage risks. The knowledge of risk is thus used to control 'danger'.

We can see all too clearly how concerns about risk management feature in recent Labour criminal justice legislation. In a risk society, governance is directed at the provision of security. Security is 'a situation in which a specific set of dangers is counteracted or minimised. The experience of security usually rests on a balance of trust and acceptable risk' (Giddens, 1990: 35–6), but where reality and perceived anxiety do not match (as in the aftermath of the James Bulger affair at the beginning of the 1990s) worries about loss of control can lead to exaggerated interventions. The legitimacy of such interventions is not a matter for discussion here, but the notion of the 'risk society' again enhances our understanding of recent changes in juvenile justice policy.

6. FUTURE PERSPECTIVES

My argument in this chapter is essentially that any explanation of the recent changes which have taken place in the youth justice system must give primacy to the influence of politics. As Roger Hood wrote in 1974:

the belief that expert advice based on criminological and penological research is the foundation for penal change is only a screen behind which ideological and political factors, perhaps inevitably, shape those attitudes which imbue legislation' (1974: 417).

The normative project of the 1990s and into the new millennium in the realm of youth justice thus appears to be a political project dominated by broad managerialist principles. What hope is there for the future? Whilst there is little space to expand upon these points here, there are a number of avenues which may offer some light in contrast to the rather bleak picture I have so far painted.

Firstly, the overall impact of the 1998 Human Rights Act on the practice of juvenile justice has yet to be assessed. Whether or not human rights law can help us reconstruct a normative theory of juvenile justice, of course, is a difficult question, but it is at least conceivable that the Government may be constrained in the unwarranted blaming and controlling of young people and their parents within the criminal justice system.

Secondly, there is the prospect of wise practice on the ground from those who have experience of dealing with young offenders and their families (the practitioner-led movement of the 1980s gives hope in this direction).

Thirdly, there is the possibility that the Government will further demonstrate its commitment to 'get tough on the causes of crime'. The social basis of crime is undeniable (Littlechild, 1997). The seeds of hope for a return to issues of social justice lie in the fact that the Social Exclusion Unit and the Community Development Foundation have created programmes to facilitate greater access for young people to the employment market, and have encouraged social improvement in socially deprived areas (Carpenter *et al*, 2000), though such developments run alongside oft-announced commitments to reduce public spending (Joyce, 1999: 488–9). Notwithstanding criticisms of the Audit Commission's Report of 1996, the emphasis on crime prevention within that report was welcome; it is perhaps time to recognise more fully the overshadowing of its recommendations by what many see as the Government's managerialist and punitive agenda. A growing body of research (Anderson *et al*, 1994; Hartless *et al*, 1995) has shown that young people are often victims 'more sinned against than sinning'. The prospect of an economic recession may of course limit positive social interventions, but at the same time limit criminal justice system interventions in a positive way (Garland, 1996).

Fourthly, renewed interest in the role of schools in promoting good citizenship may open the door to the possibility of an educative justification for both control and limits to control. Citizenship education in England has received considerable attention since 1997, resulting in the introduction of programmes of study for citizenship in secondary schools from the year 2002 (McLaughlin, 2000). Whilst there is an ongoing lively debate about the specific meaning and purposes of citizenship, what is interesting here is the location of the debates within educational circles. If 'citizenship' can be said to be linked to normative compliance, then this is possibly a development upon which we could build. An educative approach to youth offending, rather than a political and ultimately punitive one, gives grounds for optimism that a new normative theory of juvenile justice can emerge.[5]

REFERENCES

Alcock, C, Payne, S & Sullivan, M (2000) *Introducing Social Policy* (Pearson Education Limited, Harlow).

Anderson, P & Mann, N (eds.) (1997) *Safety First. The Making of New Labour* (Granta Books, London).

Anderson, S, Kinsey, R, Loader, I & Smith, C (1994) *Cautionary Tales: Young People, Crime and Policing in Edinburgh* (Avebury, Aldershot).

Ashworth, A (1997) 'Sentencing' in M Maguire, R Morgan & R Reiner (eds) *The Oxford Handbook of Criminology*, 2nd edn (Clarendon Press, Oxford).

Audit Commission (1996) *Misspent Youth* (Audit Commission, London).

Bailey, V (1987) *Delinquency and Citizenship. Reclaiming the Young Offender 1914–1948* (Clarendon Press, Oxford).

Ball, C (2000) 'The Youth Justice and Criminal Evidence Act 1999'. Part I: A Significant Move Towards Restorative Justice, or a Recipe for Unintended Consequences?' *Criminal Law Review* 211–21.

Bandalli, S (1998) 'Abolition of the Presumption of *Doli Incapax* and the Criminalisation of Children' 37 *The Howard Journal* 114–23.

—— (2000) 'Children, Responsibility and the New Youth Justice' in B Goldson (ed) *The New Youth Justice* (Russell House Publishing, Lyme Regis).

Beck, U (1992) *Risk Society* (Sage, London).

Bottoms, A E (1974) 'On the Decriminalisation of the English Juvenile Courts' in R Hood (ed) *Crime, Criminology and Public Policy* (Heinemann, London).

—— (1995) 'The Philosophy and Politics of Punishment and Sentencing' in C Clarkson & R Morgan (eds) *The Politics of Sentencing Reform* (Oxford University Press, Oxford).

Brown, S (1998) *Understanding Youth and crime. Listening to Youth?* (Open University Press, Buckingham).

Brownlee, I (1998) 'New Labour—New Penology? Punitive Rhetoric and the Limits of Managerialism in Criminal Justice Policy' 25 *Journal of Law and Society* 313–35.

Burney, E (1982) *Sentencing Young People* (Gower, Aldershot).

Carlebach, J (1970) *Caring for Children in Trouble* (Routledge, London).

Carpenter, A, Nicolson, R & Robinson, D (eds) (2000) *What If? Fifteen Visions of Change for Britain's Inner Cities* (Community Links, London).

Clarke, J (1975) *The Three R's—Repression, Rescue and Rehabilitation* (University of Birmingham, Centre for Contemporary Cultural Studies).

—— (1980) 'Social Democratic Delinquents and Fabian Families' in National Deviancy Conference (eds) *Permissiveness and Control: The Fate of Sixties Legislation* (Macmillan, Basingstoke).

[5] Thanks are due to Allison Morris, Vicky Kemp, Ido Weijers and Antony Duff for their helpful comments on an earlier draft of this chapter.

Cohen, S (1985) *Visions of Social Control: Crime, Punishment and Classification* (Polity Press, Cambridge).

Coleman, C & Moynihan, J (1996) *Understanding Crime Data* (Open University Press, Buckingham).

Criminal Justice Consultative Council (2001) *Referral Orders*, Issue 23 (Home Office, London).

Dignan, J (2000) *Youth Justice Pilots Evaluation*, Interim Report of Reparative Work and Youth Offending Teams (Department of Law, University of Sheffield).

Donzelot, J (1980) *The Policing of Families* (Hutchinson, London).

Downes, D (1998) 'Toughing it Out: From Labour Opposition to Labour Government' 19 *Policy Studies* 191–9.

Drakeford, M & McCarthy, K (2000) 'Parents, Responsibility and the New Youth Justice' in B Goldson (ed.), *The New Youth Justice* (Russell House Publishing, Lyme Regis)

Ericson, R & Haggerty, K (1997) *Policing The Risk Society* (Clarendon Press, Oxford).

Feeley, M, & Simon, J (1992) 'The New Penology' 39 *Criminology* 449–74.

Fionda, J (1999) 'New Labour, Old Hat: Youth Justice and the Crime and Disorder Act' *Criminal Law Review* 36–47.

Foucault, M (1977) *Discipline and Punish* (Penguin, Harmondsworth).

Garland, D (1996) 'The Limits of Sovereign State: Strategies of Crime Control in Contemporary Society' 36 *British Journal of Criminology* 445–71.

Gelsthorpe, L (1999) 'Youth Crime and Parental Responsibility' in A Bainham, S Day Sclater & M Richards (eds) *What is a Parent?* (Hart Publishing, Oxford).

Gelsthorpe, L & Morris, A (1994) 'Juvenile Justice 1945–1992' in M Maguire, R Morgan & R Reiner (eds) *The Oxford Handbook of Criminology*, 2nd ed, (Clarendon Press, Oxford).

—— & —— (1999) 'Much Ado About Nothing—a Critical Comment on Key Provisions Relating to Children in the Crime and Disorder Act 1998' 11 *Child and Family Law Quarterly* 209–21.

Giddens, A (1990) *The Consequences of Modernity* (Polity Press, Cambridge).

—— (1998) *The Third Way. The Renewal of Social Democracy* (Polity Press, Cambridge).

Goldson, B (ed) (1999) *Youth Justice: Contemporary Policy and Practice* (Gower, Aldershot).

Goode, E & Ben-Yehuda, N B (1994) *Moral Panics* (Blackwell, Oxford).

Graham, J & and Bowling, B (1995) *Young People and Crime*; Home Office Research Study 145 (Home Office, London).

Gramsci, A (1971) *Selections from the Prison Notebooks of Antonio Gramsci* Q Hoare & G Nowell Smith (eds & trans) (Lawrence and Wishart, London).

Hagell, A & Newburn, T (1994) *Persistent Young Offenders* (Policy Studies Institute, London).

Halsey, A H (2000) 'Further and Higher Education' in A H Halsey & J Webb (eds) *Twentieth-Century British Social Trends* (Macmillan, Basingstoke) 221–53.

Halsey, A H, Heath, A & Ridge, J (1980), *Origins and Destinations: Family Class and Education in Modern Britain* (Clarendon Press, Oxford).

Harris, R (1991) 'The Life and Death of the Care Order (Criminal)' 21 *British Journal of Social Work* 1–17.

Hartless, J, Ditton, J, Nair, G & Phillips, S (1995) 'More Sinned Against than Sinning: A Study of Young Teenagers' Experience of Crime' 35 *British Journal of Criminology* 114–33.

Holdaway, S, Davidson, N, Dignan, J, Hammersley, R, Hine, J & Marsh, P (2001) *New Strategies to Address Youth Offending. The National Evaluation of the Pilot Youth Offending Teams*; Research, Development and Statistics Directorate Occasional Paper 69 (Home Office, London).

Home Office (1997a) *Tackling Youth Crime*; Green Paper (Home Office, London).

——(1997b) *Tackling Delays in the Youth Justice System*; Consultation Paper (Home Office, London).

——(1997c) *New National and Local Focus on Youth Crime*; Consultation Paper (Home Office, London).

——(1997d) *No More Excuses—A New Approach to Tackling Youth Crime in England and Wales*; Cm 3809 (HMSO, London).

——(2000) *Criminal Statistics in England and Wales 1999* (Home Office, London).

Hood, R (1974) 'Criminology and Penal Change: a Case Study of the Nature and Impact of some Recent Advice to Governments' in R Hood (ed) *Crime, Criminology and Public Policy* (Heinemann, London).

Hood, R & Roddam, A (2000) 'Crime, Sentencing and Punishment' in A H Halsey & J Webb (eds) *Twentieth-Century British Social Trends* (Macmillan, Basingstoke).

James, A, & Raine, J (1998) *The New Politics of Criminal Justice* (Longman, London).

Jones, D (2001) 'Misjudged Youth. A Critique of the Audit Commission's Reports on Youth Justice' 41 *British Journal of Criminology* 362–80.

Joyce, P (1999) *An Introduction to Politics* (Hodder & Stoughton, London).

King, P (1984) 'Decision-makers and Decision-making in the English Criminal Law 1750–1800' 27 *Historical Journal* 25–58.

Littlechild, B (1997) 'Young Offenders, Punitive Policies and the Rights of Children', *Critical Social Policy*, Issue 53, 73–92.

McLaughlin, T (2000) 'Citizenship in England: The Crick Report and Beyond' 34 *Journal of Philosophy of Education* 541–70.

Marwick, A (1982) *British Society Since 1945* (Penguin, Harmondsworth).

Mattinson, J & Mirrlees-Black, C (2000) *Attitudes to Crime and Criminal Justice. Findings from the 1998 British Crime Survey* (Home Office, London).

Morris, A & Gelsthorpe, L (2000) 'Something Old, Something Borrowed, Something Blue, but Something New? A Comment on the Prospects for Restorative Justice under the Crime and Disorder Act 1998' *Criminal Law Review* 18–30.

Morris, A, & Giller, H (1979) *What Justice for Children?* (Justice for Children, London).

—— & ——(1987) *Understanding Juvenile Justice* (Croom Helm, Beckenham).

Morris, A, & Giller, H, Geach, H & and Szwed, E (1980),*Justice for Children* (Macmillan, London).

Muncie, J (1999a) *Youth and Crime. A Critical Introduction* (Sage, London).

——(1999b) 'Institutionalized Intolerance: Youth Justice and the 1998 Crime and Disorder Act' 19 *Critical Social Policy* 147–75.

Nathan, S (1995) *Boot Camps: Return of the Short, Sharp Shock* (Prison Reform Trust, London).

National Association for the Care and Resettlement of Offenders (NACRO) (1989) *The Children Act: Implications for Juvenile Justice* (NACRO, London).

——(2000) *A Brief Outline of the Youth Justice System in England and Wales Incorporating the Crime and Disorder Act 1998* (NACRO, London).

Newburn, T (1997) 'Youth, Crime and Justice' in M Maguire, R Morgan & R Reiner (eds) *The Oxford Handbook of Criminology*; 2nd edn (Clarendon Press, Oxford).

Office for National Statistics (2001) *Social Trends* (HMSO, London).

Pitts, J (1988) *The Politics of Juvenile Justice* (Sage, London).

Radzinowicz, L & Hood, R (1990) *The Emergence of Penal Policy in Victorian and Edwardian England* (Clarendon Press, Oxford).

Reiner, R & Cross, M (1991) *Beyond Law and Order: Criminal Justice Policy in the 1990s* (Macmillan, London).

Robson, L (2001) 'How Not to Raise a Juvenile Delinquent', *Relational Justice* (Issue 6) 6–7.

Straw, J (1998) 'New Approaches to Crime and Punishment' *Prison Service Journal* (No. 116) 2–6.

Taylor, I (1981) 'Crime waves in post-war Britain' 5 *Contemporary Crises* 43–62.

Warner, M (1994) *Making Monsters* (Vintage, London).

Young, A (1996) *Imagining Crime* (Sage, London).

4

Rehabilitation in America: The Philosophy and Methods, from Past to Present

CARTER HAY & MARK STAFFORD

B Y THE MID-1970s, there was a growing consensus in the United States that the juvenile justice system had not lived up to the ideals expected of it. And just as there were criticisms of juvenile justice, so too were there criticisms of rehabilitation. To discover how all of this came about, we review the development of the rehabilitative philosophy, exploring how it was greeted initially with hope and optimism, only to be viewed later as a bankrupt concept with little value. We then consider its resurgence in recent years.

1. FORERUNNERS OF REHABILITATION

The philosophy of rehabilitation was a product of the late 1800s and early 1900s. Prior to that time, punishment of delinquents largely was done for retribution, often by means of corporal punishments such as whipping, mutilation, branding, and even death (Sanders, 1970: 21). But corporal punishment and death were sometimes viewed as too cruel or as ineffective. As a result, English reformers suggested another kind of punishment:

> The methods now employed to dispose of delinquent children failing either to reform them or relieve society from their presence, it is certainly expedient a new experiment should be tried. . . . Now it appears to us that it would be real humanity towards these unfortunate creatures to subject them to compulsory and perpetual exile from England . . . . Abroad, in New South Wales [Australia], they often become prosperous and useful citizens; but, at home, they seem incapable of resisting the temptations presented by a luxurious and refined community (Sanders 1970: 137).

This new idea, called 'transportation,' was quickly accepted and widely used in England and France. A similar kind of punishment, which was even older than transportation, involved the removal of children to the 'hulks'—abandoned, rotting ships, unfit for service, that were anchored off shore in rivers, bays and inlets (Sanders, 1970: 70). Sometimes children served out their sentences along with adult convicts on hulks, working as tailors, shoemakers, carpenters and bookbinders. In other cases, they were confined to hulks awaiting transportation to Australia.

The important thing about the use of hulks, whipping, mutilation, branding and transportation—the primary punishments prior to the 1800s—was that those punishments did not in any sense involve a concern for rehabilitation. They were seen as inflicting deserved pain and unpleasantness. Also important is the absence of formal institutions, such as prisons. To be sure, prisons did exist, but they were uncommon and 'were uniformly considered to be merely places of safekeeping' (Sellin, 1964: xix). In short, the idea of rehabilitating law violators had not emerged on a large scale.

But this began to change. In the late 1700s, responses to crime increasingly reflected a new idea that lawbreakers, young or old, could be reformed while restraining them in a prison. The state of Pennsylvania led the way in 1790 by passing a law that led to one of the most important innovations in penal history: a prison in which convicted offenders could be confined in solitary cells as a method of reforming them (see generally McKelvey, 1936: 6–11; Barnes, 1972: 120–37; Hawkins & Alpert, 1989: 39–46). Led by the Quakers, influential reform societies, and by such people as Benjamin Franklin and William Bradford, reformers assumed that by segregating offenders from all corrupting influences and denying them all but the physical necessities of life, they could recognise the errors of their ways and refrain from committing more crimes.

The Pennsylvania system was first tried in the Walnut Street Jail in Philadelphia, but it soon failed because of overcrowding. Not discouraged, however, reformers passed new legislation to construct two new prisons, one being the Eastern State Penitentiary constructed at Cherry Hill, Pennsylvania in 1829. It included a series of massive stone corridors radiating like the spokes of a wheel from a central rotunda (Pettigrove, 1910). Each of the corridors contained a series of large cells, 8 by 15 feet, with 12-foot ceilings, into which inmates were placed in solitary confinement for the duration of their sentences. Each offender had access to his own small exercise yard, entirely walled off to 'prevent any communication between the convicts' (McKelvey, 1936: 11).

Leaders in the state of New York were impressed with the Pennsylvania system. In 1816, a law was passed permitting construction of a prison at Auburn, New York to be designed with individual cells. But whereas the Eastern State Penitentiary cells were large and permitted access to the outside, those in the new Auburn prison were only 3.5 by 7 feet, with 7-foot ceilings and no outside access. The results were troubling. Many Auburn prisoners became ill or insane. New York officials took only two years to conclude that the experiment had failed, and the result was the development of an alternative system called the Auburn system.

Although inmates in the new Auburn prison were locked up in their cells at night, they were permitted to work together during the day. But, to prevent disobedience and opposition, prisoners were to be silent at all times, march in lockstep, keep their eyes downcast and never face another prisoner. Armed with such new means of maintaining order and because working prisoners could help to pay for their own keep, Auburn officials were proud of their achievements:

> It is not possible to describe the pleasure which we feel in contemplating this noble institution. . . . We regard it as a model worthy of the world's imitation. . . . The whole establishment, from the gate to the sewer, is a specimen of neatness. The unremitted industry, the entire subordination and subdued feeling of the convicts, has probably no parallel among an equal number of criminals. In their solitary cells they spend the night, with no other book but the Bible, and at sunrise they proceed . . . in solid columns, with the lock march, to their workshops; thence, in the same order, at the hour of breakfast, to the common hall, where they partake of their wholesome and frugal meal in silence. Not even a whisper is heard. . . . When they have done eating, at the ringing of a little bell, . . . they rise from the table, form the solid columns, and return . . . to the workshops. . . . It is the testimony of many witnesses, that they have passed more than three hundred convicts, without seeing one leave his work, or turn his head to gaze at them. . . . At the close of the day, . . . the work is all laid aside at once, and the convicts return . . . to the solitary cells, where they partake of the frugal meal. . . . After supper, they can, if they choose, read Scripture undisturbed and then reflect in silence on the errors of their lives (Louis Dwight, as quoted by Barnes, 1972: 136–37).

It was not mentioned, however, that, in addition to silence, marching in lock-step and downcast eyes, whipping also was used to maintain order and to encourage prisoners to reflect on the errors of their ways.

Institutions exclusively for delinquents followed the construction of prisons by several years. Until then and even after, many juveniles were confined in the Pennsylvania, Auburn, and other prisons. Although houses of refuge and asylums, run largely by private groups, had begun to appear about 1825, the first public reformatories and training schools were not built until almost 1850:

> The Lyman School for Boys opened in Westborough, Mass, in 1846. Then came the New York State Agricultural and Industrial School in 1849 and the Maine Boys Training Center in 1853. By 1870, Connecticut, Indiana, Maryland, Nevada, New Hampshire, New Jersey, Ohio, and Vermont had also set up separate juvenile training facilities; by 1900, 36 states had done so (President's Commission on Law Enforcement and Administration of Justice, 1967a: 141).

Just as prisons were viewed as humane and progressive, so too were juvenile institutions. Of course, this meant that juveniles were not treated very differently: 'Many of the juvenile reformatories were . . . , in reality, juvenile prisons, with prison bars, prison cells, prison garb, prison labor, prison punishments, and prison discipline' (Hart, 1910: 11).

Later in the 1800s, there were changes. Perhaps the most profound change was an increasing concern for the developmental needs of children: It was believed that

> every child allowed to grow up in ignorance and vice, and so to become a pauper or a criminal, [was] liable to become in turn the progenitor of generations of criminal (Platt, 1969: 130).

Many Americans believed that, if their worst fears were to be avoided, all poor, uneducated and parentless children had to be both treated and disciplined.

2. REHABILITATION ARRIVES: ITS PRINCIPLES AND METHODS

Following the Civil War, those beliefs were reflected in the recommendations of a group of America's leading penal reformers. Meeting at the Cincinnati Prison Congress of 1870, the reformers concluded that considerable good could be accomplished if lawbreakers were made the 'objects of a generous parental care'; they should be 'trained to virtue' instead of suffering in prison (Henderson, 1910: 40).

2.1. The 'Declaration of Principles'

In a series of pronouncements, the reformers enunciated the first philosophy of rehabilitation and embodied it in a formal Declaration of Principles. The following, attributed to Enoch Wines, who also drafted the Principles, represents a preamble:

> A prison governed by force and fear is a prison mismanaged, in which hope and love, the two great spiritual, uplifting, regenerating forces to which mankind must ever look for redemption, are asleep or dead. . . . Why not try the effect of rewards upon the prisoner? Rewards, as truly as punishments, appeal to the inextinguishable principle of self-interest in his breast (Wines, 1910: 12).

Wines's Declaration of Principles not only described rehabilitation in abstract terms, but also outlined the specific methods by which it should be accomplished. The central notions were:

—*Rehabilitation*: Punishment is not the primary goal of penology; instead, it is rehabilitation:

> Whatever differences of opinion may exist among penologists on other questions . . . , there is one point on which there may be . . . almost . . . perfect unanimity, namely, that the moral cure of criminals, adult as well as juvenile, . . . is the best means of attaining the end in view—the repression and extirpation of crime; . . . hence . . . reformation is the primary object to be aimed at in the administration of penal justice (Henderson, 1910: 17).

—*Treat criminals, not crimes*: The Declaration of Principles opposed the premise of the classical school of criminology that legal punishments should match the seriousness of crimes. Instead, rehabilitation should be administered according to the needs of offenders:

> The treatment of criminals by society is for the protection of society. But since such treatment is directed to the criminal rather than to the crime, its great object should be

his moral regeneration. Hence the supreme aim of prison discipline is the reformation of criminals, not the infliction of vindictive suffering (*ibid*: 39).

—*The indeterminate sentence*: The practice of giving offenders determinate sentences, according to the seriousness of their crimes, should be replaced by indeterminate sentences:

Peremptory sentences ought to be replaced by those of indeterminate length. . . . Reformation is a work of time; and a benevolent regard to the good of the criminal himself, as well as to the protection of society, requires that his sentence be long enough for reformatory processes to take effect (*ibid*: 40–41).

—*Classification*: The practice of confining all prisoners together regardless of age, character or gender should be eliminated. Prisons should be designed to meet the needs of different kinds of prisoners:

Prisons, as well as prisoners, should be classified or graded so that there shall be prisons for the untried, for the incorrigible and for other degrees of depraved character, as well as separate establishments for women and for criminals of the younger class (*ibid*: 41).

—*Education*: Education is indispensable in rehabilitating offenders:

Education is a vital force in the reformation of fallen men and women. Its tendency is to quicken the intellect, inspire self-respect, excite to higher aims, and afford a healthful substitute for low and vicious amusements (*ibid*: 40).

—*Industrial training*: Occupational training is beneficial for practical and personal reasons:

Industrial training should have both a higher development and a greater breadth than has heretofore been, or is now, commonly given to it in our prisons. Work is no less an auxiliary to virtue than it is a means of support (*ibid*: 41).

—*Rewards*: Change is more likely to be produced by rewards than by punishments:

Since hope is a more potent agent than fear, it should be made an ever-present force in the minds of prisoners, by a well-devised and skilfully applied system of rewards for good conduct, industry and attention to learning. Rewards, more than punishments, are essential to every good prison system (*ibid*: 39).

—*Self-respect*: Punishment only degrades; correctional practices should uplift:

The prisoner's self-respect should be cultivated to the utmost, and every effort made to give back to him his manhood. There is no greater mistake in the whole compass of penal discipline than its studied imposition of degradation as a part of punishment. Such imposition destroys every better impulse and aspiration. It crushes the weak, irritates the strong, and indisposes all to submission and reform. It is trampling where we ought to raise, and is therefore as unchristian in principle as it is unwise in policy (*ibid*: 40–41).

—*Parole*: Treatment in an institution completes only half the task; offenders require help when they return to the community:

> More systematic and comprehensive methods should be adopted to save discharged prisoners, by providing them with work and encouraging them to redeem their character and regain their lost position in society. . . . And to this end it is desirable that state societies be formed, which shall co-operate with each other in this work (*ibid*: 42).

—*Prevention*: Prevention is more promising than confinement for having committed a crime:

> Preventive institutions, such as truant homes, industrial schools, etc., for the reception and treatment of children not yet criminal, but in danger of becoming so, constitute the true field of promise in which to labor for the repression of crime. It is our conviction that one of the most effective agencies in the repression of crime would be the enactment of laws by which the education of all the children of the state should be made obligatory. Better to force education upon the people than to force them into prison to suffer for crimes (*ibid*: 41–42, 44).

2.2. Central Features of the Rehabilitative Philosophy

This declaration of principles was characterised by three main features. The first was *optimism*. In contrast to the pessimistic and retributive features of prior penal philosophies, the rehabilitative philosophy involved a belief that men and women, as well as children, could be reclaimed from evil. That belief became even more optimistic with the invention of the juvenile court. By applying the principles of rehabilitation, children could be redeemed and future offending prevented.

The second feature of the rehabilitative philosophy was its focus on the *individual offender*. It was the individual's morals that required regeneration. It was the individual's characteristics for which classification, separate institutions, and indeterminate sentences were needed. It was the individual's educational deficiencies that demanded attention, and it was the individual's character from which other people required protection.

The Declaration's third feature was its belief that the *institution* is the most effective means for treating children not yet criminal, as well as for rehabilitating those who are. Throughout the 1800s, there was some (albeit ineffective) opposition to institutionalisation of children, but the idea prevailed that an institution could meet the needs of troubled children by providing everything an understanding family and well-organised community could provide, and even more:

> In the ordinary family home the [delinquent] child is often at a great disadvantage. . . . The neighborhood may be thoroughly bad. The daily journey to and from school may lead past saloons. . . . The mother may be lazy, slatternly and shiftless. The father may be drunken, vicious, improvident. . . . In the institution, however, we are able to

control absolutely the child's environment. We can create ideal sanitary conditions. . . . We can select his school teacher and his Sunday School teacher. We can bring to bear upon him the most helpful and elevating influences. The boy will never play truant, he will never be out with a gang, he will never be late to school. Under these circumstances, why should we not be able to produce satisfactory results? (Hart, 1910: 62).

The principles of rehabilitation first were applied in a new reformatory for boys and young men, ages 16 to 30. As leader of the New York Prison Association, Enoch Wines again led the way by gaining authorisation in 1869 to plan for a new reformatory at Elmira, New York. Construction was completed about 1876, and Zebulon Brockway was chosen as its first superintendent (Brockway, 1910; Scott, 1910: 90–98).

Brockway was impressed by the growth of science in the 1800s. In 1877, as a result, he drafted and gained the passage of a law implementing the principles of the Cincinnati Prison Congress: indeterminate sentences; a classification system; a programme of treatment, education, physical discipline, and work; and parole (Scott, 1910: 94–112). Although the new reformatory resembled a strict military school more than anything else (Hawkins & Alpert, 1989: 50–52; Mennel, 1973: 102–03), Brockway's general approach had lasting appeal:

> The [Elmira] Reformatory system meets a demand of enlightened public sentiment which favors the idea that young offenders . . . shall be wisely and humanely treated, be supplied with incentives and opportunities to reform, and, as far as possible, the unworthy and determined offenders shall be subjected to lengthened detention . . . and all, when released, be properly supervised until they are established in industry, respectable associations, and good behavior (Brockway, 1912: 238).

Whereas reformatories were built for older youths and young adults, industrial and training schools were constructed for younger status offenders and delinquents. New guidelines stressed the importance of locating both types of institutions in rural areas and emulating the character of a well-disciplined family. They were widespread by the time the juvenile court was established, except in the southern states, which had not yet constructed special institutions for juveniles (Bremner, 1970, vol 1: 672; Platt, 1969: 61–62). Over time, it became more difficult to distinguish among industrial schools, reformatories and training schools. Likewise, it became more difficult to distinguish among types of institutionalised children. Because the purpose of rehabilitation was to treat children, not crimes, there was little need to distinguish among them.

2.3. Concerns About Rehabilitation

These new institutions eventually became the subject of growing concern, much of it having to do with their inordinate focus on discipline and control rather than on moral guidance and education. This may have been an inevitable consequence of institutionalising individuals who did not want to be there. At any rate, reformers began to voice opposition to institutions in the early 1900s, even as more were being constructed. Hastings Hart expressed a common belief about 'institutionalism':

> In a great institution like the New York House of Refuge, with 700 boys, or Girard College, with 1700 boys, or the Catholic Protectory, with 2700 children, the child is lost in the mass. He is one of a multitude. It is almost impossible to give him that personal attention which is essential to the normal development of a child, or to give opportunity for such development. The child lacks initiative; he lacks courage; he lacks power to act for himself. In the institution someone else is doing his thinking for him, someone else is planning his life for him; and when he goes into the world, he goes at a disadvantage (Hart, 1910: 62).

Hart believed that children raised by the state are incapable of free and independent judgement, accustomed to confinement as a way of life, and comfortable only in a setting where all decisions are made for them:

> However good an institution may be, however kindly its spirit, however genial its atmosphere, however homelike its cottages, however fatherly and motherly its officers, however admirable its training, it is now generally agreed . . . that institutional life is at the best artificial and unnatural, and that the child ought to be returned at the earliest practicable moment to the more natural environment of the family (Hart, 1910: 12).

2.4. A Shift Towards the Community

It was such reasoning that led many of the first juvenile court judges to argue that juvenile corrections should be shifted toward the community. Probation, and not institutionalisation, should be the 'cord upon which all the pearls of the juvenile court are strung' (Rothman, 1979: 50).

Probation actually had earlier roots than the first juvenile courts (Diana, 1960: 189–90). It was used first in Boston in 1841 when a shoemaker, John Augustus, began to provide bail for petty adult offenders, women and children and to assist them following their court appearances. After Augustus died, the Boston Children's Aid Society and other volunteers continued his activities. Massachusetts formalised those activities in 1869 by appointing a worker from the Board of State Charities, a private agency, to investigate children's cases, make recommendations to the criminal court, and receive children for placement. In 1878, an additional law was passed permitting the employment of paid probation officers in Boston (United Nations, 1951: 29–42). A few other states, as well as Great Britain, legalised probation late in the 1800s, permitting first-time offenders to be released on good conduct (Tappan, 1960: 546). It was the juvenile court movement, however, that truly legitimised probation and gave it its impetus. 'By 1933 all states except Wyoming had juvenile probation laws' (Diana, 1960: 189). The practice has become so widespread that today far more delinquents are placed on probation than are institutionalised (Torbet, 1996).

Along with probation, parole was gradually added as a rehabilitative tool (Carter & Wilkins, 1970: 177–276). Like probation, parole has the dual purpose of casework assistance for the offender and protection of the community. But unlike probation, parole is a community service that follows institutionalisation. The idea is that delinquents who have suffered 'institutionalism' should not be released to the community without adult supervision and assistance. Instead, parole should be part of an indeterminate sentence. If delinquents are given help when they leave an institution and can successfully adjust to the community, they will be permitted to remain there. If they are unable to cope with the many demands of community life, they will be returned to the institution for further rehabilitation.

2.5. Justice Revolutionised

Prior to the application of the principles and methods of rehabilitation, the fate of an offender, juvenile or adult, was prescribed by law and decided by a judge once guilt was established: imprisonment, hard labour, a fine or some other punishment. But the rehabilitative revolution diminished judicial power and transferred it elsewhere. In the juvenile court, new laws permitted deferred sentencing until an offender could be evaluated and recommendations made to a judge. Probation officers often influenced judges' dispositional decisions. But that was only the beginning.

Once a dispositional decision was made, the court turned an offender over to probation or institutional officials for treatment. Responsibility and power were divided, not only among people close to the court, but, eventually, throughout the correctional system. The adoption of indeterminate sentences assigned new power to probation officers and correctional officials. The decisions handed down by them, in turn, led to the construction of diagnostic centres, specialised institutions, reformatories, industrial schools, farms, probation camps and cottage programmes, which were to respond to different classes of offenders rather than classes of crimes—first-time offenders, neglected children, hard-core delinquents, as well as males and females.

This resulted in such specialised roles for correctional officials as administration, care and feeding, custody, supervision, casework, education, therapy and vocational training. Then, following institutionalisation, the use of parole further divided responsibility and power by assigning them to parole boards and parole officers. They, rather than judges or correctional officials, would decide when offenders would receive their freedom.

In short, the concept of rehabilitation totally altered the classical system of justice. As a result, delinquents were made to answer for their rehabilitation, not merely to a judge, but to a host of decision-makers, all of whom were given a part in deciding their fates and judging their performances. A crucial question, therefore, is this: Were the grand and optimistic hopes of the reformers realised?

3. DISMAY OVER THE SYSTEM

For more than half of the twentieth century, there was no serious challenge to the philosophy of rehabilitation. The juvenile justice system operated in relative quiet with only occasional criticisms (Tonry, 1976). But by the late 1960s, many Americans had become suspicious of the juvenile justice system, as well as of the very notion of rehabilitation. Influential critics like Edwin Lemert argued that the 'treatment of delinquency is . . . much more akin to midwifery than medicine' (Lemert, 1967: 96). He insisted that judges, probation officers, psychologists and counsellors should recognise that, like midwives, they do not have the knowledge to diagnose ills and prescribe cures. At best, they only could assist the process of maturation and could not be expected to have much impact on its outcome. Norman Carlson, former director of the Federal Bureau of Prisons, expressed similar views in an address to the American Academy of Psychiatry and the Law in 1975, arguing that 'We cannot diagnose criminality . . . , we cannot prescribe a precise treatment and we certainly cannot guarantee a cure' (Carlson, 1975: 1).

This emerging suspicion of rehabilitation was probably due to a number of factors, not the least of which were increases in official delinquency occurring during the 1960s and 1970s. Also important was an emerging awareness that the juvenile justice system was severely under-funded. There were poorly paid and unqualified judges, inadequate numbers of probation officers, a lack of psychiatric services, inadequate foster homes and institutional care, and an ineffective parole system. As a result, the juvenile justice system provided a sort of mass-oriented, assembly line justice that fell far short of the individualised treatment envisioned by Wines, Brockway and other reformers. Cohen (1975) discovered that in one court, it took an average of 76 days for intake personnel to decide what to do with a case. If the case required judicial action, the average waiting period almost doubled to 130 days. If it was contested in court, the wait was 211 days. And when a court hearing finally took place, it often lasted no longer than 10 or 15 minutes. If the juvenile then was assigned to probation, the situation was no better. The average probation officer was expected to maintain a caseload of about 75 probationers, conduct pre-sentence investigations, maintain extensive paper work, and carry out other functions as well (President's Commission on Law Enforcement and Administration of Justice, 1967b: 4–5, 140). As a result, there was little time for dealing with the actual problems of juveniles.

3.1. 'Nothing Works'

Perhaps most damaging to the rehabilitative philosophy was an emerging perception that scientific research was proving that rehabilitation did not work. Studies pointing to negative consequences of institutionalisation, such as fear, isolation, and opposition to authority, had existed for some time (Clemmer, 1940: 109, 152–64; Schrag, 1954; Ohlin & Lawrence, 1959: 7–11; Sykes & Messinger, 1960: 13–19; Cressey, 1961; Glaser, 1964: ch. 5; Sykes, 1965: ch 5; Manocchio & Dunn, 1970; Bartollas, Miller & Dinitz, 1976: 62–69). But more troublesome for the rehabilitative philosophy was a study that would become known as the 'Martinson Report.' In 1966, the New York State Governor's Special Committee on Criminal Offenders financed a survey of correctional research to make sure that some promising leads had not been overlooked. Clearly, the commission hoped that, if isolated, some correctional programmes might be redesigned and revitalised. Three criminologists, including Robert Martinson, were commissioned to find them (see Martinson, 1974).

In pursuit of that goal, they gathered and reviewed the results of 231 evaluation studies. By 1970 they had completed their work and produced a report that shocked the Governor's Special Committee. Rather than identifying successful programmes, the report seemed to suggest that there were none. But because the Governor's Special Committee was either disbelieving, defensive, or both, it suppressed the report. Indeed, the report might still be unavailable for public scrutiny if not for the fact that it was subpoenaed as evidence for a case before the Bronx Supreme Court. It was thus freed from the controls of the state and published in a large volume entitled *The Effectiveness of Correctional Treatment: A Survey of Treatment Evaluation Studies* (Lipton, Martinson & Wilks, 1975).

'With few and isolated exceptions,' Martinson concluded, 'the rehabilitative efforts that have been reported so far have had no appreciable effect on recidivism' (Martinson, 1974: 25) In other words, *nothing works*. In another era, when optimism rather than pessimism was the order of the day, that conclusion might have gone unnoticed. But the 1970s was not such an era. Instead, reformers from different perspectives used it as a means for criticising the juvenile justice system and for suggesting that methods other than rehabilitation had to be found for responding to delinquency.

3.2. Four Reactions

One such group of reformers consisted of utilitarians who contended that, in attempting to rehabilitate delinquents, the juvenile justice system had been excessively lenient, had denied the rights of victims, had eroded discipline and respect for authority and threatened to destroy a tenuous social order (Miller,

1974: 454–55). Thus, the following reforms were advocated: (1) abolish the juvenile court (McCarthy, 1977); (2) lower the age of accountability for crime (van den Haag, 1975: 173–175); and (3) punish and incapacitate offenders (van den Haag, 1975: ch 21; Wilson, 1975: ch 8, 1983: chs 7–8).

Because the rehabilitative philosophy had failed, it was futile to attempt to control crime by trying to undo the effects of its causes (van den Haag, 1975: 77–78; Wilson, 1975: ch 3). Rather, the law's purposes should be to insure that legal punishment is certain and severe and that chronic offenders are incapacitated for long periods of time, perhaps even until age 40, when the 'impulse' to commit crimes has diminished considerably (van den Haag, 1975: 61, 70, 195, 214–15, 241, ch 21; Wilson, 1975: ch 8).

Those partial to labelling theory, by contrast, argued that increasing delinquency was due to the failures of the juvenile justice system itself. It had overcriminalised the young, labelled and stigmatised them unnecessarily, denied them their civil rights, and had not only failed to rehabilitate them, but had also been excessively punitive (National Advisory Commission on Criminal Justice Standards and Goals, 1973a: 34–36, 1973b: ch. 14; President's Commission on Law Enforcement and Administration of Justice, 1967b: 7–40). The only defensible philosophy for the juvenile justice system, therefore, was one of 'judicious nonintervention' (Lemert, 1967: 96). '*Leave kids alone wherever possible*' (Schur, 1973: 155).

A third reaction came from proponents of 'just deserts' (Fox, 1974; Fogel, 1975; Gaylin & Rothman, 1976; von Hirsch, 1976). They believed that, since nothing works, the only defensible policy is one that insures that justice is administered uniformly and that offenders are punished according to the seriousness of their offences. They suggested that our treatment-oriented system of justice has 'produced far too many instances of recorded abuse to think fairly that it is much more than simply a vehicle for abuse' (Fox, 1974: 3).

Unlike utilitarians, however, proponents of just deserts did not believe that legal punishments deter persons from committing crimes. The state should reduce the length of sentences to the point where it satisfies our sense of equity, but no more than that: ' "warnings" for crimes low on a scale of seriousness, intermittent confinement (weekends or evenings) for more serious offenses, and . . . full-time incarceration only for the most serious crimes' (Gaylin & Rothman, 1976: xxxv). In other words, social policy should be concerned 'less with the administration of justice and more . . . with the *justice of administration*' (Fogel, 1975: xv).

A final reaction—one that gained special momentum only in the past decade—came in the form of calls for restorative justice. Unlike, the utilitarian, labelling and just deserts perspectives, the restorative justice perspective is not inherently pessimistic about delinquents' capacity for rehabilitation. Proponents of restorative justice do argue, however, that a response to delinquency must be concerned with more than just rehabilitation of offenders. Like just deserts proponents, advocates of restorative justice are concerned with doing justice. However, they argue that an exclusive focus on the offender prevents justice from being served; restorative justice is concerned with achieving justice for victims of crime as well as offenders. From their perspective, the problem with a punishment-based system is that it becomes preoccupied with securing convictions and imposing punishments; in so doing, it ignores the financial, physical and emotional losses that victims have suffered. Also, when crimes are perceived as offences against the state, and when the debt to be paid will be a *debt to society*, then offenders are seldom required to face their victims, and thus 'understand the real human costs of their actions' (Zehr, 1982: 4).

Restorative justice would change this by stressing that in the wake of a crime, justice is served only when offenders provide victims with restitution that returns them to the greatest extent possible to their original circumstances (Barnett, 1981). This philosophy clearly runs into difficulty with respect to victimless crimes or very serious crimes for which restitution would be impossible. For other crimes, though, victim-offender mediation can be used to negotiate a restitution agreement that typically includes such things as an apology and replacement or repair of damaged property.

3.3. Death Reports are Premature

Despite challenges to the philosophy of rehabilitation, there were some who believed that reports of its death were premature—a feeling even expressed by Martinson (1979). In 1977, a special panel of scientists from such disciplines as sociology, psychology, psychiatry, political science, economics, penology, and applied statistics was convened by the National Academy of Sciences to examine the Martinson Report. In light of the widespread belief that correctional treatment was dead, the conclusions were striking.

To begin with, the panel observed that, although 'Lipton, Martinson, and Wilks were reasonably accurate and fair in their appraisal of the rehabilitation literature,' they were 'overly lenient' in their assessment of the quality of the research on which their conclusion was based (Sechrest, White & Brown, 1979: 5). Hence, the panel did *not* draw the same conclusion as that of the original researchers. Instead, it concluded that research on the effects of treatment programmes was so weak that existing studies could not yield reliable knowledge about the effects of rehabilitation (Martin, Sechrest & Redner, 1981: 9). They furthermore argued that if blame for the lack of knowledge was to be assigned, the scientific community was responsible for at least some of it:

> In general, techniques have been tested as isolated treatments rather than as complex combinations, which would seem more suited to the task. And even when techniques have been tested in good designs, insufficient attention has been paid to maintaining their integrity, so that often the treatment to be tested was delivered in a substantially weakened form. It is also not clear that all the theoretical power and the individual imagination that could be invoked in the planning of rehabilitative efforts have ever

been capitalized on. Thus, the recommendation in this report that has the strongest support is that more and better thinking and research should be invested in efforts to devise programs for offender rehabilitation (Sechrest, White & Brown, 1979: 3–4).

The panel was so convinced of the importance of the debate about rehabilitation that it met for an additional two years to 'suggest . . . directions for both program development and research' (Martin, Sechrest & Redner, 1981: viii). An underlying belief was that it would be premature to bury a humane ideal:

> The currently fashionable suggestion that society abandon efforts to find more effective programs to rehabilitate offenders is, we believe, irresponsible and premature . . . The promise of the 'rehabilitative ideal' (Allen, 1959) is so compelling a goal that the strongest possible efforts should be made to determine whether it can be realized and to seek to realize it (Martin, Sechrest & Redner, 1981: 17, 22).

Coming from a group of scientists supposedly known for their cold and dispassionate approach to emotional issues, those statements were remarkable. Indeed, the panel rejected

> the idea that efforts to facilitate the rehabilitation of criminal offenders . . . should be terminated. . . . This position rests on the assumptions that rehabilitation as a form of behavior change is (1) possible . . . (2) more likely to occur through the adoption of a more systematic approach to the accumulation of knowledge . . . (3) morally and socially desirable; and (4) likely, in the long run, to prove to be the most practical and cost-effective option available to the criminal justice system (*ibid*: 22–23).

4. THE CURRENT SITUATION: REHABILITATION IN THE POST-MARTINSON PERIOD

The reports issued by the National Academy of Sciences panel went a long way in tempering reactions to the Martinson Report, but the rehabilitative philosophy is still on tenuous ground. This is readily evident from the changes in juvenile justice in recent decades. There have been continued calls during the 1980s and 1990s to rethink the juvenile justice system and even abolish the juvenile court (Dawson, 1990; Federle, 1990; Feld, 1990, 1993; Ainsworth, 1991). Many states have changed their juvenile codes to de-emphasise rehabilitation and more strongly emphasise public protection, punishment, justice, deterrence and accountability (Feld, 1993: 245–46; Snyder & Sickmund, 1995: 71). For example, Texas recently revised its juvenile justice system to promote punishment as its primary purpose. The revisions lowered the age at which juveniles could be transferred to adult court, and also expanded the use of lengthy, determinate sentences for serious offenders who could not be transferred to the adult court (Mears & Field, 2000).

Similar but even more far-reaching changes have occurred in California, where a ballot initiative (Proposition 21) overhauling the juvenile justice system was supported by over 60 per cent of voters. Such changes have prompted some to complain that the juvenile court's historic emphasis on rehabilitation, the very thing that distinguished it from the adult criminal court, is rapidly disappearing. According to Butts and Mitchell,

> juvenile courts across the United States are increasingly similar to criminal courts in their method as well as their general atmosphere. . . . The two court systems appear to be moving toward complete convergence (Butts & Mitchell, 2000: 167).

Rehabilitation is faring better on the research front. In the two decades since the National Academy of Sciences panel issued its call for more and better research, evaluations of rehabilitation programmes, and subsequent meta-analyses of these evaluations, have flourished in criminology (Greenwood & Zimring, 1985; Gendreau & Ross, 1987; Lab & Whitehead, 1988, 1990; Whitehead & Lab, 1989; Andrews *et al*, 1990; Palmer, 1991; Lipsey, 1992). Many of these studies have reached favourable conclusions. For example, in a recent review of the results of 443 evaluation studies, Lipsey (1992: 94) reported that in 285 (64 per cent) there was a reduction in recidivism. Moreover, the most successful programmes showed 'effects . . . in the range of 10–20 percentage points reduction in recidivism' (Lipsey, 1992: 123).

4.1. What Works?

Studies like Lipsey's have not ended the debate on rehabilitation because different researchers interpret the research findings differently (eg, Andrews *et al*, 1990; Lab and Whitehead, 1990). What is remarkable, however, is the more balanced nature of the debate during the past decade. Generally speaking, the discussion of rehabilitation is no longer dominated by two entirely contradictory positions: one insisting that rehabilitation is uniformly good and one insisting that it is uniformly bad. Instead, there is greater recognition that some rehabilitation or prevention programmes are effective (under some circumstances and with some populations), and that others are ineffective. Andrews and his colleagues have indicated that 'the effectiveness of correctional treatment is dependent upon what is delivered to whom in particular settings' (Andrews *et al*, 1990: 372). Thus what is needed is high quality research that can help distinguish between programmes that are effective and those that are not. Schwartz and Travis recently commented on this evolving focus of rehabilitation research:

> Contemporary researchers have reopened the effectiveness debate, but the scope has been narrowed. The question is no longer 'Does treatment work?' Today, the effectiveness question is 'What are the characteristics of treatments that work?' (Schwartz & Travis, 1997: 215).

Several recent meta-analyses have begun to address that question. In particular, recidivism is reduced most by 'treatment that is delivered to high risk cases, that targets criminogenic need, and that is matched with the learning styles of offenders' (Andrews *et al*, 1990: 377). Moreover, the 'more structured and focused treatments (eg, behavioral, skill-oriented) and multimodal treatments seem to be more effective than the less structured and [less] focused approaches (eg, counseling)' (Lipsey, 1992: 123). The intensity of the treatment also matters. For high risk offenders, the most effective interventions occupy 40 to 70 per cent of their time and they last at least 23 weeks (Levrant *et al*, 1999).

Palmer (1995) reports that 'nonprogrammatic' features of a programme also affect recidivism levels. These nonprogrammatic features relate not to the core content of the treatment (eg, vocational training vs. family therapy), but rather to the structural and logistical aspects of its delivery, including such things as the caseload size for staff members and the extent of their training, the nature of staff/client interaction and the setting in which the treatment occurs (eg, home vs. institutional). For example, two major reviews have found that rehabilitation programmes in community settings are more effective in reducing recidivism than those in institutional settings (Andrews *et al*, 1990: 384–86; Lipsey 1992: 122). Palmer (1995) also points to the success of California's Community Treatment Project, arguing that such things as the small caseloads and strong skills of its counsellors were responsible for the 50 per cent reduction in recidivism that it produced among participants.

4.2. Popular Failures

Researchers concede that there still is much to learn, but it is becoming possible to identify specific programmes that are highly effective and to distinguish them from those that are not. Researchers have sometimes found that very popular programmes are generally ineffective. Boot camps are one such type of programme. A boot camp is a residential facility that is based on a military model of discipline and physical conditioning, but also includes rehabilitative components such as education, vocational training and drug and alcohol counselling. Boot camps became very popular in the 1980s, with many believing that the combination of a 'get-tough' approach and rehabilitative services would reduce recidivism. Evaluations generally have suggested otherwise. One of the more rigorous evaluations was done in conjunction with the US Office of Juvenile Justice and Delinquency Prevention (Peters *et al*, 1997). Across three programme sites, it was found that 'boot camp participants . . . were . . . no less likely to reoffend after release than [were] their control group counterparts'. In fact, in one of the sites, the level of recidivism was substantially higher among the boot camp inmates. In all sites, boot camp inmates committed new offences more quickly than youths in a control group.

Another popular programme that has not fared well in evaluations is the Drug Abuse Resistance Education (DARE) programme. Unlike boot camps, DARE is concerned with prevention rather than rehabilitation. First introduced by the Los Angeles Police Department, DARE uses uniformed police officers to teach antidrug messages in schools. DARE is overwhelmingly popular. 'It is administered in about 70 percent of the nation's school districts, reaching 25 million students in 1996, and has been adopted in 44 foreign countries' (Rosenbaum & Hanson, 1998: 381). Unfortunately, it appears to be ineffective for most students, and may actually increase drug use for some. In a comprehensive study of urban, suburban and rural students who were surveyed each year from 6th to 12th grades, Rosenbaum and Hanson found that 'students who participated in DARE were no different from students in the control group [those who did not participate in DARE] with regard to their recent and lifetime use of drugs and alcohol'; the only exception was suburban students, among whom 'participation in DARE is associated with increased level of drug use' (*ibid*: 401–02).

In their comprehensive assessment of prevention programmes, Sherman and his colleagues (1998) arrived at a similar conclusion. Many explanations for DARE's ineffectiveness have been cited, including such things as the programme's content (eg, its emphasis on providing factual information about drugs and their pharmacological effects at the expense of teaching social competency skills), teaching methods (its emphasis on lecture and discussion rather than more interactive forms of teaching), and the use of uniformed police officers who are relatively inexperienced teachers and may have less rapport with the students. Whatever the reason, the overall ineffectiveness of DARE is disappointing, and it points to the need to carefully evaluate the results of all efforts to prevent delinquency and rehabilitate delinquents.

4.3. Two Success Stories

Researchers have identified successful programmes as well. Two that merit special attention are Multisystemic Therapy (Henggeler, 1997) and the Prenatal and Early Childhood Nurse Home Visitation Program (Olds, Hill & Rumsey, 1998). Multisystemic Therapy (MST) is a home-based family services programme for serious, violent juvenile offenders. The three principal goals of MST are to (1) improve family functioning (primarily by improving parents' capacity to monitor, discipline and positively interact with an adolescent), (2) remove offenders from deviant peer groups, and (3) enhance the youth's capacity to succeed in school. A main premise is that improving family functioning is the most important because the family will be the tool used to accomplish the other two goals.

Each family that is referred to the MST programme is assigned a masters-level therapist who has been extensively trained in the MST approach and who carries a caseload of only four to six families. Also, the therapist is part of an overall treatment team that includes other therapists who are supervised by a doctorate-level staff person. The therapist will have on average about 60 hours of contact with the family over a period of about four months, but the frequency and duration of sessions are determined by family need.

Evaluations of MST have revealed positive results. In one study, 84 violent, chronic offenders were randomly assigned to either MST or 'usual services', which was a blend of institutionalisation and referral to mental health, educational and vocational services. Fifty-nine weeks after the completion of their dispositions, several differences were found between the two groups. Compared to the usual services group, the MST cases had committed about one-third the number of self-reported offences, had about one-half the number of arrests and had spent almost one-third as much time in an out-of-home placement. Moreover, because MST is a home-based approach that requires no institutionalisation, it is relatively inexpensive: about $3,500 per client, compared to $17,769 for the usual services group (Henggeler, 1997).

The Prenatal and Early Childhood Nurse Home Visitation Program is different from MST in that its focus is on prevention for at-risk families, rather than rehabilitation of serious, violent offenders. This programme targets low income, first-time parents. Participating families receive home visits from a nurse during pregnancy and then during the first two years of the child's life, with visits occurring about every week or two. Nurses' main focus is to provide the instruction and support to accomplish three goals: (1) improving health-related behaviours during pregnancy (especially with respect to nutrition and abstinence from drugs, alcohol and tobacco), (2) preventing abuse and neglect of the child during early life (in part, by providing information about how to manage frustration and how to interpret their child's signals), and (3) helping to keep the parents' lives on track. This third goal involves providing instruction and support for planning future pregnancies, reaching educational goals and finding adequate employment.

As with MST, the evaluation results for this programme have been very positive. Children from participating families fare substantially better than children from similar families who did not participate (Olds, Hill & Rumsey, 1998). By age 17, they are 60 per cent less likely to have run away, 55 per cent less likely to have been arrested, and 80 per cent less likely to have been convicted of a crime. These positive outcomes produce a substantial cost savings for public agencies. By the time the first child reaches age four, the programme has paid for itself, primarily because of the reduced number of subsequent pregnancies and the related reductions in welfare costs. By the time the first child is 15, public agencies have saved about $4 for every $1 spent on the programme, primarily because of reductions in crime, welfare and health care costs.

4.4. Public Support

It is unknown at this point whether the success of programmes like MST and The Prenatal and Early Childhood Nurse Home Visitation Program will translate into a more rehabilitative and preventive approach to delinquency. One thing is clear, however: contrary to the typical claims of US politicians, the US public generally supports rehabilitation for juvenile offenders. Schwartz *et al*, (1992), for example, found that when respondents in a national survey were asked about the main purpose of the juvenile court, 78 per cent supported rehabilitation. Similar levels of support for rehabilitation have been found with other samples, including those taken from Tennessee (Moon *et al*, 2000), Oregon (Doble Research Associates, 1995), and Ohio (Applegate, Cullen & Fisher, 1997). Support for rehabilitating juveniles is strong even in states known for a punitive approach to crime, including Texas (Makeig, 1994) and California (Steinhart, 1988). Support for prevention may be high as well. In their study of Tennessee respondents, Moon *et al* (2000) found that when given the choice between spending money to build prisons or to fund prevention-oriented programmes, close to 90 per cent of respondents chose prevention.

A point to emphasise is that these survey results do not suggest that Americans are opposed to punishing juveniles. Many studies find support for tougher penalties for juvenile offenders (Moore, 1994; *The Public Perspective* 1997). Moon *et al* (2000) conclude that when all of the studies are taken together, the best interpretation is that support for rehabilitation is higher than expected, but that Americans generally support punishment *and* rehabilitation for delinquents.

5. CONCLUSION

The development of the rehabilitative philosophy has been scarcely linear. From the late 1800s until the 1960s, it received almost unqualified support. It was viewed not only as just and civilised, but as the most effective way to decrease delinquency. In the 1960s and 1970s, however, those views changed, as rehabilitation went from receiving unqualified support to receiving almost unqualified rejection. Rehabilitation was viewed as a naive, antiquated relic of the past, and harsh punishment became a more favoured response to delinquency. The period since 1980 has struck a middle-ground between these two extreme views. There is an increasing recognition that rehabilitation is neither uniformly good nor uniformly bad. Rather, some rehabilitation programmes are effective while others are not, and research is needed to distinguish them.

Of special importance for the future may be the rise of restorative justice. Some see it as a philosophy and practice that can bridge the gap between the duelling philosophies of rehabilitation and punishment. Proponents of punishment embrace restorative justice's emphasis on holding delinquents accountable to their victims. Proponents of rehabilitation, on the other hand, see rehabilitative potential in restorative justice's emphasis on delinquents acknowledging the human costs of their behaviour. Moreover, through apology and restitution, delinquents are given a potentially transformative opportunity to gain 'atonement' (compare Duff, ch 6 in this volume).

By 1995, 24 states had adopted or were considering juvenile justice reforms that emphasised restorative justice (Freivalds, 1996). Moreover, the number of victim-offender mediation programmes has increased steadily in recent years (Umbreit *et al*, 2000). It is difficult to know the implications of this trend for the rehabilitative philosophy. On the one hand, restorative justice programmes may limit criticism that the juvenile court is too soft on delinquents; such criticism was damaging to the rehabilitative philosophy in the 1960s and 1970s. On the other hand, some view restorative justice as a threat to the rehabilitative philosophy. Levrant *et al* (1999) argue that restorative justice's potential for rehabilitation has been overstated, and that in practice, these programmes in the United States often emphasise retribution at the expense of restoration or rehabilitation.

In sum, the future of the rehabilitative philosophy in the United States is unclear. There are signs of resurgence, but there also are signs of threat. If the past is any indication, the status of rehabilitation will remain tenuous in the coming decades.

REFERENCES

Ainsworth, J E (1991) 'Re-Examining Childhood and Reconstructing the Legal Order: The Case for Abolishing the Juvenile Court' 69 *North Carolina Law Review* 1083–133.

Allen, F A (1959) 'Criminal Justice, Legal Values and the Rehabilitative Ideal' 50 *Journal of Criminal Law, Criminology and Police Science* 226–32.

Andrews, D A, Zinger, I, Hoge, R D, Bonta, J, Gendreau, P & Cullen, F T (1990) 'Does Correctional Treatment Work?: A Clinically Relevant and Pyschologically Informed Meta-Analysis' 28 *Criminology* 369–404.

Applegate, B K, Cullen, F T, & Fisher, B S (1997), 'Public Support for Correctional Treatment: The Continuing Appeal of the Rehabilitative Ideal' 77 *The Prison Journal* 237–58.

Barnes, H E (1972), *The Story of Punishment*, 2nd edn (Patterson-Smith, Montclair, NJ).

Barnett, R (1981) 'Restitution: A New Paradigm for Criminal Justice' in B Galaway & J Hudson (eds) *Perspectives on Crime Victims* (Mosby, St. Louis) 245–61.

Bartollas, C, Miller, S J & Dinitz, S (1976) *Juvenile Victimization: The Institutional Paradox* (John Wiley and Sons, New York).

Bremner, R H (ed) (1970) *Children and Youth in America: A Documentary History* (Harvard University Press, Cambridge, Mass).

Brockway, Z R (1910) 'The American Reformatory Prison System' in C R Henderson (ed) *Prison Reform and Criminal Law* (Charities Publication Committee, New York) 88–107.

—— (1912) *Fifty Years of Prison Service: An Autobiography* (Charities Publication Committee, New York).

Butts, J A, & Mitchell, O (2000) 'Brick by Brick: Dismantling the Border Between Juvenile and Adult Justice' in C M Friel (ed) *Boundary Changes in Criminal Justice Organizations*; Criminal Justice 2000 Vol. 2 (National Institute of Justice, Rockville, Md) 167–213.

Carlson, N (1975) 'Giving Up the Medical Model?' 6 *Behavior Today* 1.

Carter, R M & Wilkins, L T (eds) (1970) *Probation and Parole: Selected Readings* (John Wiley, New York).

Clemmer, D (1940) *The Prison Community* (Christopher, Boston).

Cohen, L E (1975) *Juvenile Dispositions: Social and Legal Factors Related to the Processing of Denver Delinquency Cases* (US Government Printing Office, Washington, DC).

Cressey, D R (ed) (1961) *The Prison: Studies in Institutional Organization and Change* (Holt, Rinehart & Winston, New York).

Dawson, R O (1990) 'The Future of Juvenile Justice: Is It Time to Abolish the System?' 81 *Journal of Criminal Law and Criminology* 136–55.

Diana, L (1960) 'What Is Probation?' 51 *Journal of Criminal Law, Criminology and Police Science* 189–208.

Doble Research Associates (1995) *Crime and Corrections: The Views of the People of Oregon* (Doble Research Associates, Englewood Cliffs, NJ).

Federle, K H (1990) 'The Abolition of the Juvenile Court: A Proposal for the Preservation of Children's Legal Rights' 16 *Journal of Contemporary Law* 23–51.

Feld, B C (1990) 'The Punitive Juvenile Court and the Quality of Procedural Justice: Disjunctions Between Rhetoric and Reality' 36 *Crime and Delinquency* 443–46.

—— (1993) 'Criminalizing the American Juvenile Court' in M Tonry (ed) *Crime and Justice: A Review of Research*, vol 17 (University of Chicago Press, Chicago) 197–280.

Fogel, D (1975) *We Are the Living Proof: The Justice Model for Corrections* (Anderson, Cincinnati).

Fox, S J (1974) 'The Reform of Juvenile Justice: The Child's Right to Punishment' 25 *Juvenile Justice* 2–9.

Freivalds, P (1996) 'Balanced and Restorative Justice Project' *Office of Juvenile Justice and Delinquency Prevention: Fact Sheet* (Office of Juvenile Justice and Delinquency Prevention, Washington DC).

Gaylin, W & Rothman, D J (1976) 'Introduction' in A von Hirsch, *Doing Justice: The Choice of Punishments* (Hill & Wang, New York) xxi–xli.

Gendreau, P & Ross, R R (1987) 'Revivification of Rehabilitation: Evidence from the 1980s' 4 *Justice Quarterly* 349–407.

Glaser, D (1964) *The Effectiveness of a Prison and Parole System* (Bobbs-Merrill, Indianapolis).

Greenwood, P 1 & Zimring, F E (1985) *One More Chance: The Pursuit of Promising Intervention Strategies for Chronic Delinquent Offenders* (Rand, Santa Monica, Calif).

Hart, H (1910) *Preventive Treatment of Neglected Children* (Russell Sage, New York).

Hawkins, R & Alpert, G P (1989) *American Prison Systems: Punishment and Justice* (Prentice-Hall, Englewood Cliffs, NJ).

Henderson, C R (ed) (1910) *Prison Reform and Criminal Law* (Charities Publication Committee, New York).

Henggeler, S W (1997) 'Treating Serious Antisocial Behavior in Youth: The MST Approach' *Office of Juvenile Justice and Delinquency Prevention: Juvenile Justice Bulletin* (Office of Juvenile Justice and Delinquency Prevention, Washington, DC).

Lab, S P & Whitehead, J T (1988) 'An Analysis of Juvenile Correctional Treatment' 34 *Crime and Delinquency* 60–83.

—— (1990) 'From "Nothing Works" to "The Appropriate Works": The Latest Stop on the Search for the Holy Grail' 28 *Criminology* 405–17.

Lemert, E M (1967) 'The Juvenile Court—Quest and Realities' in President's Commission on Law Enforcement and Administration of Justice, *Task Force Report: Juvenile Delinquency and Youth Crime* (US Government Printing Office, Washington, DC) 91–106.

Levrant, S, Cullen, F T, Fulton, B & Wozniak, J F (1999) 'Reconsidering Restorative Justice: The Corruption of Benevolence Revisited?' 45 *Crime and Delinquency* 3–27.

Lipsey, M W (1992) 'Juvenile Delinquency Treatment: A Meta-Analytic Inquiry into the Variability of Effects' in T D Cook *et al* (eds) *Meta-Analysis For Explanation: A Casebook* (Russell Sage Foundation, New York) 83–127.

Lipton, D, Martinson, R & Wilks, J (1975) *The Effectiveness of Correctional Treatment: A Survey of Treatment Evaluation Studies* (Praeger, New York).

Makeig, J (1994) 'Most in Poll Favor Rehabilitation for Youthful Offenders' *Houston Chronicle*, 19 February 30A.

Manocchio, A J & Dunn, J (1970) *The Time Game: Two Views of a Prison* (Sage, Beverly Hills).

Martin, S E, Sechrest, L B & Redner, R (eds) (1981) *New Directions in the Rehabilitation of Criminal Offenders* (National Academy of Sciences, Washington, DC).

Martinson, R (1974) 'What Works? Questions and Answers About Prison Reform' 35 *The Public Interest* 22–54.

——(1979) 'New Findings, New Views: A Note of Caution Regarding Sentencing Reform' 7 *Hofstra Law Review* 243–58.

McCarthy, F B (1977) 'Should Juvenile Delinquency be Abolished?' 23 *Crime and Delinquency* 196–203.

McKelvey, B (1936) *American Prisons: A Study in American Social History Prior to 1915* (University of Chicago Press, Chicago).

Mears, D P & Field, S H (2000) 'Theorizing Sanctioning in a Criminalized Juvenile Court' 38 *Criminology* 983–1020.

Mennel, R M (1973) *Thorns and Thistles: Juvenile Delinquents in the United States, 1825–1940* (University Press of New England, Hanover, NH).

Miller, W B (1974) 'Ideology and Criminal Justice Policy: Some Current Issues,' in S L Messinger *et al* (eds), *The Aldine Crime and Justice Annual, 1973* (Aldine, Chicago) 453–73.

Moon, M M, Sundt, J L, Cullen, F T & Wright, J P (2000) 'Is Child Saving Dead? Public Support for Juvenile Rehabilitation' 46 *Crime and Delinquency* 38–60.

Moore, D W (1994) 'Majority Advocate Death Penalty for Teenage Killers', *Gallup Poll Monthly*, September: 2–6.

National Advisory Commission on Criminal Justice Standards and Goals (1973a) *A National Strategy to Reduce Crime* (US Government Printing Office, Washington, DC).

——(1973b) *Courts* (US Government Printing Office, Washington, DC).

Ohlin, L E & Lawrence, W C (1959) 'Social Interaction Among Clients as a Treatment Problem' 4 *Social Work* 3–13.

Olds, D, Hill, P & Rumsey E (1998) 'Prenatal and Early Childhood Nurse Home Visitation', *Office of Juvenile Justice and Delinquency Prevention: Juvenile Justice Bulletin* (Office of Juvenile Justice and Delinquency Prevention, Washington, DC).

Palmer, T (1991) 'The Effectiveness of Intervention: Recent Trends and Current Issues' 37 *Crime and Delinquency* 330–46.

——(1995) 'Programmatic and Nonprogrammatic Aspects of Successful Intervention: New Directions for Research' 41 *Crime and Delinquency* 100–31.

Peters, M, Thomas, D, Zamberlan, C & Caliber Associates (1997) *Boot Camps for Juvenile Offenders* (Office of Juvenile Justice and Delinquency Prevention, Washington, DC).

Pettigrove, F G (1910) 'The State Prisons of the United States Under Separate and Congregate Systems' in C R Henderson (ed.), *Penal and Reformatory Institutions* (Charities Publication Committee, New York) 27–67.

Platt, A M (1969) *The Child Savers: The Invention of Delinquency* (University of Chicago Press, Chicago).

President's Commission on Law Enforcement and Administration of Justice (1967a) *Task Force Report: Corrections* (US Government Printing Office, Washington, DC).

——(1967b) *Task Force Report: Juvenile Delinquency and Youth Crime* (US Government Printing Office, Washington, DC).

Rosenbaum, D P & Hanson, G S (1998) 'Assessing the Effects of School-Based Drug Education: A Six-Year Multilevel Analysis of Project DARE' 35 *Journal of Research in Crime and Delinquency* 381–412.

Rothman, D J (1979) 'The Progressive Legacy: Development of American Attitudes toward Juvenile Delinquency' in L T Empey (ed) *Juvenile Justice: The Progressive Legacy and Current Reforms* (University Press of Virginia, Charlottesville) 34–68.

Sanders, W B (ed) (1970) *Juvenile Offenders for a Thousand Years: Selected Readings from Anglo-Saxon Times to 1900* (University of North Carolina Press, Chapel Hill).

Schrag, C (1954) 'Leadership Among Prison Inmates' 19 *American Sociological Review* 37–42.

Schur, E M (1973) *Radical Nonintervention: Rethinking the Delinquency Problem* (Prentice-Hall, Englewood Cliffs).

Schwartz, I M, Kerbs, J J, Hogston, D M & Guillean, C L (1992) *Combatting Juvenile Crime: What the Public Really Wants* (Center for the Study of Youth Policy, Ann Arbor, MI).

Schwartz, M D & Travis, L F III (1997) *Corrections: An Issues Approach*; 4th edn (Anderson Publishing, Cincinnati, Oh).

Scott, J F (1910) 'American Reformatories for Male Adults' in C R Henderson (ed) *Penal and Reformatory Institutions* (Charities Publication Committee, New York) 89–120.

Sechrest, L, White, S O & Brown, E D (eds) (1979) *The Rehabilitation of Criminal Offenders: Problems and Prospects* (National Academy of Sciences, Washington, DC).

Sellin, T (1964) 'Introduction: Tocqueville and Beaumont and Prison Reform in France' in G de Beaumont & A de Tocqueville, *On the Penitentiary System in the United States and its Application in France* (Southern Illinois University Press, Carbondale) xv–xl.

Sherman, L W, Gottfredson, D C, MacKenzie, D L, Eck, J, Reuter, P & Bushway, S D (1998) 'Preventing Crime: What Works, What Doesn't, and What's Promising', *National Institute of Justice: Research in Brief* (National Institute of Justice, Rockville, Md).

Snyder, H N & Sickmund, M (1995) *Juvenile Offenders and Victims: A National Report* (Office of Juvenile Justice and Delinquency Prevention, Washington, DC).

Steinhart, D (1988) *California Opinion Poll: Public Attitudes on Youth Crime* (National Council on Crime and Delinquency, San Francisco).

Sykes, G M (1965) *The Society of Captives: A Study of a Maximum Security Prison* (Atheneum Press, New York).

Sykes, G M & Messinger, S L (1965) 'The Inmate Social System' in *Theoretical Studies in Social Organization of the Prison* (Social Science Research Council, Pamphlet No. 15) 5–19.

Tappan, P W (1960) *Crime, Justice and Correction* (McGraw-Hill, New York).

The Public Perspective: A Roper Center Review of Public Opinion and Polling (1997) (The Roper Center, Storrs, CT).

Tonry, M H (1976) 'Juvenile Justice and the National Crime Commissions' in M K Rosenheim (ed) *Pursuing Justice for the Child* (University of Chicago Press, Chicago) 281–98.

Torbet, P M (1996) *Juvenile Probation: The Workhorse of the Juvenile Justice System* (Office of Juvenile Justice and Delinquency Prevention, Washington, DC).

Umbreit, M S, Greenwood, J, Fercello, C & Umbreit, J (2000) *National Survey of Victim-Offender Mediation Programs in the United States* (US Department of Justice, Washington, DC).

United Nations (1951) *Probation and Related Measures* (Department of Social Affairs, New York).

van den Haag, E (1975) *Punishing Criminals: Concerning a Very Old and Painful Question* (Basic Books, New York).

von Hirsch, A (1976) *Doing Justice: The Choice of Punishments* (Hill & Wang, New York).

Whitehead, J T & Lab, S P (1989) 'A Meta-Analysis of Juvenile Correctional Treatment' 26 *Journal of Research in Crime and Delinquency* 276–95.

Wilson, J Q (1975) *Thinking About Crime* (Vintage Books, New York).

—— (1983) *Thinking About Crime*, rev. ed. (Vintage Books, New York).

Wines, F H (1910) 'Historical Introduction' in C R Henderson (ed) *Prison Reform and Criminal Law* (Charities Publication Committee, New York) 3–38.

Zehr, H (1982) *Mediating the Victim/Offender Conflict* (Mennonite Central Committee, Akron, Pa).

Part II

Education and Punishment

5

Not Punishing Children, but Committing Them to Restore

LODE WALGRAVE

1. ON PUNISHMENT

PUNISHMENT IS THE intentional infliction of a deprivation (hard treatment, pain) on someone, because he[1] has supposedly committed a wrong (von Hirsch, 1993: 9). Three elements are crucial: the hard treatment inflicted, the intention that the punished person should suffer and the link between the infliction of pain and the wrong previously committed. If one of these elements is lacking, there is no punishment.

1.1. The Context of Punishment

Punishment occurs in very different contexts, in which behaviour is judged according to normative standards by a powerful agent. Children are punished by their parents in families, by their teachers in schools. Employees are punished by their employers, football players by referees, and so on. Citizens are punished by judges who are given legal power to decide whether their behaviour is legally wrong and to impose a corresponding hard treatment on the wrongdoer.

The context of punishment is crucial to understanding its impact. The deepest differences may exist between punishment in the family and punishment by the criminal justice system.

A family punishment is a private affair: why punishment is imposed by parents and how it is experienced by the child is primarily to be understood within the relationship between the actors involved. In well functioning families, hard treatment is imposed in a context of affection and support. The child experiences the daily commitment of his parents to his well being, their love and care, and he therefore basically trusts that, even if his parents impose hard treatment, this is done for his good. The parents are given moral authority to distinguish right from wrong and to attach the appropriate consequences to them. Even if

---

[1] For practical reasons, I shall use the male form as the general form. This should not be understood as any kind of hidden or open sexism.

the child feels a punishment to be unfair, he will not reject his parents, because he accepts that they essentially want what is good for him. The child understands that the negative moment is not a definitive split, but only a suspension of the loving relationship. This usually amounts to a kind of reintegrative shaming, as described by John Braithwaite (1989): the action is shamed, not the person, and after shaming, gestures of reintegration will confirm the child as part of the parents' loved world.

Punishment by the judiciary is fundamentally different. Punishment is now a public affair. Unlike punishment in families, it is not about a relationship between the punisher and the punished. At least three parties are now involved: the state, the offender and the victim (Ashworth, 1986; 2000). The punisher, the judge, is considered to be a neutral agent. The judgement is addressed not only to the offender, but also to the public and to the victim. Because imposing a punishment is an intrusion into rights and freedoms, it may only be done in strictly limited cases, and within strict procedures. Sentencing procedures and possible sentences are therefore highly formalised.

This takes us far from the conditions of family punishment. Moreover, and contrary to the love and care evidently experienced in most families, many offenders have suffered a career of social exclusion and failure. They view society and its (judicial) representatives as hostile and unjust. Unlike the parents in relation to the child, the judge has no moral authority in the eyes of the offender. The judge is perceived as a professional who is paid to do his job—a job which further excludes the offender. The punishment is seen as the confirmation or reinforcement of the negative relationships that already existed.

Some authors do compare the 'educative punishments' in youth courts with punishments imposed in families, but this seems wrong.[2] The type of context, the relationship between punisher and punished, the parties involved, the 'sentencing procedures', the impact on the person punished, all are too different to put them on a par. Learning psychology has identified conditions for making reward and punishment effective, and the operations of the courts are far from fulfilling these (Van Doosselaere, 1988). In punishing, the State does not and cannot act as a 'good parent' towards offenders.

1.2. Ethical Problems in Punishing

Punishment poses a fundamental ethical problem (Fatic, 1995). In most moral systems, the deliberate and coercive imposition of suffering on another person

---

[2] True, not all parents are equal, as are not all judges. Some parents are very problematic punishers and provoke understandable resistance in their children. Some judges are charismatic open minded persons and succeed in achieving constructive dialogues with the offenders. I have described here what in my mind typically happens, in view of the structural and functional characteristics of families and parents, and of courts and judges.

is considered to be unethical and socially destructive. Punishment '. . . involves actions that are generally considered to be morally wrong or evil were they not described and justified as punishments' (de Keijser, 2000: 7). So, what kind of exceptional circumstances or arguments would make the deliberate infliction of pain morally acceptable?

In family situations, the ethical issues are not normally so prominent. Punishment is primarily seen as an educative instrument to teach the child that certain behaviour is wrong, so that he will not repeat that behaviour. It is implicitly accepted that the parents' love and care are generally sufficient to safeguard a morally 'good' punishing practice. Ethical limitations appear only in problematic cases, where punishments seem to be inappropriate, for instance because they are too severe. Then, public welfare agencies may intervene.

The problem is different in criminal justice, though it seems hard to avoid the punishment of offences . Even abolitionists end up by reformulating a kind of 'hidden' penal law in their alternative accounts (Blad, 1996). Nils Christie, for whom the 'reduction of man-inflicted pain on earth' is the central value to pursue, and who therefore combats the punitive criminal justice system, finally accepts that 'absolute punishment' may be needed in some cases to express the grief and mourning caused by certain crimes (Christie, 1981). But why this is so remains unanswered. 'Punishing today is a deeply problematic and barely understood aspect of social life, the rationale for which is by no means clear' (Garland, 1990: 3).

1.3. Two Types of Penal Theories

Penal theories are predominantly of two types: retributivist or deontological, and consequentialist or instrumental. Retributivism flows from the Kantian principle that punishing the wrongdoing is a 'categorical imperative', and it is not primarily interested in questions about the possible goals or effects of punishment. Consequentialists, by contrast, reflect on the purposes for which the criminal justice system exists, and derive constraints for the system from the goals that they posit.

Though several versions of the basic retributivist approach exist (see von Hirsch, 1998), they all share more or less the same drawbacks (Fatic, 1995; Braithwaite & Pettit, 1990; Walgrave, 2001). First, a purely deontological theory is untenable. It inevitably hides goals which are ultimately consequentialist. If, for example, punishment is said to be necessary to confirm moral rules, this concern to preserve morality is inspired by a concern to maintain life in community. Advancing a system of punishment for purely moral principles, without asking any questions about its impact on those involved and on social life in general, would show a rigid and asocial attitude which would be immoral itself. After all, if criminal justice does not (at least implicitly) serve some goal, what should we fear from abolishing this expensive machinery of pain causation?

Secondly, the portrayal of punishment as a confirmer of the system of rules leaves us no room to question the morality of the system itself. Punishment may be used, or misused, to enforce any legal system, even if the legal rules are themselves immoral. This issue arises not only for penal justice in obviously totalitarian regimes, but for laws in Western democratic States. Why, for example, is penal law predominantly geared to public order, personal security and property, and not to social peace, solidarity and socio-economic equity?

Finally, given that the deliberate infliction of pain is in principle ethically questionable, alternative ways to express social rejection of the offence should be thoroughly explored. Everyday life, and experience of restorative processes, show that these alternatives do exist (see infra, ss 3–4). Maintaining punishment as the a priori means of expressing blame is therefore in itself morally highly doubtful. In order to keep punishment as the a priori means of responding to crime, it should be underpinned by better reasons than retributivism can offer.

Does consequentialism provide these reasons? In fact, pure consequentialism is not tenable either. It must always be limited by ethical principles. Otherwise, the end would justify the means. For example, widespread use of the death penalty could be promoted with the argument that its application is the only absolute guarantee against recidivism, and that it does not need large investments. The mere fact that most civilised states have abolished the death penalty shows a basic deontological consideration of respect for human life limiting the instrumental aims of criminal justice policy. Pure consequentialism would lead to the expansion of authoritarian social control to the extent that it would itself be uncontrollable. It would be insatiable (Braithwaite & Pettit, 1990: 78–80).

The consequentialist pretensions of penal justice can be empirically tested. Deterrence research has demonstrated that the general preventive impact of penal law is weak. 'Deterrent literature fails to find any strong compelling arguments that the law and sanctions have any major impact on the level of offending' (Lab, 1992: 116). There are much more effective methods of prevention (Lab, 1992 ; Tonry & Farrington, 1995).

The claim that punishment as such would have resocialising, rehabilitating or individually deterring effects on offenders has never been demonstrated. Recent years have witnessed a significant rise in 'What works' research, consisting mostly of meta-evaluations of all kinds of already evaluated programmes for (young) offenders (and their families). One of the conclusions is that 'punishment-based programmes . . . on average lead to a 25% *increase* in re-offending rate as compared with control groups' (McGuire & Priestly, 1995:10, emphasis added). The assumption that offences have to be punished therefore appears to be an obstacle to the rehabilitation of offenders, rather than an opportunity or a direct means to rehabilitate them.

1.4. Rejecting the Punishment Paradigm in Criminal Justice

Garland writes that punishment is 'an expression of state power, . . . a vehicle for emotional expression, an economically conditioned social policy . . . a set of symbols which displays a cultural ethos and help create a social identity' (Garland, 1990: 287). It is nevertheless quite a negative idea that these functions can only be achieved through inflicting pain on those who have committed offences. The fact that pain is inflicted in a rational, controlled manner by a legal authority is still more negative, because it has lost the excuse of emotional indignation and anger. Criminal punishment is a well-considered negative act that refuses to consider the context that has caused the offence.

For society at large, penal criminal justice intervention offers a strong confirmation of legal order and of legal safeguards for those involved, but public safety is badly served by it. Punitive justice stigmatises, excludes, responds to violence with counter-violence and does not contribute to reconciliation or to peace. Pure punishment carries the seeds of more discord and unhappiness, and thus of more crime and criminalisation.

Nor does penal criminal justice offer much comfort to the victim (Dignan & Cavadino, 1998). Victims are typically used as witnesses, and are then left alone with their losses and grievances. Moreover, the priority given to the penal procedure and the penal sanction usually hinders the opportunities for victims to be compensated and/or restored.

In penal law, the offender is recognised as a bearer of rights, but the sanction itself is a senseless infliction of suffering that does not contribute to public safety, or to the victim's interests. It is a needless intrusion into the offender's rights and freedom, which adds an additional threat to his social future.

1.5. Censure, Punishment and Communication

The necessity to censure the offence does not entail the necessity to punish it. The relation between reprobation and punishment should be considered in two directions. First, not all punishments express blame. Many professional criminals and white collar criminals consider it not as blame, but as a rationally balanced risk to take when they go for a benefit by criminal action. For juveniles involved in subcultures, being arrested and condemned is often a reason for pride in relation to their peers. Some scholars even argue that the *decrease* of social blaming in community provokes the need to *increase* penal punishment as an 'objective risk' for potentially criminal behaviour (Boutellier, 1996).

But, second, do we need punishment to express blame? Braithwaite (1989) and Braithwaite & Pettit (1990) uncouple this relation, as does von Hirsch (1993). Moral disapproval is expressed in everyday life by parents and teachers, by churches and other authoritative agencies, without any punishment being imposed, while still having great impact on behaviour. Victim-offender mediation and restorative conferencing include intense reprobation of the offence, but are not punishments: the act is blamed, moral disapproval is expressed, without hard treatment being deliberately inflicted on the one who committed the act. What is essential is that the disapproval is communicated in such a way that it is understood and accepted by those concerned—the offender, the victim and the community at large.

The communicative aspect of social responses to crime is indeed crucial, as pointed out by Duff (1986, 2001) and by Weijers (2000). The problem with their approaches is, however, that they cramp the communication into the a priori structure of punishment, which keeps the communication poor in content and difficult to achieve. The communication after the offence can and should be more complete and rich than is possible through punishment. Disapproval must make clear to the offender that his behaviour was unacceptable and socially destructive, but should at the same time avoid further exclusion by communicating the belief that he is able to reintegrate as a responsible member of society; the communication must offer the victim reassurance of his rights to protection and support by the community; society as a whole must receive confirmation of the norm and of the authorities' determination to enforce the norm and to protect citizens from victimisation.

Pursuing communication includes pursuing adequate conditions for communication. Most offenders are not affected by moralising sermons, but are sensitive to the concrete suffering of their victims. Offenders may be open to communication if they themselves experience respect and understanding. These and other conditions are difficult, if not impossible, to achieve in court, in confrontation with the judge who will in the end decide upon the kind and degree of hard treatment. In court, most offenders do not listen, but try to get off as lightly as possible. They do not hear the invitation, but experience the threat.

As I will argue, most restorative settings are much more apt for good communication.

2. A SPECIAL SYSTEM FOR JUVENILES?

How far do these critical comments on judicial punishment apply to the specialised procedures for dealing with offending children? In Western industrialised societies juvenile justice systems subordinate punishment to rehabilitative goals. Belgium even abolished punishment for juveniles below the age of 18 (with a few exceptions). Mostly, however, juvenile justice provides special types of punishment, aiming at re-educating offenders.[3]

This shift is supported by two types of argument. First, minority is taken to diminish guilt, since minors are 'less capable of understanding and willing' (Gatti

---

[3] For a survey of European systems, see Mehlbye & Walgrave, 1998.

& Verde, 1998: 360). This 'excuse de minorité' (Gazeau & Peyre, 1998: 223) leads to a lightening of punishments as compared to those imposed on adults. Secondly, it is believed that young offenders can, more than adults, still be influenced positively. Punishments or other measures imposed should therefore be educational.

Because juveniles are considered to be less culpable, the troublesome behaviour is not primarily seen as a 'wrong' which must be punished, but as a mistake, due to problems in the juvenile's ongoing socialisation. Because parents obviously have not corrected these problems, the State takes the *'parens patriae'* position, meaning that the State will take care of the further development and welfare of the juvenile. By enhancing the young offender's welfare, it is believed, his 'need' or 'tendency' to commit offences will be diminished.

Two clusters of criticisms are advanced against this approach: (1) it is at odds with basic legal safeguards, to which all citizens, including juveniles, are entitled; and (2) it is generally inefficient.

2.1. Legal Problems with Juvenile Justice

In *in re Gault* (387 US 1 [1967]), the US Supreme Court offered the first severe legal critique of the *'parens patriae'* conception of juvenile justice. Since then, analogous objections have been advanced all over the world. The basic problem is that the attempt to address the needs of the offender rather than the wrongfulness of the offence shifts the focus of the intervention from the offence to the offender. It is not the offence, committed in the past, that determines the content and intensity of the intervention, but the welfare of the offender, as a future aim. Whereas penal justice is retrospective, juvenile justice is prospective. Sentencing does not rely on an already available criterion for deciding upon the appropriate amount of deprivation of liberty, but seeks a future goal. Clinical and pedagogical interpretations and expectations, rather than legally established facts, prevail in sentencing (Feld, 1999: 28–30). Re-educative and clinical considerations and speculations are joined with the interventionist power of the judge. It thus becomes hard to safeguard due process principles, and proportionality to the seriousness of the crime is a secondary or even absent consideration. With the argument that their welfare must be preserved, young offenders are subjected to longer sentences than they would undergo were they adults, and the net of judicial control over juveniles widens dramatically. In many juvenile justice systems, youth courts' competencies are not limited to interventions against young offenders, but also include 'preventative' interventions in so called 'risk families', or towards juveniles who have committed no crime, but who are considered to be 'at risk'. This is what is rightly rejected by Braithwaite and Pettit as 'preventionism', because it makes the system and its interventions 'insatiable' (Braithwaite & Pettit, 1990: 46–8, 78–80).

It is in fact a mission impossible, to try to combine the humane goal of responding to the needs of juveniles and their families with the societal need for just and fair trials. The constraints of formal procedural rules hinder the possibilities for flexibility and rich human dialogue which the therapeutic ambitions require, and vice versa. As the US Supreme Court said, 'The child receives the worst of both worlds: he gets neither the protections accorded to adults nor the solicitous care . . . postulated for children' (*Kent v US* 383 US 541, 556 [1966]; quoted in Feld, 1993: 198).

In the face of these problems, two types of positions have so far been adopted. The first is to give up the impossible combination, and to return to a more explicit penal framework. One of the most forceful defenders of such a move is Feld (1999). On the basis of a thorough analysis of what happens to juveniles under the treatment-oriented juvenile justice regime in most American states, he concludes that juveniles would both legally and in fact be better off if they were subjected to the traditional criminal justice system, including effective rights of defence and proportionate punishments. In his view, criminal justice would then provide a 'youth discount' in the amount of punishment inflicted. This is not the position I would accept. Feld's suggestion would indeed hand over the juveniles to the a priori punitive response, which I criticised above.

Another way of responding to the juridical problems in juvenile justice is typified by several international organisations. They have reaffirmed their belief in a specialised juvenile justice system to address the specific needs of juveniles, but have at the same time laid down minimum rules and recommendations as to the legal guarantees to be assured for minors.[4] The so-called Beijing rules are often quoted as an important set of guidelines to improve the quality of jurisdiction towards juveniles (Doek, 1991: 206)· Nevertheless, ambivalence persists. It is easy to state that the judicial reaction 'should be in proportion to both the offender and the offence' (statement 5.1), but it is very difficult in practice to combine these two proportionalities. How can we 'allow appropriate scope for discretion at all stages of proceedings' (statement 6.1), and at the same time assure 'the principles of fair and just trial' (statement 14.1)? The proclamation of basic principles for the special treatment of juveniles cannot avoid its basic problem, ie the impossible combination of welfare ambitions with juridical rules guaranteeing constraints of justice.

In the last few years, a third response to these juridical problems with juvenile justice has emerged, involving a radically different way of doing justice. I will explain this in ss 3–4.

2.2. Efficiency Problems with Juvenile Justice

The instrumentalist ambitions of juvenile justice can be empirically checked. It becomes evident that a century of juvenile justice cannot claim any triumphant

---

[4] See eg *United Nations Standard Minimum Rules for the Administration of Juvenile Justice (Beijing Rules* 1985), the *United Nations Standard Minimum Rules for Juveniles deprived of their Liberty* (1990), and several Council of Europe Recommendations.

results. First, it has not contributed to a general feeling of security. This may be one of the reasons why most countries are now 're-penalising' their juvenile justice systems (Schüler-Springorum, 1999).

Secondly, and more importantly, court-ordered measures and treatments generally have no significant positive impact on individual integration or re-offending. In recent years, a lot has been published under the label 'What works'. Based mostly on meta-analyses, these studies suggest that under some conditions (proper staff training and expertise, proper implementation and assessment) some programmes do work (Lipsey, 1992; McGuire & Priestley, 1995). They have provoked a new rise in treatment-optimism that goes far beyond the scope of the balanced 'What works' publications. Many treatment programmes are now advocated which have in fact been shown not to work.

All in all, it seems that cognitive-behavioural programmes such as behavioural therapy, relaxation techniques or social skills training have some positive outcomes, manifested in, inter alia, an estimated reduction in re-offending of 10 per cent to 12 per cent (McGuire & Priestley, 1995). Structured, responsibilising programmes were more effective than others. However, it is difficult to generalise these conclusions. (1) The studies measure only quantifiable aspects of the interventions, and seldom include possibly important context-oriented interventions, such as 'community building' and its impact on the social environment. (2) The evaluations usually isolate the intervention from its social and human context: accurate scientific monitoring, a pioneer mentality, charismatic individuals, exceptionally good co-operation by police and judiciary, etc. The gap between such pioneering experiments and more generalised routine practices seriously reduces the value of the original experiment. (3) The meta-analyses also show a great diversity of problems underlying patterned crime, for which a diversity of appropriate treatment programmes should be offered. The heart of a treatment-oriented system should thus consist of a diagnostic dispatching centre, in order to ensure appropriate referrals. The feasibility of such centres is still to be demonstrated. (4) The 'what works' analyses fail to pose essential questions on the socio-ethical acceptability of sometimes long and intensive restrictions of liberty, which seem disproportionate to the often limited seriousness of the offences committed, and which are of doubtful efficiency.

That does not mean that treatment, re-education or other types of rehabilitation-oriented initiatives for youthful offenders are useless. On the contrary. Many delinquents are societally vulnerable, enjoy only poor social opportunities and have unfavourable social prospects. An ethically motivated society should consider it an obligation to offer them additional support and new opportunities for integration into conforming social life.

But welfare work is no task for the criminal justice system. The criminal justice system's function is to control the citizens' respect for legal obligations and prohibitions, and to intervene with legalised force if they do not. Other institutions and agencies exist to offer opportunities for support and promoting welfare. Welfare matters become the business of the justice system only if disagreements emerge and coercive decisions are considered to be necessary. But in a constitutional democratic state, it is crucial to keep the use of force under the strict control of legal safeguards. It is difficult, if not impossible, to combine this with a welfare perspective. For this reason, and because enforced treatment is itself seriously hindered by the use of force, everything possible must be done to keep welfare oriented work outside the reach of the criminal justice system.

2.3. The Need to Look for a Radical Renovation

The ongoing dilemma between welfare orientation and juridical correctness seems to have led to a deadlock. Judicial coercion needs strict legal rules, and welfare orientation needs openness, informalism and flexibility. The idea that juveniles are subjected to 're-educative punishments', while comparing this punishment model to family sanctioning, does not resolve the dilemma. As argued above, comparing family punishment with judicial punishment is playing with words, but does not reflect reality. It is, as van de Kerchove calls it, a 'mystification du langage' (1976–1977). Instead of trying to find new rhetorics to justify the unjustifiable, many scholars believe that juvenile justice and justice in general should look for totally new ways of doing justice after the occurrence of a crime. An increasing number of them believe that it can be found by developing the restorative justice paradigm as a fully-fledged systemic alternative (see eg Barnet,t 1977; Galaway & Hudson, 1990; Zehr, 1990; Messmer & Otto, 1992; Walgrave, 1994, 2000b; Bazemore & Umbreit, 1995; Van Ness & Heetderks Strong, 1997; Bazemore & Walgrave, 1999a).

3. IN SEARCH OF RESTORATIVE JUSTICE

According to the restorative justice paradigm, the function of (juvenile) justice is not to punish, not even to (re-)educate, but to provide the conditions for reasonable reparation or compensation for the harm caused by the offence. Though based on ancient principles (Weitekamp, 1999; Schafer, 1977), restorative justice has only recently re-emerged in our modern societies. It is rooted in a diversity of trends and movements, such as victim movements, communitarianism, indigenous emancipation movements, critical criminology and abolitionism (Faget, 1997: 23–38). Critical criminology focused in part on the juvenile justice system (Walgrave, 1994; Bazemore & Walgrave, 1999b).

These movements have given rise to a steadily growing number of experiments all over the world, most of which are focused on juveniles. To explain this would need a sociological analysis, but several possible reasons can be tentatively advanced. (1) As we saw in s 2, Western juvenile justice systems are currently under great pressure, so that movements towards renovation are more likely to occur there. (2) Youthful offending is in general considered to be less serious than adult crime. It may therefore be viewed as less risky to try out new models on juveniles. (3) Juvenile justice procedures are more flexible than adult procedures, so that restorative experiments can more easily be fitted in the judicial system or made complementary to it. (4) There is probably rather more public tolerance towards juvenile offending. It may therefore be politically more feasible to promote experiments with juveniles.

Victim-offender mediation in its different versions, family group conferencing, community service in some settings, all have in common (1) a definition of crime as an injury (concrete and societal) to victims, (2) an intervention primarily oriented towards restoration of that injury, (3) the acceptance of the offender's accountability and his active and direct involvement in the restorative action, and (4) the judicial framework, to supervise the operations of these modes of intervention.

These practices are sustained by an increasing flux of socio-ethical and juridico-theoretical reflection and of empirical research, leading to the awareness that much more is going on than just a few interesting techniques—that restorative justice could lay the foundations of a fully fledged alternative to both the punitive and the rehabilitative models of responding to crime.

At present, the concept of restorative justice has different definitions and interpretations (McCold, 1998). This diversity is not surprising, given the diversity of its philosophical roots and connections. But if the words 'restorative' and 'justice' have a meaning, it must be possible to find some principles which should be common to all conceptions and experiments that define themselves as being part of restorative justice (Bazemore & Walgrave, 1999b).

Bazemore and I see restorative justice as: 'every action that is primarily oriented towards doing justice by restoring the harm that has been caused by a crime' (1999b: 48). This definition provokes the key questions and major lines of discussion about restorative justice. (1) What is the harm caused by a crime? (2) Who is to be considered as suffering that harm? (3) How can that harm be restored? (4) What is justice and how can it be done?

3.1. The Harm

A focus on the harm done by the offence is the key to understanding restorative justice and to distinguishing it from the traditional retributive and rehabilitative justice models. This is why we call restorative justice another paradigm. According to the restorative justice paradigm, the problem posed by a crime is to be considered through the harm it has caused and the primary function of the response to it is not to punish or to rehabilitate, but to repair or compensate for that harm. In fact, restorative justice can partly function in the absence of a known offender: since the main goal is to restore the harm, individuals or agencies can provide support, assistance and compensation to victims, without an offender being involved. However, if the offender is known, his accountability must be taken seriously and his contribution to the restorative action will make it much more restorative.

In principle all kinds of harm are considered, including material losses, physical injuries, psychological consequences, relational troubles and social dysfunctions, in so far as they have been caused by an offence.

3.2. The Victim

Whom we should consider as suffering the harm is a matter of discussion among restorative justice advocates. All agree that the injuries and losses inflicted on the concrete victim are at the centre of the restorative action. Most authors also include community in their accounts, but it is difficult then to define such community and to make concrete the kind of harm that it has suffered.

Fierce disagreement exists about the question whether society should also be considered a victim. Some fear that recognising society as a victim will cause a shift back to the retributive situation, wherein the state has set itself up as the main victim, pushing the concrete victim into a subordinate position. We believe, however, that society inevitably has a role to play in the settlement of a crime. It is therefore better to specify that role accurately in order to avoid the feared dominance of the state. It is one of the most delicate challenges in the enterprise of restorative justice, to conceive the role of the State (or government) in such a way that it does not impede the restorative process, whilst still playing its norm-enforcing role.

3.3. The Restoration

Restoration is achieved by a process and its outcome. The possible reparative outcomes include a wide range of actions such as restitution, compensation, reparation, reconciliation, apology. They may be direct or indirect, concrete or symbolic. Depending on the nature of the victimisation under consideration, they may be addressed to the concrete victim, to his intimates, to a community or even to society. Several types of victim restitution or community service seem to be archetypes of such actions, but creative practitioners still invent new versions of them.

Different processes exist to aim at such restorative outcomes. The most important distinction is based on voluntariness. The processes of voluntary negotiation and agreement, direct or indirect, between the offender and his victim, whether as individuals or backed by their intimates (victim-offender mediation, restorative group conferences and the like) are generally accepted as being restorative, and there is no doubt that the restorative calibre of compensatory actions is much higher if they are voluntarily accepted than if they are imposed. Some proponents therefore insist on voluntariness as a necessary feature of restorative justice processes, and reject all kinds of pressure and coercion. Others however, including myself, would allow for some coercive juridical procedures under the arch of restorative justice.

3.4. Doing Justice

'Justice' has two meanings. On the one hand, it refers to a feeling of equity, of being dealt with in a just way, according to a subjective balance of rights and wrongs (in Dutch: *'gerechtigheid'* or *'rechtvaardigheid'*). On this reading, restorative justice aims at the optimal satisfaction of all parties involved. Victims feel that their victimisation has been taken seriously and that the compensation and support are reasonably in balance with their sufferings and losses. Offenders feel that their dignity has not been unnecessarily hurt and that they have been given the opportunity to make up for their mistakes in a constructive way.

But justice also refers to legality (in Dutch: *'recht'*, *'gerecht'* or *'justitie'*). On this reading, restorative justice requires that the restorative process and its outcomes respect the legal safeguards to which all citizens are entitled. Even voluntary settlements in the aftermath of an offence must respect the legal rights of the victims and offenders. Participation must in no way be imposed, and agreements must be accepted and reasonable in relation to the seriousness of the harm and to the accountability and the capacities of the parties.

In a coercive procedure, all legal guarantees such as legality, due process and a proportionate maximum of sanction must be observed. This aspect of justice provokes a debate on the role of the State and its justice system in the restorative justice process.

4. FOR A MAXIMALIST SYSTEM OF RESTORATIVE JUSTICE

The points of disagreement among restorative justice advocates and researchers that I noted above reflect a fundamental debate about the position of restorative justice.

4.1. Communication as the Basis of Restorative Justice

Many have turned to restorative justice out of dissatisfaction with the functioning of the formal criminal justice system. They observe the benefits of informal, voluntary settlements, and try to develop as large a space for such practices as possible. There is no dispute about the enormous value of such processes.

The key to understanding this is communication. After a crime has been committed, there is a need for communication. Something went wrong in the social interactions among individuals, people have been victimised, legal rules have been infringed and messages have to be exchanged in order to find out what went wrong and why, and how it can be constructively resolved. In restorative justice, the need for communication is taken very seriously and processes are developed to promote communication and facilitate communicative outcomes. The communicative strength in restorative processes lies in their focus on the harm and suffering caused, concretised in the victim. The offender is confronted directly with the negative consequences of his behaviour and with the person who suffered those consequences most concretely. Most offenders are deeply touched by this confrontation, and feel emotionally (sometimes more than they understand cognitively) the reason why their behaviour should be blamed. Such direct confrontation has a much higher communicative potential than a moral-ising address by an authoritarian agent, referring to an abstract victim and abstract rules. Whether or not the confrontation works positively depends on, among other things, how the other participants in the process frame it. They may blame the act, but should not threaten the actor. They should not reject the offender, but should encourage him to make up for the wrongs committed, and offer 'gestures of reintegration' (Braithwaite, 1989: 55). Restorative procedures aim to promote such dynamics by creating a context of mutual respect, wherein communication is not pre-structured by formal rules, but is left open to hori-zontal exchanges of messages, and driven by the commitment of the participants to finding a solution which is reparative for the victim, reintegrative for the offender and constructive for social life as a whole. It is for the sake of commun-ication that restorative justice advocates reject the a priori choice of formalist penal procedures which aim to impose hard treatment.[5]

4.2. Divergence

Despite agreement on this basic position, there is divergence among restorative theorists as to its scope. The communicative process described above will only occur when it is accepted voluntarily by the parties. Victim and offender, for example, must be aware that they have a common interest in at least minimal mutual understanding, and in coming to an agreement, based on common val-ues and possibly shared benefits. This is obviously not always the case, to say the least. After many crimes, one of the parties is not willing to participate vol-untarily, or to comply with freely accepted agreements on compensation or restitution. What divides restorative justice advocates is the question of how we should deal with this problem.

---

[5] Penal justice advocates, on the contrary, accept the formal procedures and punitive outcomes a priori, and try to find some space for communication within them. The communication-based just-ifications of traditional criminal justice lack credibility because of the anti-communicative proced-ures, structures and scope of possible reactions inherent in criminal justice systems.

Some prominent scholars are anxious to preserve the benefits of informal voluntary settlements, and therefore exclude any intrusion by formalised state institutions (Fattah, 1993; McCold, 2000). They prefer to keep restorative justice as a form of diversion from the criminal justice system, rather than run the risk of losing the benefits of its informality (Dünkel, 1996; Marshall, 1996). These theorists want to withdraw as many cases as possible from the criminal justice system, but they exclude the system itself from their reflections and experiments. They leave the cornerstone of the social response to crime to traditional punitive or rehabilitative approaches. In the diversionists' view, the traditional system must take over when voluntary settlements cannot be achieved.

For many, including me, the diversionist option is not sufficient. First, because it would probably select the less serious cases for restorative solutions, whereas the victims of the most serious crimes are most in need of reparation and restoration. Secondly, because it leaves the existing criminal justice system out of the discussion, and fails to offer any alternative to the retributive and purely rehabilitative systems of responding to crime. Earlier in this chapter, I argued that we need a fully fledged alternative. This is especially true with regard to juvenile justice, where restorative justice could help to avoid the shift towards a renewed punishment-based approach.

The maximalist version recognises the crucial advantages of informal restorative processes, especially because of their communicative and peacemaking potential, and agrees with the 'diversionists' that we must maximise the space for such processes. But 'maximalists' explore the possibility of going further, and of reorienting the judicial process itself towards restoration, instead of punishment or rehabilitation. This position provokes many questions, of which I will deal briefly with three: (1) Does coercion not undermine the possible restorativeness to the extent that the 'justice' is no longer restorative? (2) What is the difference between juridically imposed restoration and punishment? (3) How can we combine these enforced restorative obligations with legal safeguards?

4.3. Coercion in Restorative Justice

Voluntariness in restorative processes is a very important value, because it greatly improves the restorative calibre of the response to a crime. A heartfelt apology can have a much deeper restorative impact than a material restitution which has been imposed. But given that in many cases voluntariness is not achieved, does that mark the limit of restorative justice? It does not. Courts can impose restorative obligations (or sanctions), such as material restitution or compensation to the victim, work for a Victims' Fund, or community service.

These sanctions certainly do not completely fulfil the aims of the restorative justice approach, but they are still preferable to forced punitive or rehabilitative interventions.

There is, first of all, the material benefit. The mere fact that something is actually done for the victims and for the community is certainly more beneficial than a retributive response.

Secondly, there is a reintegrative advantage. Even if the offender does not freely agree to undertake a restorative measure, he might in the longer term understand the sanction in a constructive way, and the chances for him to be re-accepted by the community are greater than after a retributive punishment. Moreover, the carrying out of restorative sanctions within the community is educational for the community itself.

Finally, even coercive restoration gives our response to crime a more principled coherence. Even if individual victims or offenders do not fulfil the constructive character of the restorative response, the state's mission should be to stick to the ethical principle of restoration, and to act as far as possible in accordance with it (Walgrave, 1999: 144).

4.4. Coerced Restorative Sanctions and Punishment

My acceptance of enforced restorative sanctions, imposed according to judicial procedures as a result of assessed accountability for the consequences of wrong behaviour, raises questions about the remaining differences between such restorative sanctions and traditional punishments. I have explained elsewhere why there are still key differences (Walgrave, 2001a, 2001b).

First, the two concepts belong on different levels. Whereas punishment is a means which can be used to enforce any system of rules, restoration is a goal which can be served by different means.

Secondly, whereas pain in punishment is deliberately inflicted for the sake of pain, pain in restoration is not intentional. Obligations to repair may be hard to comply with, but they are not meant to be hard. This is not to say that restorative obligations can be imposed irrespective of the possible burdens they inflict on the offender. The amount of the burden is, however, only a reason to diminish the obligation, never a reason to augment it, as it could be when the aim is to impose a proportionate retributive punishment.

Thirdly, the difference in intention makes the key difference with regard to ethics. As I noted in s 1.2, the intentional character of the pain inflicted in punishment poses a fundamental ethical problem. This is not the case for imposed restorative obligations.

Court-ordered restorative obligations may therefore be considered as sanctions in their own right, distinct both from punitive sanctions and from treatment-oriented measures. They are imposed for the sake of a social-ethical objective, namely to contribute to the quality of social life which was impaired by the offence.

4.5. Reflections on Legalising Restorative Justice

Maximalist restorative justice is not restricted to voluntary processes. It also includes the use of coercion, to be implemented by a 'restorative justice system'. Such a judicial system should offer all legal safeguards.[6] Some think that the legal problems involved in restorative justice are insurmountable. This makes them very sceptical of the feasibility of a restorative justice system (Ashworth, 1993; Feld, 1999). Others, however, take up the challenge, and reflect on the possible insertion of restorative justice into the principles of the democratic constitutional state (Van Ness & Heetderks Strong, 1997; Braithwaite & Parker, 1999; Van Ness, 1999; Walgrave, 2000a). I believe that the possibility of developing restorative justice into a fully fledged alternative should be thoroughly explored. The litmus test for it is to find a way to combine maximal scope for voluntary informal processes with legal safeguards applicable both to these processes and to judicially imposed restorative sanctions.

The few published reflections on that subject so far have enlisted a series of prescriptions to which penal law is subject, such as legality, due process, proportionality, and have then examined whether these constraints also apply to restorative justice, possibly in an adjusted form (Warner, 1994; Walgrave & Geudens, 1996; Van Ness, 1999).

However, the restorative justice paradigm might need to include specific deontological principles of its own; the deontological principles of penal law may not be simply transferable to a restorative justice system. Despite similarities, the aims and principles of restorative justice are different, and penal justice prescriptions may have to be reviewed (Walgrave, 2000a, 2001a).

Coercive judicial responses, under both a punitive and a restorative model, set clear limits to social tolerance, justify the intervention by reference to the past (to the seriousness of the crime committed or of the harm caused), include public interests as one reason for the intervention, are based on the accountability of the offender, can use force upon him, and may be painful.

As mentioned earlier, an essential difference between them lies in intention: whereas in punitive justice, hard treatment is an a priori aim, it is only a possible side effect in restorative justice, if the completion of the restoration makes it unavoidable. Another difference is that sentencing in restorative justice does not depend only on the seriousness of the crime or the harm and the degree of guilt (or accountability), as it does in traditional criminal justice. In restorative justice, a third criterion is added, namely to whom and how far the obligation will

---

[6] Voluntary sessions also need to be checked on their respect for legal rights (Warner, 1994; Wright, 1998; Trépanier, 1998). The voluntariness of the participation, the power balance in the negotiations, the reasonableness of the agreed compensation and the authenticity of the commitment to comply are elements to be checked and assured. This is not to say that legal formalism should intrude into the voluntary restorative process, but that this process should take place in a 'legalised context'.

be beneficial. The restorative sanction is meant to be beneficial for the victim, constructive for community (society) and possibly also reintegrative for the offender.

The further development of legal principles for restorative justice will have to consider yet more differences between the restorative and the penal model.

—The procedure must provide easy exits from the system towards informal processes for dealing with the aftermath of a crime in the community, because these processes have far more restorative potential than the formal system. The principle of subsidiarity is taken more seriously here than it is under the existing criminal law approach.
—The procedure will have to provide more space for the contribution and the interests of the victim, without, however, giving the victim any decisive power.
—The investigation must focus not only on assessing the facts and guilt, but also on defining the harm, suffering and social unrest caused by the offence. It must also seek possible ways to negotiate suitable repair for these harms.
—The sanction should not consist primarily of hard treatment, but must aim at restoring, as far as is possible, all the kinds of harms that were caused. This could be done, for example, by requiring restitution or compensatory work for victims, or work for a Victims' Fund, or community service.
—The 'volume' of the sanction must be determined retrospectively, by reference to the harm caused and the responsibilities of the agent; but its content must at the same time be determined prospectively, with a view to restoration in the future.

These few reflections offer only some indications of how it might be possible to legalise restorative justice. Restorative justice appears to be a promising track in the search for a better way of dealing with the aftermath of offences. It focuses on the core problem of an offence, namely the harm caused by it, tries to find socially constructive solutions for that problem, and seems at the same time to offer sufficient clues for constructing the legal safeguards that are necessary in a democratic constitutional state.

But restorative justice is a project under construction. The major challenge in developing restorative justice is to find a way to integrate it into the principles of a democratic constitutional state, whilst preserving as far as we can the human profundity and richness of the individual, emotionally based exchanges and commitments that restorative justice appears to make possible.

5. CONCLUSION

In my view, the a priori demand for punishment as a response to crime is ethically highly problematic and socially destructive, and should therefore be avoided. The educative arguments in favour of punishing children in a juridical system are empirically misplaced. Using the juvenile justice system primarily to try to re-educate young offenders is not realistic, and causes too many problems with regard to legal safeguards.

Therefore, the search must be for a third way, which would offer a better basis for the preservation of legal rights, and at the same time lead to constructive outcomes for all parties concerned. Based on the evidence thus far available, there are good reasons to further explore the potentials of restorative justice.

Focusing on the harm and suffering, and not on the offender's culpability for the offence or on his person, leads to questioning the existing two-track model in criminal justice, one track for adults and one for juveniles. For a victim, indeed, it makes no difference whether he has been robbed or beaten up by a boy of 16 or by a young adult of 21. The harm has to be repaired, and the offender has to make his reasonable contribution to this reparation. What counts as 'reasonable' may differ in degree, but is not intrinsically different. In fact, the acceptance of a separate justice system for juveniles is never a self-evident option. If it is accepted that the intrinsic qualities of a category of offenders can justify the maintenance of a separate system, there are no fundamental reasons not to invent other systems for the elderly, for females/males, for immigrants/autochthonous people. These categories also mark some systematic differences in life experiences and prospects; in their interpretations of needs and deeds. Like adults, children are entitled to all legal safeguards, and therefore need a system that retrospectively focuses on the offence or on its consequences. Conversely, adults' criminality is also often an expression of specific life circumstances, and adults should also be treated with respect and in a way that is as little destructive as possible of their future social integration. Guilt and culpability are not linked to a specific age threshold, but develop gradually. Age is only one of the indicators of differences, and often not the decisive one. I believe that, in the longer term, the abolition of the specialised juvenile justice system should be considered, but only if a general criminal justice system has been developed which provides constructive sanctions, and is flexible enough to sentence according to capacities and strengths (Walgrave, 2000a).

REFERENCES

Ashworth, A J (1986) 'Punishment and Compensation: Victims, Offenders and the State' 6 *Oxford Journal of Legal Studies* 86–122.
—— (1993) 'Some Doubts about Restorative Justice' 4 *Criminal Law Forum* 277–99.
—— (2000) 'Victims' Rights, Defendants' Rights and Criminal Procedure' in A Crawford & J Goodey (eds), *Integrating a Victim Perspective within Criminal Justice* (Ashgate, Aldershot) 185–204.
Barnett, R (1977) 'Restitution: a New Paradigm of Criminal Justice' in R Barnett & J Hagel (eds) *Assessing the Criminal* (Ballinger, Cambridge) 349–84.
Bazemore, G & Umbreit, M (1995) 'Rethinking the Sanctioning Function in Juvenile Court: Retributive or Restorative Responses to Youth Crime', 41 *Crime and Delinquency* 296–31.

Bazemore, G & Walgrave, L (eds) (1999a) *Restorative Juvenile Justice: Repairing the Harm by Youth Crime* (Criminal Justice Press, Monsey).

—— & —— (1999b) 'Restorative Juvenile Justice: in Search of Fundamentals and an Outline for Systemic Reform' in Bazemore & Walgrave (1999a) 45–74.

Blad, J (1996) *Abolitionisme als Strafrechtstheorie* (Gouda Quint, Arnhem).

Boutellier, H (1996) 'Beyond the Criminal Justice Paradox. Alternatives between Law and Morality' 4 *European Journal on Criminal Policy and Research* 7–20.

Braithwaite, J (1989) *Crime, Shame and Reintegration* (Cambridge University Press, Cambridge).

—— & Parker, C (1999) 'Restorative Justice is Republican Justice' in Bazemore & Walgrave (1999a) 103–26.

—— & Pettit, P (1990) *Not Just Deserts: A Republican Theory of Criminal Justice* (Oxford University Press, Oxford).

Christie, N (1981) *Limits to Pain* (Norwegian University Press, Oslo/Oxford).

de Keijser, J (2000) *Punishment and Purpose. From Moral Theory to Punishment in Action*, PhD thesis, University of Leyden.

Dignan, J & Cavadino, M (1998) 'Which Model of Criminal Justice Offers the Best Scope for Assisting Victims of Crime?' in E Fattah & T Peters (eds) *Support for Crime Victims in a Comparative Perspective* (Leuven University Press, Leuven) 139–68.

Doek, J (1991) 'The Future of the Juvenile Court' in J Junger-Tas, L Boendermaker & P van der Laan (eds) *The Future of the Juvenile Justice System* (Acco, Leuven) 197–210.

Duff, R A (1986) *Trials and Punishments* (Cambridge University Press, Cambridge).

—— (2001) *Punishment, Communication, and Community* (Oxford University Press, New York).

Dünkel, F (1996) 'Täter-Opfer Ausgleich. German Experiences with Mediation in a European Perspective' 4 *European Journal of Criminal Policy and Research* 44–66.

Faget, J (1997) *La Médiation. Essai de Politique Pénal* (Erès, Ramonville (F)).

Fatic, A (1995) *Punishment and Restorative Crime-Handling. A Social Theory of Trust* (Avebury, Aldershot).

Fattah, E (1993) 'From a Guilt Orientation to a Consequence Orientation. A Proposed New Paradigm for the Criminal Law in the 21st Century' in W Küper & J Welp (eds) *Einträge zur Rechtswissenschaft* (Müller Juristische Verlag, Heidelberg) 771–92.

Feld, B (1993), 'Criminalizing the American Juvenile Court' in M Tonry (ed) *Crime and Justice: a Review of Research*, vol 17 (University of Chicago Press, Chicago) 197–280.

—— (1999) 'Rehabilitation, Retribution and Restorative Justice: Alternative Conceptions of Juvenile Justice' in Bazemore & Walgrave (1999a) 17–44.

Galaway, B & Hudson, J (1990) 'Towards Restorative Justice' in B Galaway & J Hudson (eds) *Criminal Justice, Restitution and Reconciliation* (Willow Tree, Monsey) 1–3.

Garland, D (1990) *Punishment and Modern Society* (Clarendon Press, Oxford).

Gatti, U & Verde, A (1998) 'Italy' in J Mehlbye & L Walgrave (eds) *Confronting Youth in Europe. Juvenile Crime and Juvenile Justice* (AKF, Copenhagen) 355–88.

Gazeau, F & Peyre, V (1998) 'France' in J Mehlbye & L Walgrave (eds),*Confronting Youth in Europe. Juvenile Crime and Juvenile Justice* (AKF, Copenhagen) 217–50.

Lab, S (1992) *Crime Prevention. Approaches, Practices and Evaluations*, 2nd edn (Anderson, Cincinnati).

Lipsey, M (1992) 'The Effects of Treatment on Juvenile Delinquents: Results from Meta-Analysis'. Paper presented at the National Institute of Mental Health on Research to Prevent Violence, Bethesda.

Marshall T (1996) 'The Evolution of Restorative Justice in Great Britain' 4 *European Journal of Criminal Policy and Research* 21–43.

McCold, P (1998) 'Restorative Justice: Variations on a Theme' in L Walgrave (ed) *Restorative Justice for Juveniles. Potentials, Risks and Problems for Research* (Leuven University Press, Leuven) 19–53.

—— (2000) 'Towards a Holistic Vision of Restorative Justice: a Reply to Walgrave' 3 *Contemporary Criminal Justice Review* 357–414.

McGuire, J & Priestly, P (1995) 'Reviewing "What Works": Past, Present and Future' in J McGuire (ed) *What Works: Reducing Reoffending* (J Wiley, Chicester/New York) 3–34.

Mehlbye, J & Walgrave, L (1998) *Confronting Youth in Europe. Youth Crime and Juvenile Justice* (AKF, Copenhagen).

Messmer, H & Otto, H U (eds) (1992) *Restorative Justice on Trial* (Kluwer Academic Publishers, Dordrecht/Boston).

Schafer, S (1977) *Victimology. The Victim and his Criminal* (Prentice Hall, Reston).

Schüler-Springorum, H (1999) 'Juvenile Justice and the "Shift to the Left"' 7 *European Journal of Criminal Policy and Research* 353–62.

Tonry, M & Farrington, D (eds) (1995) *Building a Safer Society. Strategic Approaches to Crime Prevention; Crime and Justice: A Review of Research*, vol 19 (University of Chicago Press, Chicago).

Trépanier, J (1998) 'Restorative Justice: A Question of Legitimacy' in L Walgrave (ed) *Restorative Justice for Juveniles. Potentials, Risks and Problems for Research* (Leuven University Press, Leuven) 55–73.

van de Kerchove, M (1976–1977) 'Des Mesures Repressives aux Mesures de Sûreté et Protection. Réflexions sur le Pouvoir Mystificateur du Langage' 4 *Revue de Droit Pénal et de Criminologie* 245–79.

Van Dooselare, D (1988) 'Du Stimulus Aversif à la Cognition Sociale. L'efficacité de la Sanction selon un Modèle de Psychologie Expérimentale' 3 *Déviance et Société* 269–87.

Van Ness, D (1999), 'Legal Issues of Restorative Justice' in Bazemore & Walgrave (1999a) 263–284.

Van Ness, D & Heetderks Strong, K (1997) *Restoring Justice* (Anderson, Cincinnati).

von Hirsch, A (1993) *Censure and Sanctions* (Clarendon Press, Oxford).

—— (1998) 'Penal Theories' in M Tonry (ed) *The Handbook of Crime and Punishment* (Oxford University Press, New York/Oxford) 659–82.

Walgrave, L (1994) 'Beyond Rehabilitation. In Search of a Constructive Alternative in the Judicial Response to Juvenile Crime' 2 *European Journal on Criminal Policy and Research* 57–75.

—— (1999) 'Community Service as a Cornerstone of a Systemic Restorative Response to (Juvenile) Crime' in Bazemore & Walgrave (1999a) 129–54.

—— (2000a) 'Restorative Justice and the Republican Theory of Criminal Justice. An Exercise in Normative Theorizing on Restorative Justice' in J Braithwaite & H Strang (eds) *Restorative Justice: from Philosophy to Practice* (Ashgate, Aldershot) 165–83.

—— (2000b) *Met het oog op Herstel* (Leuven University Press, Leuven).

—— (2001a) 'Restoration and Punishment. On Favourable Similarities and Fortunate Differences' in G Maxwell & A Morris (eds) *Restorative Justice for Juveniles* (Hart Publishing, Oxford) 17–37.

Walgrave, L (2001b) 'Restoration and Punishment: Duet or Duel? In Search of Social Ethics for Restorative Justice'. Paper presented at the symposium *Restorative Justice. Aims and Limits*, Toronto, 11–12 May 2001 (publication forthcoming).

Walgrave, L & Geudens, H (1996) 'The Restorative Proportionality of Community Service for Juveniles' 4 *European Journal of Crime, Criminal Law and Criminal Justice* 361–80.

Warner, K (1994) 'Family Group Conferences and the Rights of the Offender' in C Alder & J Wundersitz (eds) *Family Group Conferencing and Juvenile Justice. The Way Forward or Misplaced Optimism?* (Australian Institute of Criminology, Canberra) 141–52.

Weijers, I (2000) *Schuld en Schaamte. Een Pedagogisch Perspectief op het Jeugdstrafrecht* (Bohn Stafleu Van Loghum, Houten/Diegem).

Weitekamp, E (1999) 'History of Restorative Justice' in Bazemore & Walgrave (1999a) 75–102.

Wright, M (1998) 'Victim/offender Conferencing: the Need for Safeguards' in L Walgrave (ed) *Restorative Justice for Juveniles. Potentialities, Risks and Problems for Research* (Leuven University Press, Leuven) 75–91.

Zehr, H (1990) *Changing Lenses: a New Focus for Crime and Justice* (Herald Press, Scottsdale).

6

Punishing the Young

ANTONY DUFF

1. INTRODUCTION: JUVENILE OFFENDERS AND CRIMINAL RESPONSIBILITY

I FIND MYSELF IN both agreement and disagreement with each of the other contributors to Part II of this volume. I agree with Ido Weijers (ch 7) that a process of moral communication, which aims to bring offenders to realise the significance of what they have done, should be central to the criminal law's response to juvenile offenders (and, indeed, to adult offenders). However, whereas he argues that the criminal trial, rather than punishment, is the proper locus for such moral communication, I believe that it should be central to punishment as well as to the trial. I agree with Lode Walgrave (ch 5) that our responses to crime, both juvenile and adult, should seek 'restorative justice'—restoration, reparation and reconciliation. However, whereas he urges us to seek restoration *rather than* punishment, I believe that the kind of 'restoration' which crime makes necessary is to be achieved *through* punishment—though this will involve giving a very particular account of the proper meaning and aims of criminal punishment.

Another question, which divides Walgrave and Weijers, is whether we should maintain a separate system of juvenile justice. If the question was whether juveniles should be subjected to the kind of criminal process of trial and punishment to which adults are in fact subjected, it would be easy to answer 'No'—simply on the grounds that *no one* should be subjected to that process. But if the question is, more properly, whether juveniles should be subjected to the kind of criminal process to which adults *should* be subjected, any adequate answer must wait upon a clearer account of the kind of criminal process that is suitable for adults—an account which I cannot provide here. However, I will say a little more about this question in s 3.

The main part of this paper (s 2) will be devoted to sketching an account of punishment, as an appropriate response to crime which is both 'restorative' and (in one sense of that much abused term) 'retributive'; I will then argue that punishment as thus understood is a proper response to juvenile crime (s. 3). Before that, however, a little ground-clearing is necessary.

1.1. 'Juvenile' Offenders and 'Contra-factualism'

For present purposes, we should understand 'juvenile' offenders to be those who are neither so immature that they can certainly not be held criminally responsible, nor so mature that they are certainly as fit as any other adult to be held criminally responsible. What should count as 'maturity' in this context will depend on what it is to be held criminally responsible, and on what conditions must be satisfied if such holdings are to be just. I say a bit more about this in s 1.2 below, but by way of very rough summary we could say here that maturity is a matter of one's capacities for rational thought and action—in particular, in this context, the capacity to grasp and be moved by the values and reasons by which one's actions should be guided, and to guide one's own actions accordingly; and the capacity to understand what one has done, and others' responses to it, in the appropriate normative terms. (To talk of capacities for rational thought, and of understanding, should not be taken to imply that maturity is an essentially or primarily *intellectual* matter: there is an ineliminable emotional dimension to rational practical thought, and to understanding values, reasons for action, and the responses of others; and maturity thus requires emotional as well as intellectual development.)

Given the variations in child development, any specification of a precise age range within which young people should be counted as 'juveniles' in this sense is of course to a significant degree arbitrary: but we could think of young people between the ages of about 14 and 19. Given their lack of maturity, it would not be absurd to treat them as not being (yet) criminally responsible, in the way that it would be absurd to treat a fully mature adult as not being criminally responsible: but simply to deny their criminal responsibility would ignore or deny the extent to which they have matured. Given the maturity they have achieved, it would not be absurd to treat them as criminally responsible, in the way that it would be absurd to treat a younger child as criminally responsible: but to treat them as unqualifiedly responsible would seem to ignore or deny the extent to which they have not yet achieved full maturity.

Weijers argues that juvenile offenders should be subjected to a special, separate criminal process which treats them as responsible agents, but which, we must recognise, still involves an element of 'contra-factualism': in holding the juvenile offender 'responsible as a citizen before the law' (this volume: 141), we must recognise that we are still to a degree treating him 'as if' he is fully responsible, when in fact he is not (we should treat him thus in order to help him become what we pretend he already is—a fully responsible citizen). But this implies that we, and the courts which hold juveniles criminally responsible, are engaged in *deception*—in the pretence that the offender has achieved a responsible maturity that we know he in fact lacks; and it implies that there is a determinate fact of the matter about the degree to which the juvenile is a responsible agent—a fact 'contra' which we act insofar as we engage in 'contra-factualism'.

Each of these implications is problematic: the first is morally problematic, since we should not want our criminal process to involve such deception or pretence; the second is conceptually problematic, since a person's responsibility is a matter not of determinate (or of determinable) fact, but of how she can properly be treated by others. What we should rather recognise is that in treating juvenile offenders as criminally responsible, we are engaging in a modest kind of social construction.

We should of course aim to develop practices within which we can recognise the nuanced character of the juveniles' stages of development—within which we can do justice both to the extent to which they are mature enough to be held responsible for their wrongdoings, and also to the extent to which they are not yet fully mature. But insofar as we do hold them criminally responsible, we are to an extent constructing, or constituting, them as criminally responsible agents—partly in order to help or induce them to take on responsibility for their own lives and actions: we are going *beyond* the facts, in that the facts of their development do not force us to hold them responsible as we do adults. We are not, however, as 'contra-factualism' suggests, going *against* the facts: for it is not a fact that the juvenile is not criminally responsible.

None of this yet shows that we *ought to* treat juvenile offenders as criminally responsible, or what that should involve. Before we can tackle that normative question, however, we must recognise that it is not one question but several: for we must distinguish four different aspects or implications of criminal responsibility, and ask of each of them whether it is appropriate to treat juvenile offenders as in that respect or to that extent criminally responsible.

1.2. Four Aspects of Criminal Responsibility

We must ask, first, how far it is appropriate to see juvenile offenders as *culpable wrongdoers*: how far should their youth or the psychological characteristics typically associated with youth affect our understanding of the nature or seriousness of the wrongs they have done, or of their culpability for those wrongs? (This question, like the others, might permit no general answer, covering all kinds of offence: for instance, insofar as culpable wrongdoing requires an ability to understand the nature of the wrong one is doing, juveniles might be *less* culpable for *more* serious wrongs; it might be easier to hold them culpably responsible for theft than for murder. See von Hirsch, 2001 on some of the ways in which youth can affect criminal culpability.) We should note, however, that this question, as a question about *criminal* responsibility, concerns their culpability for *criminal* wrongdoings, and that we must therefore ask what is distinctive about crimes as particular kinds of wrongdoing. It is one thing to ask whether Jane is culpable for, for instance, deliberately breaking her brother's toy, as a moral wrong; it is another thing to ask whether she is culpable for criminal damage, as a criminal wrong. What the difference is between these questions, and what more is involved in being culpable for a crime, depends on how we should understand the idea that crimes are 'public' wrongs—an issue that I cannot pursue here (but see Marshall & Duff, 1998; Duff, 2001: ch 2.4): but if culpability requires an understanding of the nature of the wrong for which one is culpable, criminal responsibility or culpability requires an understanding of the nature of the relevant crime as a wrong.

This leads into the second question: insofar as juveniles are culpable wrongdoers, by or to whom should they be called to *answer* for their wrongdoing? Up to a certain age, we suppose that it is their parents' responsibility to call them to account (insofar as they can be called to account at all): it is their parents to whom they are answerable; the state should intervene only if the parents fail to discharge their responsibilities. We must of course ask *why* that should be so: does it reflect a view of parents as owning their children, or of what is possible or useful in terms of the child's moral development? We should also note that the parents are not the *only* people with standing in this context. They do not even have sole responsibility for punishing their children, since schools also punish their pupils, whilst others have moral standing to call young wrongdoers to informal account—if a boy vandalises my car, I can call him, as well as his parents, to account for this. But the question that concerns us here is that of when and why it becomes appropriate to hold juvenile wrongdoers answerable to and before the law, through a legal process that at least resembles that through which adults are properly called to answer for their crimes. This question has to do partly with the extent to which we should understand their wrongdoings as crimes, as kinds of wrong that should be the criminal law's concern. But it also has to do with the extent to which they should be expected to understand and play their proper part in the process—to understand that they are being called to answer for an alleged wrongdoing, to understand the nature of that wrong and to recognise the court's authority (see Weijers, this volume: 141). Here again, the answer to our question might depend in part on the nature of the crime. It is often said that whilst we might try to divert young offenders from the criminal process when their crimes are relatively minor, they must be tried in court for the most serious crimes—which is why the two boys (of 10 and 11) who killed James Bulger were tried for murder in a criminal court. I suspect, however, that it makes more sense to try a juvenile for theft than for murder: for it is more likely that she can understand the character of theft as a wrong than that she can really understand what murder is.

Third (or, more precisely, as another aspect of the second question), when the law should take an interest in juveniles' criminal wrongdoing, what kind of interest should it take? Should their offences be salient, as wrongs for which they must be called to answer; or should they be relevant only as one amongst other kinds of possible evidence of a welfare need? The Scottish system of Children's Hearings embodies the latter view (see Martin & Murray, 1976): the fact that a child has committed an offence is one among other possibly sufficient kinds of evidence that she needs special welfare measures of the kind that the Panel can provide; the Panel does not call children to account for their wrongdoings, but tries to diagnose their welfare needs. A system of juvenile criminal courts embodies the former view: whether or not those convicted in such courts are then *punished* (see below), the criminal process is one which calls them to answer a charge of wrongdoing.

Fourth, if juvenile offenders should be called to answer, by the law and the courts, for their criminal wrongdoings, should they also be *punished* by the law for those wrongdoings? An affirmative answer to the third question by no means entails an affirmative answer to this question: we could imagine a system of criminal trials that called those accused of crimes to answer the charges against them, and convicted those who were proved guilty, but that did not lead to any further punishment (beyond that which is already involved in being condemned by a criminal conviction). Furthermore, if we do give an affirmative answer to this question, we must then ask how far the punishment of juveniles should serve the same aims, or involve the same material modes of punishment, or be determined by the same criteria, as those imposed on adult offenders.

I clearly cannot tackle all these questions here, and will focus on the fourth. Suppose that a juvenile offender is properly held responsible for his commission of a crime, in that he has been duly tried and convicted through a suitable version of a criminal trial: should he then be punished for that crime? If so, how should he be punished: what modes of punishment, with what aims, could be appropriate for juvenile offenders?

To answer these questions I will begin by sketching a general account of punishment, and arguing against the increasingly prevalent view that in our responses to crime we should seek 'restoration' rather than punishment (s 2); I will then argue that this account also shows how criminal punishment can be appropriate for juvenile offenders (s 3).

(Note that I am not supposing that the juvenile has been subjected to the kind of criminal trial to which adult offenders are now subjected. This is partly because, as I noted earlier, we must ask not whether juveniles should be subjected to the criminal processes to which adults are in fact subjected, but whether they should be subjected to the kind of criminal process to which adults *should* be subjected; and the criminal trials to which adults are now too often subjected are not procedures through which citizens are properly called to answer charges of wrongdoing. But it is also because a trial process appropriate for adults might still need to be adapted to the juvenile's capacities. It might still be (justly) objected that I am begging too many questions by taking some kind of criminal trial for granted, since those who argue that juvenile offenders should not be subjected to criminal punishment often argue that they ought to be diverted from the criminal process altogether, and object to the orthodox trial process as strenuously as they object to punishment (as do Morris and Walgrave in this volume). Although I believe that the criminal trial can and should be a procedure through which citizens, both adult and juvenile, are called to answer for their alleged wrongdoings, I cannot defend that belief here: but see Duff, 1986: ch 4, and 2001: 72, 189–90; also Weijers' account of the trial as a communicative process in this volume: 146–52.)

2. CRIMINAL PUNISHMENT: RESTORATION AND RETRIBUTION

The 'restorative justice' movement has found some of its most fertile soil in the context of juvenile crime: most famously in the Australasian Family Group Conference system (Morris, this volume: ch 8; Maxwell & Morris, 1993; Hudson *et al*, 1996), and now perhaps also in England, through the provisions of the Youth Justice and Criminal Evidence Act 1999 (Ball, 2000). Now a striking feature of 'restorative justice', as it is often portrayed by its advocates (and by some of its critics), is that it is supposed to offer an *alternative* to 'retributive justice', and so to punishment: *rather than* punishing offenders, we should seek restorative processes of mediation, reparation and reconciliation (see eg Walgrave, this volume: ch 5; Christie, 1981: 11; Braithwaite, 1999: 60; Dignan, 1999: 48; for further references, and apt criticism, see Daly & Immarigeon, 1998: 32–4; Zedner, 1994). I will argue that a suitable account of criminal punishment, as a mode of moral communication, undercuts this contrast: in our responses to crime we should indeed aim for restoration, reconciliation and reparation, but those aims are properly to be achieved *through* punishment which is in a significant sense retributive (for a fuller version of this argument see Duff, 2001).

There are many different kinds of 'restorative justice' programme: I will focus on victim-offender mediation programmes as one way of trying to achieve restoration. These themselves come in different forms (see Matthews 1988; Marshall & Merry, 1990; Daly & Immarigeon, 1998; von Hirsch & Ashworth, 1998: ch 7; Braithwaite, 1999; Dignan, 1999): I will not discuss these variations here, but will instead set up two simple models, of 'civil' and of 'criminal' mediation. Actual schemes will no doubt include elements of each model: but the contrast between them will help me show how mediation can be appropriate *as a mode of punishment*.

2.1. Civil and Criminal Mediation

Civil mediation is a matter of negotiation and compromise, aimed at resolving some conflict. I am in conflict with my neighbour: she objects to my late night parties, while I complain about her early morning home improvements. We call on a mediator to help us resolve our conflict, so that we can find some way of living together as neighbours. The mediation process might include explaining to each other why we find the other's behaviour so aggravating, and each coming to admit that we have been in the wrong in various ways. But we will also probably recognise that it is unproductive to harp on each other's past wrongdoings: we must look to the future, and negotiate a mutually acceptable *modus vivendi*. That will involve negotiating a compromise between our conflicting lifestyles: we might agree that I will not hold more than one late night party a fortnight, and that she will avoid noisy home improvements before 9.00 am. It might also include agreeing to pay compensation for any past damage (damage to her hedge by my guests, damage to my walls by her hammering), and an exchange of apologies for any past wrongs: but the compensation will be focused purely on any material damage that was done; and the apologies might be both formal (we do not aim to become the sort of close friends between whom apologies are worthwhile only if sincere) and general (we do not list and apologise for each wrong).

Now some such process of civil mediation is very often the appropriate way of dealing with conflicts, including conflicts which involve criminal conduct that *could* be prosecuted—so long as the wrongs involved were not that serious, and our relationship was one of rough equality. Sometimes, however, such a process is inappropriate: if mediation is appropriate at all, what is required is what I call *criminal* mediation.

Criminal mediation, unlike civil, is precisely focused on a *wrong* that has been done. A woman has been regularly beaten up by her husband, or her house has been vandalised and burgled (see Hulsman, 1991); the parties agree to a mediation process. It matters, first, that the relevant facts be established, either at a trial before the mediation or as its first stage: that this was what the criminal law defines as a serious assault, or burglary and criminal damage. The process will include discussion and mutual explanations of those facts: the victim will explain how the crime affected her; the offender can explain how he came to commit it. But whilst his explanations might appeal to excusing or mitigating factors (which might not all be formally recognised by the law), he should not be allowed to argue that his conduct was justified—that husbands have the right thus to 'chastise' their wives; or that the crime was partly her fault—that she 'provoked' him by not providing meals on time, or 'encouraged' him by leaving her windows open. The criminal law, under whose aegis the mediation takes place, defines what counts as a crime, and as a justification: whatever else is negotiable during the mediation, the wrongfulness of the offender's crime is not (compare Dobash & Dobash, 1992: ch 7, on the CHANGE project for violent men).

Part of the point of the criminal mediation process consists precisely in this exchange of explanations. The victim can explain her suffering to the offender— an explanation that will consist not in a neutral account of how the crime affected her, but in one that expresses and tries to communicate to the offender her hurt and anger, and that condemns his crime as a wrong; she will also have a chance to come to understand (which will not be to condone) the offender's action from his perspective. The offender will be vividly confronted, through his victim's voice, with his crime: but he will also have a chance to explain himself. However, more is hoped for and intended than this.

The most ambitious hope is for a reconciliation between victim and offender. If they are, as might be true of the burglar and his victim, related only as fellow citizens, they might have no further dealings with each other: but reconciliation is still valuable, as restoring the bonds of citizenship, of mutual respect and concern, which the crime damaged. If they are related more closely than that, as in the case of domestic violence, reconciliation *might* enable them to repair and maintain their marriage: but even if that is impossible, there is still value in a reconciliation that enables them to part on morally satisfactory terms. We must, however, be clear what kind of 'reconciliation' is required, and what it can or must involve.

Given that the wrongfulness of the crime is not negotiable, one thing that reconciliation cannot properly involve is some compromise between the conflicting 'desires' of victim and offender: a compromise that might, for instance, allow the husband occasionally to beat his wife, or the burglar to steal from the victim's car but not from her house. Whatever else they might negotiate, the offender's commitment to refrain from repeating the crime must be a non-negotiable demand.

Reconciliation will also require some kind of reparation: some attempt by the offender to 'make up' to the victim for what he did to her. Now this might involve something materially similar to the kind of compensation that results from civil mediation: the burglar might repair or pay for the damage he caused, or replace the goods he stole. But compensation of this kind will not always be possible; nor, even when there is some material loss that can be repaired, will such material compensation suffice by or in itself. For what needs 'repairing' or 'making up for' is not just such material harm as was caused (which might anyway be irreparable), but the *wrong* that was done to the victim; and what *that* requires is, minimally, an apology which expresses both the offender's repentant recognition of the wrong done and his commitment to avoid its repetition.

2.2. Apology and Moral Reparation

Apologies do not always presuppose wrongdoing: I may apologise to another for some harm that I inadvertently and non-culpably did to her, thus expressing my regretful recognition of the harm she suffered at my hands. Apologies for wrongdoing, however, involve more than this. They purport to express not merely regret at the harm that I caused, but remorse for the wrong that I did, my repudiation of that wrong as something I now wish I had not done, and my implicit commitment to strive to avoid doing such wrong in future. They thus also seek forgiveness from, and reconciliation with, the person whom I wronged. Even if the wrong did not threaten to *destroy* our relationship (as lovers, friends, colleagues, fellow citizens, or just fellow human beings), it was inconsistent with the normative bonds by which that relationship is defined: it created a flaw, if not a rupture, in the relationship. Such flaws can be ignored or forgotten: but they can be removed or remedied only by an apology made by the wrongdoer and accepted in a spirit of forgiveness by the victim.

It is also worth noting that apologies can have a ritual or formalised character; and that—especially in less intimate relationships—an apology whose sincerity is doubtful or unknown can still have value. I might apologise to the person I wronged, not because I truly repent my action, but because that is what is expected or demanded of me; and whilst between friends or lovers apologies are worthwhile only if sincere, between strangers it might be enough that the apology is made—that the ritual is undertaken.

Sometimes, however, a mere apology is not enough. If I have seriously wronged another person, I cannot expect to resolve the matter merely by apologising to him: something more is due to him, from me. This is not because a serious wrong usually involves material harm for which compensation must also be paid: some such wrongs (serious betrayals of friendship or marriage, for instance) involve no such harm; some such harms (the harm involved in a rape, or in fraud committed by a friend, for instance) cannot be repaired by material compensation. The point is that the victim cannot reasonably be expected to forgive me, to treat the matter as closed, merely on receipt of a verbal apology, however sincere, and that the wrongdoer cannot reasonably expect to close the matter thus: the wrong goes too deep for that. It goes too deep for the victim: a mere apology cannot heal the moral wound done by the wrong. It goes too deep for the wrongdoer, whether or not she realises it: to think that she could just apologise, and then return to her normal life, would be to portray the wrong as a relatively trivial matter which did not seriously damage the victim or their relationship.

The wrongdoer, we think, owes the victim something more than a mere apology; and she deserves to suffer something more than merely having to apologise. But what is this 'more'?

This 'more' need not be something separate and distinct from an apology. What 'more' is owed to the victim is something that recognises and addresses the seriousness of the wrong he has suffered. The 'more' the wrongdoer should suffer has to do with the pains of remorse: with the painful recognition of the wrong she has done, and of its implications for the victim, for their relationship, and for her own moral life. Their lives and their relationship have been ruptured by the wrong: the victim's life as someone who is respected and cared for in the light of the values (supposedly) intrinsic to their relationship; the wrongdoer's life as a moral agent bound by those values; their relationship as one structured by those values. What repairs those ruptures, however, is not an apology *and* some further and separate reparative measure, but an apology of a kind that takes and addresses them seriously; and this can be achieved by a mode of reparation that itself expresses the wrongdoer's apology.

Suppose that the burglar in a criminal mediation process agrees to pay for the damage he caused or to help to repair it himself; or that the violent husband agrees to take on some extra domestic duty that hitherto had been his wife's. These can both be reparative measures. What gives them their significance as reparation, however, is not their material content (the damage might equally be paid for by the victim's insurance; such a shift in domestic responsibilities cannot by itself make up for the violent assaults), but their meaning as forceful expressions of apology: the wrongdoer shows that he means what he says in apologising, that he takes his wrongdoing seriously, by undertaking this burdensome task for the victim's benefit.

This then is the significance of reparation in a criminal mediation process: it serves not primarily as material repair or compensation for such material harm as was done, but as a way of adding weight and force to the apology by which offender and victim are to be reconciled. The reconciliation that is sought, as far as the criminal law is concerned, is not reconciliation as spouses or friends (that is not the criminal law's business), but as fellow citizens: whatever happens to any more intimate relationship that existed between them, the aim of the mediation process held under the aegis of the criminal law is that they should recognise and accept each other as fellow citizens who can live together, if not in friendship, at least in civic peace.

One further point should be noted. I have talked of reparation as a means of expressing an offender's *already* repentant understanding of the wrong he has done: he agrees to undertake the reparation because he realises that this is how he can 'make up' to his victim for the crime he committed—a realisation that might itself have been achieved partly through the mediation process. That is the ideal towards which criminal mediation aspires: but the reparative burden that the offender undertakes can also serve as a *means to* the repentant understanding which it should in the end *express*. The mediation process itself might not bring the offender to a fully repentant understanding of his crime—such an understanding is often hard to achieve and to hold on to. He might nonetheless agree to undertake the reparation proposed by the mediator, and the very process of undertaking it might focus his attention more firmly on the nature and implications of the wrong for which it is undertaken; the process helps to induce what it then expresses.

We can thus see criminal reparation of this kind as a species of secular penance: a burden undertaken by a wrongdoer which aims to induce and to express her repentant and apologetic understanding of the wrong done, and through which she seeks reconciliation with those she has wronged.

2.3. Criminal Mediation and Reparation as Punishment

Criminal mediation focuses on the character and implications of the wrong that was done, and seeks a reparative apology for that wrong. Despite this focus on the past wrong, it might look more like an alternative to punishment—which is how advocates of mediation as a restorative response to crime typically portray it—than a mode of punishment. I think, however, that we should see it as a *punitive* process: as, indeed, a *paradigm* of punishment, since it involves a kind of penal process which is best suited to the ends that punishment should serve.

Consider first how punishment is standardly defined: as something intentionally painful or burdensome, imposed on an alleged offender for an alleged crime by some body with the authority to do so—and, we might add, intended to communicate censure for that crime (see Scheid, 1980; and Feinberg, 1970).

Criminal mediation is intended to be *painful* or *burdensome*, in both its procedure and its outcome. It does not simply aim to 'deliver pain', to make the wrongdoer suffer: what matters is not so much *that*, but *what* he suffers. But it aims to bring him to confront and recognise the wrong he has done; and that process is meant to be painful (which is to say, in part, that it *will* be painful if it succeeds in awakening the offender's moral sensibilities). It aims to bring him to remorse for his crime—if he recognises what he has done as a wrong, he will feel remorse for it; and remorse is essentially painful. The reparation to which the process leads must also, if it is to give real weight to the apology it is meant to express, be burdensome; if it was not, it would not have its appropriate apologetic meaning. These kinds of pain or burden are *integral* to criminal mediation and reparation, not mere side-effects of it (contrast Christie, 1977: 10; Walgrave, 2001, and in this volume: 108).

Criminal mediation and reparation are focused *on* offenders and are *for* their crimes. Only the offender can be intelligibly required to undertake criminal mediation with the victim; and the focus of the process is precisely on the past crime and what is needed to 'repair' the moral harm it did. This focus on the wrong done also makes censure central to criminal mediation: it is implicit in the process, as one that the offender ought to undertake because of the wrong he has done; it is typically explicit in what the victim says to him; and it might be harder to avoid or to dismiss than is the formal censure communicated by a conviction in court—the offender can 'receive a kind of blame that it would be very difficult to neutralise' (Christie, 1977: 9).

What of *authority*? Even if mediation took place outside the reach of the criminal law and courts, we could say that the victim has the moral authority to demand reparation and apology from the offender, whilst the mediator has—is given—authority over the proceedings. I would argue, however, that criminal mediation, since it is required by and focused on a crime, should be conducted under the supervision and authority of the criminal courts. It must be determined that the (alleged) offender committed what the law defines as a crime against the victim; there must be a procedure for determining that the outcome agreed by the parties—the reparation to be undertaken by the offender—is appropriate both in kind and in severity; and there must be provision for offenders who will not play their part in the process. These matters are best dealt with by a criminal court.

But, it might be said, what precludes portraying criminal mediation as punishment is that it is not *imposed* on the offender: he must agree to take part in the process, and undertake the reparation for himself. However, matters are not that simple.

First, punishments can be self-imposed: I can punish *myself* for some wrong I have done, by imposing some penitential burden on myself. Thus even an

offender who willingly enters into mediation, and undertakes the agreed reparation, could be said to be punishing himself—subjecting himself to this burden
for the crime he committed (see Adler, 1992: ch 2).

Second, offenders could be *required* to enter into mediation, and to undertake
the agreed measures of reparation—required, for instance, by a criminal court.
This would not constitute a strict *imposition*, since it would still be up to them
to do, or to refuse to do, what they were required to do. But the same is true of
most punishments imposed by our courts: the offender is required to pay a fine,
or to undertake community service, or to report to a probation officer—or even,
in some countries, to report at weekends to serve parts of a prison term; and it
is up to her to do, or not to do, what she is thus required to do. There are of
course sanctions against such refusals—offenders are not allowed just to get
away with refusing their punishment; and the final sanction is always something
strictly imposed on the offender regardless of her will—she is taken to prison,
her fine is deducted from her salary. But criminal mediation could have the same
structure: the court could specify mediation leading to reparation as the appropriate disposal for the case, and would have back-up sanctions for any offender
who refused to play his proper part in the mediation process.

However, my claim that criminal mediation and reparation should be seen as
a process of punishment is not simply a definitional claim: it is that this process
can serve the appropriate aims of criminal punishment.

First, mediation is a *communicative* process: it consists in communication
between victim and offender about the nature and implications of the crime as
a wrong against the victim, and aims to bring the offender to face up to the
wrong she has done. The reparation undertaken by the offender also serves a
communicative purpose: it communicates his apology for the wrong he did to
the victim. But it is a process of *punitive* communication: it censures the
offender for his crime, and it involves an intentionally burdensome reparation
for that crime. I believe that criminal punishment must be understood and justified as a communicative enterprise in which a political community communicates with its members as responsible moral agents; criminal mediation is
certainly such an enterprise.

Second, criminal mediation is *retributive*, in that it seeks to impose on (or to
induce in) the offender the suffering she deserves for her crime. She deserves to
suffer censure for what she has done: mediation aims to communicate that censure to her, in such a way that she will come to understand why it is deserved.
She deserves to suffer remorse for what she has done: mediation aims to induce
such suffering in her by bringing her to recognise the wrong she has done. She
ought to make apologetic (and thus necessarily burdensome) reparation for that
crime to its victim: mediation should lead to such reparation. By seeing criminal
mediation as a kind of punishment, we can thus make plausible sense of the retributivist's intuition that the guilty deserve to suffer, by showing just what they
deserve to suffer, and why. What they deserve to suffer is not just pain, or a burden, but that particular kind of painful burden which is integral to the recogni-

tion of guilt: they deserve to suffer that because it is an appropriate response to their wrongdoing; and criminal mediation aims to impose or induce that kind of suffering.

Third, the reparative burden the offender undertakes is a species of penal *hard treatment*. That is to say, it is intentionally burdensome; and while it serves a communicative purpose, it is burdensome—making demands on the offender's money, time, or energies—independently of its communicative meaning. Now a familiar problem for those who justify punishment in communicative terms, as communicating the censure that offenders deserve, is that they must explain why that communication should involve penal hard treatment: why not communicate censure simply through a formal declaration, or through a purely symbolic punishment which is painful or burdensome *only* in virtue of its censorious meaning? The example of reparation as part of a process of criminal mediation provides the start of an answer to this question. For the hard treatment involved in the reparation is now integral to the communicative purpose of criminal mediation as a punishment: it is the means by which the offender makes apologetic reparation to the victim. (It is also, I have suggested, a vehicle through which he can deepen and strengthen his own repentant understanding of the wrong he has done.)

Fourth, whilst criminal mediation is retributive, looking back towards the past crime, it is also future-directed. Its most direct aim is reconciliation between victim and offender through apologetic reparation by the offender. But it also aims to dissuade the offender from further crimes: to bring her to a remorseful recognition of the wrong she has done will be to bring her to see why she should not commit such wrongs again. We can thus meet the consequentialist concern that punishment must aim to do some good. (But this is not to posit a consequentialist justifying aim for criminal mediation or punishment, since on this account the means are as important as—indeed are not separable from—the end; see Duff, 2001: 112–24.)

My account clearly has something in common with Walgrave's (this volume: ch 5), since he too favours a system which involves censure ('intense reprobation': 94), apology (104) and 'restorative sanctions' which can be court-imposed rather than undertaken voluntarily by the offender (107–8). He insists, however, that he is offering an alternative to punishment, whereas my argument is that this should still be seen as a punitive process. He insists on this in part because he is offering an alternative to the orthodox *practice* of criminal punishment—to the familiar criminal processes of trial and punishment in which the moral communication that we agree is important can find little room to flourish, but also because he denies that the restorative process is or should be intended to be painful or burdensome (p. 108): the appropriate restorative measures might in fact and foreseeably be burdensome or painful for the offender, but this is no part of their purpose. I have argued that 'intense reprobation', and an attempt to bring the offender to confront what she has done, *are* intended to be painful, in that they are intended to induce in the offender a

necessarily painful recognition of the wrong she has done: but what is also crucial to my argument, and what also distinguishes Walgrave from me, is that the
'reparation' or 'restoration' that is needed is not just or primarily for the *harm*
that was caused, but for the *wrong* that was done. Whilst I agree with Walgrave
that reparation or restoration of harm caused need not be, or be intended to be,
burdensome or painful, I have argued that the kind of moral reparation which
can make up for a wrong must be, and must be intended to be, painful or burdensome. My argument against Walgrave would thus be that he is wrong to
focus as he does on the repair of harm, and that he should pay more attention
than he does to the significance of wrongdoing and to the question of what can
repair or make up for that.

2.4. Extending the Model

Criminal mediation of the kind described above is, I suggest, an appropriate
kind of response to various types of crime, *and* an appropriate paradigm of
criminal punishment—a paradigm very different from those that dominate the
current debate. To transform or extend this into a *complete* account of criminal
punishment would, of course, require me to discuss the different modes of
process and of punishment that could be appropriate when direct mediation
between offender and individual victim is impossible or inappropriate. I cannot
do that here, but should at least indicate the directions in which I would seek to
extend the model I have offered here.

I suggested that criminal mediation should be conducted under the aegis and
authority of a criminal court. Now when there is an identifiable victim, when
both victim and offender are willing to take part seriously in the mediation
process, and when they can—with the help of a mediator—agree on a suitable
mode of reparation, the court's role might not be prominent. It still has an
important role—as a guarantor of the individual interests of victim and
offender, to ensure that neither exploits or coerces the other; but also as
guardian of the public interest. For crimes are still public wrongs which concern
the whole political community, and which merit public condemnation and censure. One role for the court is to ensure that the relevant facts are recognised and
accepted, and the character of the wrongdoing, as a crime, identified; to make
clear that this is not a private matter between victim and offender, but a public
matter (that the community as a whole recognises the wrong the victim suffered,
and condemns the wrong the offender committed); and to ensure that the
reparation agreed by victim and offender is indeed appropriate to the wrong
done. But the court's role becomes larger when no direct mediation between
offender and victim is possible.

Suppose, first, that the offender refuses to take part in such a process; or
refuses to agree to an appropriate mode of reparation. The court could *require*
her to hear (though of course it cannot force her to *listen to*) what the victim has

to say, and could specify the reparation that she must make. The point of such a requirement would be partly to assure the victim that the community takes seriously the wrong he has suffered, but also to try to bring the offender to recognise that wrong as something for which she *ought* to apologise. She is in effect required to apologise; and the hope is that what begins as an apology undertaken neither willingly nor sincerely will become an apology willingly offered as an expression of a genuine repentance. I will say more about this shortly.

Suppose second that no direct victim is available to take part in a mediation process: the direct victim might be unwilling or unable to take part; or there might be no direct individual victim—the only direct victim might be the community as a whole (as with various kinds of tax evasion), or some subset of it (as with various crimes of endangerment). In such cases, if there is to be anything resembling 'victim-offender' mediation, someone must represent and speak for the victim: this too is a role that can properly be played by the court—by the judge or magistrate, or by a suitable official, such as a probation officer, appointed by the court.

In such cases we could say that there is still a process of criminal mediation, but between offender and community rather than between offender and an individual victim. Suppose, for instance, that after an offender has been convicted (and a conviction itself is a communicative action that censures him for the wrong that was proved against him), sentence is deferred for a report from a probation officer appointed to the case. Part of the probation officer's task is to begin trying to persuade the offender to face up to the wrong he has done: this is analogous to the discussion between offender and victim in criminal mediation. The other part of her task, at this stage, is to work out a sentence to propose to the court. Now I would suggest that, just as in criminal mediation the reparation is ideally discussed and agreed between the offender and the victim (within the framework and constraints laid down by the court), so the proposed sentence should ideally be discussed and agreed between probation officer and offender (for a similar idea, see Cavadino & Dignan, 1998): but what is more important at the moment is the significance of the sentence once it is proposed to and imposed by the court.

Suppose that the probation officer recommends a 'Community Service Order', requiring the offender to spend a specified number of hours on some kind of unpaid work that benefits the community (the nature of the work might depend on the nature of the offence, as when a vandal is ordered to help repair the effects of vandalism). Now Community Service Orders are precise public analogues of the reparation that might result from a criminal mediation process: they enable the offender to make apologetic reparation to the whole community for the wrong that he has done to the whole community; and to require him to undertake this work, whether or not he is willing to do so, is to require him to make such a forceful apology. If the Order is imposed on an unwilling and unrepentant offender, it cannot constitute a *sincere* apology: but by requiring the offender to make it, the court makes clear to the victim that it takes the wrong done to her seriously, and tries to bring the offender to recognise and repent that wrong.

Both the reparation agreed as a result of criminal mediation, and the Community Service Order imposed as a punishment by a criminal court, have this dual character. They provide a way in which an already repentant offender can give forceful expression to her repentance and to the sincere apology which she sees to be needed; and a way of trying to persuade a not-yet-repentant offender to recognise and repent the wrong he has done. This is, I suggest, how we should understand criminal punishment more generally, as a system of secular *penance* which aims at the three 'R's of *repentance, reform* and *reconciliation*.

A penance is a burden imposed on a wrongdoer because of her past wrongdoing. It might be self-imposed, by one who undertakes it voluntarily; it might be required of, or imposed on, an as-yet-unrepentant wrongdoer. Its initial aim is to induce or strengthen repentance: it aims to focus the wrongdoer's attention on the wrong, and to bring her to see it and understand it as a wrong. This is important even for a wrongdoer who has already begun to repent. Repentance (at least in the case of serious wrongs) requires time and attention, a focusing of our thoughts which is not easily achieved and from which we are all too easily distracted: penance provides a structure within which we can confront, and think through, the wrong we have done. This is one function of punishment: to communicate, in a forceful way that it is hard for the offender to ignore, the censure she deserves for her crime; to try to persuade her to confront, recognise and repent the wrong she has done.

In aiming at repentance, penance also aims at reform: more precisely at the wrongdoer's *self*-reform. To repent the wrong I have done is to commit myself to avoiding its commission in future, to finding a way of being able to avoid repeating it. Unless I am (rightly) confident that it was an aberration which reveals no lasting flaw in my character, I cannot just repent it, apologise, and then forget about it: I must ask myself how I must change if I am to avoid such wrongdoing in future, and set myself to bring about such a change. This might be something I can do for myself, or something I will need help to achieve: we can see criminal punishments as providing a vehicle through which offenders can come to seek their own self-reform; and, in some cases, as offering the help they might need in doing so—this is most obviously true, for instance, of probation and of the programmes to deal with particular kinds of offending behaviour that might be attached to probation.

Finally, through penance the wrongdoer can seek reconciliation with those whom he has wronged—in the case of criminal punishment, with his victim and his fellow citizens. For by undertaking or undergoing the penance he has, as is often said, 'paid for' his crime: by which it is meant that he has either actually offered sincere, apologetic reparation for his crime; or, if he has not yet repented, he has undergone a burdensome penance that sufficiently reflects the character and seriousness of his crime. As his fellow citizens, we owe it to the truly repentant wrongdoer, who has undergone appropriate penance, to restore the bonds of community with him. (We also owe it to the offender who has not, or might not have, repented to treat him *as if* he has repented—as if the punishment he has undergone did constitute a sincere apology from him: I cannot discuss this point here, but see Duff, 2001: 121–25.)

There is still much more to be said about the modes of punishment that would figure in a communicative system of penitential punishments: about the central role of probation in such a system (see Duff, 2001: ch 3.5; Bottoms & McWilliams, 1979); about the (limited) roles that would be played in such a system by such familiar sanctions as imprisonment and fines (see Duff, 2001: ch 4). But I hope I have said enough to give some idea of the ideal conception of punishment that I favour, and to clarify the aspects of that conception which are most relevant to the punishment of juvenile offenders.

3. PUNISHING JUVENILES

I have argued that in our responses to crime we should seek restoration and reconciliation, but that this does not mean that we should pursue such aims *instead of* punishment: rather, when what makes reconciliation and restoration necessary is the commission of *crime*, it is *through* punishment, as a mode of penance, that those goods are achieved. The same is true, I think, when we are dealing with the crimes committed by juveniles.

The worried thought that perhaps we should not subject juveniles to criminal punishment might well reflect (when it does not just reflect the thought that perhaps we should not subject *anyone* to criminal punishment) both the thought that we should not subject them to the *kinds* of punishment that we often inflict on adults—most obviously imprisonment; and the thought that, rather than simply trying to 'make them suffer' (whether as retribution or as a deterrent), we should try so to rehabilitate them that they will be able in future to lead more flourishing lives, and to repair their relationships with those affected by their crimes. Hence, perhaps, the popularity of 'restorative justice' programmes for juvenile offenders. However, we can now see that those thoughts are best understood as thoughts not about *whether* we should punish juveniles, but about *how* we should punish them.

If juvenile offenders are capable of taking responsibility for their actions, we should treat them as responsible agents: as agents who, inter alia, can and should be called to account for the wrongs that they do. We owe this to them both out of respect for their moral standing as agents who can take responsibility, and out of concern for their moral development into fully responsible members of the community. Now if we are to treat them as responsible agents, we must try to bring them to face up to and recognise the wrongs they have done, as wrongs; to see the need for apologetic reparation to those whom they have wronged—the need to restore the relations that their crime damaged; and to embark (with our help) on the necessary task of self-reform. But these are, I have argued, precisely the aims that criminal punishment should serve: we should punish juvenile offenders because this is what is due to them as responsible agents, and because this should help them develop into more fully responsible agents. (There is thus more room in the case of juveniles than in the case of adults to talk of punishment as education: see Zedner, 1998; Duff, 2001: ch 3.4.1.)

This does not mean, however, that we should draw no distinctions at all between juvenile and adult offenders. In deciding just how to punish juveniles, three general questions arise.

First, are juveniles, in virtue of their youth, typically less culpable than adults for crimes which are otherwise similar?

Second, should we adopt different kinds of *procedure* in dealing with juveniles: different kinds of trial, for instance in special youth courts; or different kinds of mediation process (for instance including members of their families); different procedures for negotiating sentences? The reasons for doing so would have to do with the extent to which juveniles can be expected to understand and participate in the ordinary adult proceedings, and the extent to which they might need special help or support in taking part in such proceedings.

Third, should the modes of punishment to which juveniles can be sentenced be different from those available for adults? Should some modes of punishment be ruled out, for instance; should there be some special modes of punishment for juveniles? (In discussing this question, we must attend both to the *effects* of different modes of punishment, and to their *meanings*.)

I cannot discuss these questions in any detail here—I will be content if I have persuaded anyone to agree that we should punish juveniles for the sake of the values and goals to which I have appealed, and thus that these are the questions we must go on to ask. It seems plausible that the answer to the first question must be, very often, 'Yes' (see von Hirsch, 2000); and that the answer to the second question is also likely to be 'Yes'—although much depends on what procedures are appropriate for adult offenders (in particular, how far it is appropriate for them to maintain formal criminal procedures which emphasise the formality and majesty of the law, procedures which would then be less suitable for juveniles; see Weijers, ch 7 in this volume). The answer to the third question must obviously again be 'Yes', at least in that the content of a Community Service or Reparation Order needs to be appropriate to the offender's age and capacities; but also, and more significantly, if we think that certain modes of punishment are quite inappropriate for juvenile offenders.

The obvious candidate here is imprisonment. Given both its severity and its meaning (as *excluding* the offender from ordinary life and community), imprisonment has anyway only a very limited role to play in a communicative system of punishment of the kind I favour: it is appropriate only for crimes which, in virtue of their intrinsic character and their persistence, are so destructive of the very bonds of community that we can properly think that the offender has made it morally impossible for us to continue to live in community with him (at least for a time). We might be tempted then to think (I am tempted to think) that imprisonment can never be an appropriate punishment for juveniles: for it is destructive of the relationships on which a juvenile's moral development depends, and communicates an exclusionary judgement that we should not be ready to make on a juvenile. However, I am not sure that we should take such a view, although we should certainly maintain a very strong presumption against imprisonment for juveniles.

To reject imprisonment for juveniles need not, of course, be to reject *detention*: we could still argue that some juvenile offenders should be detained for their own protection or for the protection of others. But to take that view of juveniles is to cease to see them as responsible agents—which might be appropriate, but might instead constitute a refusal to allow them the moral standing that they can properly claim. I would rather cling, for as long as possible, to a view of juveniles as responsible agents: because this pays them the respect which is their due; because it can protect them against the otherwise intrusive power of the state; and because it can help them take responsibility for themselves and their lives. An implication of this is that I might have to accept that in some extreme cases imprisonment (in a suitable prison) is the only morally possible punishment for a juvenile's crimes.

Those would, however, be extreme cases: in the vast majority of cases juvenile offenders would receive sentences whose material content might not be very different from the kinds of response favoured by Walgrave and others who oppose the punishment of juveniles: I would argue, however, for the reasons already given, that we should understand and impose these as appropriate *punishments* for the *wrongs* the juvenile offenders have done. So long as we think of punishment only as what is done to offenders within our existing penal practices, or simply as an imposition or infliction that is intended to make wrongdoers suffer, we will rightly think that juvenile offenders should not be subjected to it. Indeed, we should think, as abolitionists do, that *no one* should be subjected to it. However, if we therefore turn away from punishment to look for essentially *non*-punitive ways of dealing with or responding to juvenile offenders, we turn our backs on morally interesting and fruitful possibilities which flow from the attempt (sketched above) to reconceptualise punishment as a communicative enterprise that addresses the wrongdoer (adult or juvenile) as someone for whom we care, and whom we respect, as a fellow member of our political community.

REFERENCES

Adler, J (1992) *The Urgings of Conscience* (Temple University Press, Philadelphia).
Ball, C (2000) 'Part I: A Significant Move towards Restorative Justice, or a Recipe for Unintended Consequences?' *Criminal Law Review* 211–22.

Bottoms, A & McWilliams, W (1979) 'A Non-Treatment Paradigm for Probation Practice' 9 *British Journal of Social Work* 159–202.

Braithwaite, J (1999) 'Restorative Justice: Assessing Optimistic and Pessimistic Accounts' in M Tonry (ed) *Crime and Justice: A Review of Research*, vol 25 (University of Chicago Press, Chicago) 1–127.

Cavadino, M & Dignan, J (1998) 'Reparation, Retribution and Rights' in A von Hirsch & A J Ashworth (eds.), *Principled Sentencing*, 2nd edn (Hart Publishing, Oxford) 348–58.

Christie, N (1977) 'Conflicts as Property' 17 *British Journal of Criminology* 1–15.

—— (1981) *Limits to Pain* (Martin Robertson, London).

Daly, K & Immarigeon, R (1998) 'The Past, Present, and Future of Restorative Justice' 1 *Contemporary Justice Review* 21–45.

Dignan, J (1999) 'The Crime and Disorder Act and the Prospects for Restorative Justice' *Criminal Law Review* 48–60.

Dobash, R E & Dobash, R P (1992) *Women, Violence and Social Change* (Routledge, London).

Duff, R A (1986) *Trials and Punishments* (Cambridge University Press, Cambridge).

—— (2001) *Punishment, Communication and Community* (Oxford University Press, New York).

Feinberg, J (1970) 'The Expressive Function of Punishment' in his *Doing and Deserving* (Princeton University Press, Princeton, NJ) 95–118.

Hudson, J, Morris, A, Maxwell, G & Galaway B (eds) (1996) *Family Group Conferences: Perspectives on Policy and Practice* (Criminal Justice Press, Monsey, NY).

Hulsman, L (1991) 'The Abolitionist Case: Alternative Crime Policies' 25 *Israel Law Review* 681–709.

Marshall, S E & Duff, R A (1998) 'Criminalization and Sharing Wrongs' 11 *Canadian Journal of Law & Jurisprudence* 7–22.

Marshall, T F & Merry, S (1990) *Crime and Accountability: Victim/Offender Mediation in Practice* (HMSO, London).

Martin, F M & Murray, K (1976) *Children's Hearings* (Scottish Academic Press, Edinburgh).

Matthews, R (ed) (1988) *Informal Justice* (Sage, London).

Maxwell, G & Morris, A (1993) *Family, Victims and Culture: Youth Justice in New Zealand* (Social Policy Agency and Institute of Criminology, Victoria University of Wellington, Wellington NZ).

Scheid, D E (1980) 'Note on Defining "Punishment"' 10 *Canadian Journal of Philosophy* 453–62.

Von Hirsch, A (2001) 'Proportionate Sentences for Juveniles—How Different than for Adults?' 3 *Punishment & Society* 221–36.

Von Hirsch, A & Ashworth, A J (eds) (1998) *Principled Sentencing*, 2nd edn (Hart Publishing, Oxford).

Walgrave, L (2001) 'Restoration and Punishment. On Favourable Similarities and Fortunate Differences' in G Maxwell & A Morris (eds), *Restoring Justice for Juveniles* (Hart Publishing, Oxford) 17–37.

Zedner, L (1994) 'Reparation and Retribution: Are They Reconcilable?' 57 *Modern Law Review* 228–50.

—— (1998) 'Sentencing Young Offenders' in A J Ashworth & M Wasik (eds) *Fundamentals of Sentencing Theory* (Oxford University Press, Oxford) 165–86.

7

The Moral Dialogue: A Pedagogical Perspective on Juvenile Justice

IDO WEIJERS

1. INTRODUCTION

WHAT IS SO special about young people who break the law that they should be dealt with separately by our justice system? They are, of course, young and immature; they still have to learn what society will allow them to do and what it will not allow. So, first, we do not hold them as fully responsible for their actions as adults, and second, we accept that their punishments should be less severe. They are, at least, typically less culpable than adult offenders, because they are—as we have come to realise more clearly—less mature: although at 17 their raw intellectual abilities are comparable to those of adults, 17-year-old adolescents lack the experience of adults, and their capacities for judgement are heavily influenced by a lack of future-orientation and of risk-aversion, and by impulsivity and suggestibility especially in relation to their peers (Scott, Reppucci & Woolard, 1995; Steinberg & Cauffman, 1996; Cauffman & Steinberg, 2000; Grisso, 2000).

Youth's lesser culpability does not by itself warrant a separate juvenile justice system. However, there is more to it than that. A separate juvenile criminal justice system is also based on the modern idea that we should deal in a different way with young people who have overstepped the mark. So we have special sanctions and institutions, and special court procedures. The idea is that the process, the sanctions and the institutions should be geared to the juvenile's limited understanding and inexperience, and should aim to bring out the best in him. A separate juvenile justice system aims at more than a minimum recognition of the immaturity and reduced culpability of the young offender. The process and the sanctions are designed to teach him something and to help him towards maturity. We have a separate juvenile justice system because we believe that the criminal prosecution of juveniles must not confine itself to retribution for the offence, or to setting a deterrent example, or to preventing further crimes. Juvenile justice is distinguished from adult criminal justice by its educational approach.

For three quarters of a century after the introduction of the juvenile court at the beginning of the last century, the principle that the juvenile justice system should serve educational ends was undisputed. However, as we saw in part I of this book, serious cracks have appeared in this consensus since the early 1970s. The rights and responsibilities of young offenders, it has been argued, must be respected, giving them greater legal protection. The distinctions between juvenile and adult criminal law should be minimised, and educational interventions with juvenile offenders should give way to a more orthodox criminal law approach which will roll back the traditional 'paternalistic' approach to juvenile offenders (Trépanier, 1999). The question then arose: how much of the 'educational mission' of juvenile justice should be preserved?

What is remarkable, however, is that it has never really been made clear just what that educational mission should involve. Special therapies and training programmes were developed, but no leading theoretical concepts of an educational approach to juvenile delinquents have been worked out as a basis for concrete practices, nor can any be deduced from our existing practices. Juvenile justice lacks a pedagogical foundation: we have never come further than the idea that young offenders should be dealt with in a different way. It is true that from the late 1920s there has been a cautious breakthrough in psychological thinking in the sphere of treatment. Under the influence of a model of therapeutic intervention, juvenile delinquency increasingly came to be seen as an individual psychological problem: the court did its best to show more understanding and sympathy, and the young offender was treated as the victim of problems of upbringing rather than as an autonomous individual, fully responsible for himself. Demonstrating understanding and seeking to serve the 'interests of the child' thus became the main rationale for the far-reaching powers of the juvenile court, supported by the assumption of a self-evidently harmonious co-operation between court, prosecutor, lawyers, forensic experts and probation workers. This notion of the 'best interests of the child', however, which supposedly justified various departures from the adult criminal process, remained amorphous and poorly developed. And despite all the debate and changes since the 1970s, we still have little more than this amorphous notion to help us understand the educational dimension of the criminal law's reaction to young offenders.

In this paper I will offer an interpretation of a pedagogical foundation for the criminal prosecution of young people, and a principled defence of a special juvenile justice system, in particular of a special juvenile court (for a fuller account of my argument, see Weijers, 2000). It is not the exceptions to the procedural rules of general criminal law (such as closed doors, compulsory appearance and compulsory legal representation), nor even the special sanctions in themselves, that mark out the educational approach. Whilst each of these features of the juvenile system is indeed an essential condition for realising an educational approach, on their own they do not identify the educational dimension of the juvenile justice system. The definitive aspect of the educational approach is, I will argue, the moral appeal made to the young delinquent during the criminal proceedings. That is the crux of my case. The key to an educational form of juvenile justice, in response to a serious offence, lies in the attempt to get the young person to realise the moral significance of what he has done, the pain inflicted on the victim, and the harm his behaviour has done to the community and to himself as a moral being. From an educational perspective everything turns on appealing to the young person's sense of morality, his sense of empathy, guilt and remorse. Our response to his wrongdoing has to teach him a concrete moral lesson. This holds generally for bringing up children: pedagogically, the core of our reaction as a parent or a teacher to the serious wrongdoing of a child or adolescent must be a moral dialogue with the young person. This should also be central to the juvenile justice system.

I develop this argument in four stages. First, in s 2, I demonstrate the complexity of the problem of how the criminal justice system should respond to juvenile delinquency; I define that problem as the double paradox of juvenile justice. Second, I argue for a communicative approach to criminal justice, which seeks a balance between the traditional justifications of retribution and prevention under an over-arching accent on the communicative dimension of criminal law (s 3). Crucial to a communicative approach is the moral dialogue in court; I draw on my experience with the Dutch juvenile court to explore the educational possibilities that such a dialogue can provide. Third, I discuss, very briefly, the implications of my thesis for the Anglo-Saxon and the continental juvenile court traditions (s 4). These traditions imply structural differences between so-called adversarial and inquisitorial procedures, which turn out to have far-reaching implications for the very possibility of realising any moral dialogue in court. In s 5, I offer a deeper analysis of the character of the moral dialogue in the juvenile court. At its core is a focus on the moral consequences of the wrongdoing: it tries to stimulate the young offender's self-reflection, by discovering and connecting itself to what he cares about. I argue that this can be understood as a practical ethics of care. Finally, I argue that this kind of moral dialogue aims to appeal at feelings of empathy, regret and remorse.

2. A DOUBLE PARADOX

Juvenile criminal law displays a fundamental complexity. Two philosophical questions play a constant role in the background when it comes to the criminal prosecution of young people: why punishment, and why punishment for minors? The historical dynamics of juvenile justice can be understood as a continually changing response to this complex combination of a problem of legal philosophy and a pedagogical problem (Weijers, 1999).

As we saw in the Introduction and in chapters 5 and 6, it seems impossible to find any generally accepted answer to the question 'Why punishment?' in the philosophy of law. Juvenile criminal justice, however, raises a second, quite different problem, which can be regarded as a typical problem in the philosophy of education: to find an answer to the question of young people's responsibility and autonomy.

2.1. Retribution and Prevention

Criminal law is concerned with the relationship between the state and a citizen with legal rights and duties. Punishment can only be justified, in the context of the criminal law, if and because it falls under the auspices of the state. There is broad consensus on an initial answer to the question of why certain acts should be prohibited by law and labelled crimes—that the state has a duty to make clear that these acts cannot be accepted by society. However, differences of opinion immediately arise over whether this is the complete answer, or only part of it. Some think that it goes without saying that we should add that the state has a duty to ensure that fewer crimes are committed, and that the criminal law must serve this purpose. Others, however, see this as an addition that obscures the core of the concept of criminal law. In this debate the deontological principle of retribution is set against the utilitarian principle of social good. According to an increasing number of participants in this debate, the discussion turns on the question of the relationship between these two principles and on finding a balance between them. As Hart wrote, 'any morally tolerable account of this institution [of criminal punishment] must exhibit it as a compromise between distinct and partly conflicting principles' (Hart, 1968: 1).

The tension between the principles of effective prevention and of appropriate retribution is responsible for a criminal law paradox, which seems hard to solve, even if we accept that both justifications have fundamental shortcomings and recognise that we need a combination which balances the strengths of both traditions. The problem with such compromises is that acknowledging that both justifications fall short still does not remove the conceptual tension between the two principles. The question is whether, and to what extent, the search for a compromise between deserved punishment and useful punishment can succeed in tempering the centrifugal force between effective deterrence and proportionate retribution.

Given the small risk of being caught for any crime in our complex, open society, the deterrent effect of a punishment that is proportionate to individual guilt is generally very low. The point is not just that subtle distinctions and considerations in sentencing pass the public at large by. It is also utterly unrealistic to expect that anyone who is reasonably well-informed, and who therefore knows the small risk of arrest, will be effectively deterred from committing offences by a threat of proportionate punishment. Really effective deterrence, in fact, seems to demand that the principle of proportionality be abandoned. That is the centrifugal force in one direction, which pretends not to hear all the objections raised against such a radical, one-sided approach.

On the other hand there is the growing demand for 'just deserts', regardless of the social effect of the sanctions. All demands for sanctions to be effective would reinforce arbitrariness and injustice and must therefore be rejected on principle. That is the centrifugal force in the other direction.

Here we come up against the paradox of criminal law. On the one hand, there is a very plausible case to be made that these two approaches ought to complement each other and that each one in its pure form is inadequate, or even misses its target completely. On the other hand, no workable compromise, preserving both principles, seems possible (see Goldman, 1979). I will argue in s 3, however, that we should first focus on and elaborate the common ground lying behind this paradox, which will lead us to emphasise the communicative dimension of our criminal law systems.

2.2. Responsible and Dependent

Juvenile justice is also faced with a second paradox. Justifying the punishment of a minor requires one to answer the question: how responsible is he? How should the criminal justice system deal with a child or young person who has committed a crime, given that, as a minor, the offender is considered to be not yet (or not yet fully) responsible? Criminal justice for young people will always have to take account of the dilemma that, while they are developing towards responsibility, they are presumed to be dependent and not yet fully responsible.

Of course, this dilemma is not specific to criminal justice. It is a general dilemma for education and upbringing, which every parent and teacher has to face over and over again. From an educational perspective, what matters in relation to the responsibility of the child is to help the child to learn to take responsibility for his actions, and in the end, for his life. The child's responsibility is essentially a concept in inverted commas: it has to be taken in the spirit of play or 'as if'; it is a responsibility that is on trial and subject to reservations. Aspects and forms of responsibility which have been tested as the child develops lose their character as play and become fixed points of real responsibility in the process of growing up. We assume we can count on them, just as we assume with reading and writing that the child can spell. Child and parent shake off the conditions attached to the child's responsibility bit by bit during the course of their relationship. Juvenile responsibility is essentially an ambiguous concept; it is also a dynamic and relational concept, which refers to a goal that is made concrete and changes during the upbringing process. Parenting goals are typically vague and open. They cannot actually be tested against explicitly defined criteria, as is customary with teaching goals for example. Nor do parenting goals have any central, definitive criterion. A goal like responsibility allows for individual variation and is open to change over time (Levering, 1991). Very broadly speaking, three phases can be distinguished here, which involve changing parental views of the child's developing responsibility.

The first stage is that of the new-born child. An interaction arises between infant and parents immediately after the birth, a continuous, mutual eliciting of responses, in which the child's responses are interpreted and met in an active and explicit way by the parents. The typical, fundamentally unequal communication pattern of this early interaction is the core of the educational relationship: a serious game of 'as if', in which the parents address the child as if he already understands what they are saying to him, as if he is already a person. The parents act as if the child was already acting with intention (Marková, 1982). The parents' behaviour, and the conceptual framework within which they are evidently operating, can be labelled 'contra-factual': they appeal to principles which have yet to be realised; they speak to the child as the person he has yet to become (Spiecker, 1982).

A second phase begins roughly when the child starts talking and reasoning. Contra-factualism now takes on a more direct significance as a prelude to independence by 'introducing an attitude that makes independence possible', as Mollenhauer put it (1986: 130–1). The parenting relationship in this second phase is also characterised by a game of 'as if', but both parent and child display far more active and explicit roles in their interaction. Now, the parent continually allows the child moments of being responsible for his own actions, scope to do things for himself, and the child for his part never ceases to take the initiative to do this. The child is wrestling free from his original responsiveness in a rapidly increasing number of spheres of action. He practises exercising responsibility in relation to his parents: they start to give him responsibilities directly related to his actions—'you can do that yourself'; and he practises taking it—'I can do it myself'.

Finally, a long last phase can be distinguished, which coincides with the beginnings of the child's moral development. Now, explicit appeals are made to the child's moral interests and sense of responsibility, which is now extended and broadened in various moral dimensions. The 'as if' aspects are pushed further into the background, without the contra-factualism disappearing altogether. That only happens when the upbringing process comes to an end, when the young person becomes an adult. In this third phase, responsibility becomes associated with questions about who the child wants to become, what he cares about, who he wants to belong to and what he believes in. In other words, the practical moral development of the child coincides with a movement away from the 'as if' playing with responsibility within the parent-child relationship, to a practical reflection on his own actions, on his personal history and future, in short, on the personal identity of the adolescent. The upbringing process can be considered to have come to an end when the young person is able to continue his personal development outside the parental relationship in a new, broader sphere of relationships. The challenges now facing him and those that he sets himself are taken up and reflected on in a perspective that contains more meaningful reference points than the parent-child relationship. From the perspective of upbringing, being an adult means that the relationship with one's parents becomes just one aspect of a whole range of considerations that come into play in one's actions and in the development of personal identity.

From a pedagogical perspective a minimum requirement for a criminal justice approach is that the child must be able to realise that the wrong he has done is not only a misdemeanour against his parents. In other words, the child must be able to realise, at least partially, the social importance of his wrongdoing. Pedagogically, juvenile justice may be viewed as an area of responses to a young person's wrongdoing where criminal justice and parental corrections overlap. Whereas (sane) adult offenders are considered fully responsible to the community for their wrongdoing, juvenile justice has to do with offenders who are at the same time eligible for punishment by their parents; this displays our recognition that their wrongdoing is still partially a misdemeanour against their parents. Bringing adolescents to court implies that we hold them responsible for their misconduct both to their parents and to the community.

The young offender thus seems to be held responsible as a citizen before the law, whilst being at the same time still subject to the reservation of contra-factualism. Again the young person has to learn something. He now has to learn what citizenship means, what being held responsible to the community rather than his parents implies, in accordance with his special legal status in a wide range of fields (driving license, alcohol license, compulsory education, right to contract, right to marry, right to have sexual relations with adults, etc). Everywhere one finds some kind of transitional stage, where the responsibility of the adolescent as a family member develops into their responsibility as a member of the social community, including all the rights and duties of citizenship. We must therefore acknowledge that in dealing with a young offender we are not dealing with a fully mature adult, but with someone who has yet to learn a full awareness of the social and moral implications of his actions as a citizen before the law of the community, and who must be helped to do so. Here is the basic justification for a special juvenile justice system: this system's special task, on behalf of the community, is to help the young offender to understand the moral implications of what he has done.

2.3. Diminished Responsibility

The basic justification for special criminal sanctions and procedures for young offenders is thus found in what Zimring has described as their diminished responsibility (Zimring, 2000). In three significant respects, young offenders display limited, or not fully developed, capacities which reveal their immaturity and seem to make special sanctions and procedures appropriate.

First, research shows that youths younger than 14 are clearly incompetent to stand trial. They cannot fully understand the legal process, nor fully appreciate the significance of legal procedures and outcomes for their own situation. They cannot communicate information in the way that adult offenders are supposed to do, or use adult reasoning in making decisions, or make psychosocially mature judgements (Woolard *et al*, 1996; Grisso, 2000).

Second, as Grisso concludes, although by about 14 to 15 years of age some youths appear to have developed legally relevant cognitive abilities that approximate those of older adolescents, many others continue to develop more slowly and will achieve their adult capacities at a later age, nearer to the late teens (Grisso, 2000: 163). This developmental delay is especially evident in young offenders. Lawyers can play an important role in assisting young offenders towards competence, in particular by developing what Emily Buss defines as 'professional friendship' (Buss, 2000). This will not be enough, however, since delinquent juvenile populations generally contain a high proportion of adolescents with intellectual deficits, learning disabilities, emotional disorders and reduced educational and cultural opportunities.

Third, the young offender's immaturity is also revealed in his limited ability to foresee and give appropriate weight to the long-range consequences of his actions during the criminal process (Scott *et al*, 1995; Steinberg & Cauffman, 1996). The young defendant in court is not the calculating adult he is sometimes supposed to be.

These limitations in young offenders' cognitive and psychosocial capacities are significant in themselves, but take on added importance in relation to the functioning of the criminal court. Much more than for adults, children's and adolescents' competence in criminal law procedures is, like all their capabilities, context-sensitive and interactive (Eggermont, 1994; Masten & Coatworth, 1998). The point is that to enable young offenders to demonstrate their maximum, almost adult, competence in court, they need to be helped by special supporting procedures, rituals, questions and explanations, and by people who develop something like a 'professional friendship', or special 'professional concern'. We should certainly hold young offenders responsible for their wrongdoing, even if it is a diminished responsibility, but the context and operations of the court must offer them as much support as possible to help them become as responsible as they can. It is along these lines that my argument in the rest of this chapter will be developed.

3. MORAL DIALOGUE

A first step to the solution of the paradox of criminal law involves recognising a presumption shared by both retributivist and consequentialist perspectives. The common ground that both kinds of justification share can be found in the communicative dimension of criminal justice. If punishment is to work either as a form of repayment or as a deterrent, the message which, according to each justification, it is to convey must come across clearly. Delinquents, potential delinquents and the public at large should not see the punishment imposed for a crime as revenge or as an arbitrary response, but should value it as a well-thought-out sanction that on the one hand balances the loss of rights suffered by others because of the crime, and on the other hand should prevent the offender from repeating these crimes in the future. There is an implicit assumption in every case that the punishment makes clear that the community condemns the offence. This is the communicative dimension of criminal justice that is incorporated in both justifications: punishment, in whatever form, implies that the public is pointing out to the person being punished that his behaviour is something to be condemned.

Our punishments and our criminal proceedings do not confine themselves to setting purely physical or mechanical limits. Above all they articulate moral limits. They refer to the boundaries of good and evil and affirm them. In this sense our punishments are essentially articulations of the values and norms of our legal order and of the limits it lays down. The sanctions that various crimes and minor offences carry under our criminal law, and the actual use of punishment, confirm what we consider to be morally unacceptable, telling both those who are considering committing such acts and those who have committed them that they are wrong.

3.1. Punishment as Moral Communication

A number of penal theorists have drawn attention to the communicative dimension of criminal justice (Feinberg, 1970; Morris, 1981; Hampton, 1984; Duff, 1986). I will not discuss the clear differences between these authors here (see Weijers, 2000: ch 2). I will instead draw from them one coherent argument for a communicative justification of punishment, and then make a critical comment.

The communicative argument ascribes a distinctive purpose to punishment: that purpose is future-oriented, but is formulated in terms of reparation—moral reparation—rather than of effective crime-prevention. The purpose of punishment, on this view, is to make good the wrong done, not only in a material sense but above all in a moral sense. Crime is seen first and foremost as creating a moral flaw in the perpetrator's relations with his community; as an infringement of the legal order as far as his personal participation in it is concerned. This infringement of the legal order and this flaw in social relations created by the offence can only be repaired if the offender regrets and condemns his action, and tries to arrange his own life in such a way as to avoid repeating it. Unlike the tradition of deterrence, in which the offender is made the object of sanctions in the hope that the sanctions will deter him and other potential offenders from committing crimes, this argument portrays punishment as an encouragement for the offender to change himself, because this is in the offender's own self-interest. Only by renouncing what he has done, by expressing remorse and by doing everything he can to change, can the offender hope to take his full place again as a citizen, a family member, a friend, colleague, neighbour and acquaintance.

Although punishment is certainly not a blessing, on this view it is better to be punished if you commit a crime than not: punishment is something good that replaces something that is unequivocally bad for the person convicted of a crime, even if that person often does not realise it (see Duff, 1996: 49). Notwithstanding their common ground in the communicative dimension of criminal justice, deterrent and retributivist theories both ignore this aspect of punishment. Both see punishment simply as inflicting pain. If, however, apart from expressing disapproval, punishment typically also facilitates reparation, through the link between punishment and regret, there is a positive side to it. Punishment, acknowledgement of guilt and regret, enable the convicted person to play a full part in the community again. Since criminal convictions and punishment aim to bring offenders to recognise and repent their crimes by censuring them for those crimes, Duff argues that the communicative approach appeals both to a retributivist notion of censure and to a consequentialist concern for crime-prevention: viewing punishment as a communicative enterprise offers a unitary justification of punishment that undercuts the traditional opposition between retribution and deterrence. 'The punishment that is deserved for the past crime is itself the intrinsically appropriate way of pursuing the forward-looking goals that punishment should serve' (Duff, 2001: 89; see also ch 6, s 2.3 in this volume).

3.2. The Focal Point of the Communicative Approach

I fully agree with this emphasis on communication; as I will make clear later, this approach can help us solve the double paradox of juvenile justice. My critical comment concerns the focal point of the communicative approach: whereas others focus on punishment itself, I think that this approach is primarily relevant to the offender's appearance in court. It is first of all in the criminal court proceedings (and in restorative justice sessions) that we can find room for the idea that punishment can and should be something that benefits the person being punished. The communicative idea is primarily relevant to the interaction between the magistrate (and the prosecutor) and the offender and only secondarily to the implementation of sanctions.

Whereas Duff claims that the communicative approach provides the justification not only of the proceedings but also of the actual infliction of the penalty (the hard treatment), I have some doubts. According to Duff, hard treatment should be seen as a worldly form of penance that aims to evoke remorse, repentance and atonement (1998: 165). He speaks of the offender

> who before her punishment is unrepentant, but who is brought by her punishment to repent her crime, to accept her punishment as an appropriate penance for that crime, and to try to reform herself and to reconcile herself with those she wronged' (2001: 116; see also ch 6 in this volume, s 2.2).

It is doubtful not only whether this is a realistic image of punishment in general, but also whether it could become that in the future; indeed, this image seems to lack the strength of the communicative idea itself. What gives that idea its strength and inspiration is its emphasis on criminal law as a process of moral communication. But only under very specific conditions can the implementation of punishment be valued as a morally communicative process. As Duff recognises, imprisonment can hardly be seen as a communicative process that brings offenders to repentance, since the crux of imprisonment is social isolation. An emotional and moral hardening seems to be the usual effect of imprisonment. In so far as some prisoners do come to repentance, this seems to be more related to reflections on what has been said in the courtroom than elicited by their imprisonment as such. But it is also questionable how far community service, as a punishment, can generally be seen as a communicative process, apart from some very carefully chosen projects involving activities whose character is highly relevant to the offence, which might thus be understood as 'communication-prone'. But even in these cases there is typically little or no direct communication about the offence or its moral consequences. We should also ask ourselves, if we really want sentences to be such vehicles of patterns of moral communication, by whom they could be properly imposed, and with what legal justification. On the other hand, learning penalties, with special courses like aggression training, may come closer to the communicative idea, precisely because there is an intensive dialogue concerning the wrongdoing. However, these dialogues have to do with coping, with learning how to handle what experts think are the offender's problems. Even when the offender identifies these problems, such as addiction or beating, as his own, these courses are not primarily moral dialogues, but lessons in coping.

I agree with Duff, that we should not (only) refer to existing practices, but should look at how these practices should and could be. My point is that, in general, in so far as punishment brings about feelings of repentance, regret and remorse, it is by reference to what has been put forward in the courtroom (and/or in a restorative session). Thus, the focal point of any communicative approach to criminal law should, I suggest, be the moral dialogue in court. In principle, this is the context in which we should really be able to observe a process of moral communication and persuasion taking place—if not directly then indirectly. The dialogue in court can function (and the court purports to function) as a moral reference point in the life of the young offender. So I interpret the communicative perspective as applying primarily to criminal proceedings in court, and as offering guidance on how such proceedings can be best designed, and only secondarily offering guidance on how punishment can best be implemented. This perspective can provide us with an over-arching idea that enables us to balance the two traditional justifications for sentencing.

A focus on the moral communication in court implies that both the amount and the kind of retribution (the proportionality) and the character of the preventive sanctions are explicitly justified to the offender, as convincing conclusions of the dialogue in court. A communicative approach means, I suggest, first, that the dialogue in court remains the central reference-point in the implementation of the sanctions, and second, that the character of the implementation is as communicative as possible. This perspective may offer an inspiring point of departure for a pedagogical vision of youth justice, first by the way in which it focuses attention on the educational interaction between the judge (and public prosecutor) and the accused, and second, by its communicative focus on the practical arrangements for juvenile sanctions. I will concentrate on the first aspect, the dialogue in court.

4. JUVENILE COURT TRADITIONS

If this vision sounds attractive, is it also realistic, or realisable? On the basis of my experience with the Dutch juvenile court, I think it is, given certain conditions. We have undertaken a long series of observations in Dutch courtrooms, placing ourselves in the modest research tradition of 'rituals in court' (Hoefnagels, 1970; Carlen, 1976; Komter, 1998; van Rossum, 1998), followed by a series of observations in England. (For the observations in England see Hokwerda, 2000. For a more detailed discussion of these observations, see Weijers & Hokwerda, 2001.) Comparing the Dutch and the English juvenile court procedures, we have found fundamental, structural differences which have to do with the differences between adversarial and inquisitorial court procedures (see Fairchild & Dammer, 2001). These different patterns turn out to have far-reaching implications for the possibility of realising any kind of moral dialogue in court.

From a pedagogical point of view we discerned three relevant dimensions of educational communication in juvenile court: general attitude, explanation and moral communication. The first dimension concerns the interest shown in the life and ideals of the offender, the focus on the offender instead of his lawyer, body language, etc.. The second dimension concerns both the explanation of rituals and the amount of legal jargon. These two dimensions taken together come close to what Emily Buss calls 'professional friendship' (Buss, 2000). I will concentrate here, however, on the last dimension, of moral communication. We identified different patterns of rituals in the juvenile court, which offer different possibilities for moral communication. In the adversarial criminal process the prosecutor and the defender are the actors who mainly steer the process. Both are addressing the magistrate(s), and if the young offender participates in their exchange of points of view at all, he does so only marginally, and to serve the ends of the defence or the prosecution. Usually, it is only at the end of the sitting of the court that the chair of the bench turns to the young offender to explain the court's decision and to warn him not to repeat his offence.

By contrast, in the Dutch juvenile court system the judge is the steering actor. Whereas in an English court the charge is first read out, and the judge then asks the offender if he pleads guilty or not, the Dutch judge simply first asks the young offender to tell his side of the story. This is usually followed by an exchange of questions and answers about the causes of, and the motives for, the wrongdoing. Later, having read the expert's report, the judge usually asks the young offender what he thinks of this report; this is again followed by a discussion of how the young offender sees himself. Another rule is that the judge must make inquiries about the young offender's personal circumstances, about his family situation and his school career, his hobbies and his plans for the future. And finally, she gives the young offender the last word.

These structural differences make clear that, whereas the Dutch inquisitorial procedure in juvenile courts is equipped from the start as a dialogue between the judge and the offender, in the United Kingdom the adversarial juvenile court procedure seems to minimise any form of dialogue between judge and offender. To make room for a moral dialogue to develop between judge and offender within the adversarial system would require a fundamental revision of this system itself. It is hard to imagine any moral dialogue with the offender within a procedural structure that actually drives his participation to the margins. The easiest way to introduce a moral dialogue seems then to lie outside the courtroom, as a variant of diversion, in the form of mediation, restorative justice, Family Group Conferencing, etc. (see Hudson *et al*, 1996; Bazemore & Walgrave, 1999; Walgrave, 2000; and Walgrave, ch 5 and Morris, ch 8 in this volume).

The search for a moral dialogue about the crime—a dialogue that should include the perspective of the victim, the parents and the young offender himself as an active moral agent—thus motivates moves to divert young offenders from the adversarial criminal justice process into alternative, non-criminal procedures. In the inquisitorial tradition though, the need for diversion seems to be far less. In fact, at least in the Dutch juvenile court tradition, the session in court has a strong dialogical structure and character, independently of the specific communicative skills and expertise of the individual judge.

5. WHAT YOU CARE ABOUT

In this section I want to say a little more about the character of the moral dialogue that the juvenile criminal process should involve, and about its relation to an ethics of care.

5.1. Community and Care

One strength of a communicative approach is that it allows 'the community'—family, friends and colleagues—to form intermediary moral chains between the offender and the legal system. Dismay, abhorrence, aversion, guilt, regret and forgiveness, in short the moral and communicative dimensions of the law, come into play, personified as it were, through the communities which give concrete meaning to these concepts. Punishment for a serious offence, provided that the offender acknowledges his guilt and is sorry for what he has done, enables him to become once more a fully participating citizen in the political community, through the more local communities of which he wishes to remain or become a member. A communicative approach involves a change in the nature of criminal justice itself: in dealing with the moral impact of the offence, proper attention is paid to the personal significance of being part of a community, and this happens on the invitation of and through dialogue with an objective and disinterested court representing the state.

A second strength of a communicative approach is the moral and educative attention paid to the victim. This involves the appeal that is made to a moral understanding of the wrong that was done; the growth in the offender's awareness that he is responsible for this; his learning to put himself in the victim's position; the development of his sense of guilt towards the victim; and the development of his awareness that punishment, acceptance of guilt and remorse offer the prospect of restoring his place as a fully participating member of society. (However, the communicative approach in court does not necessarily require the direct, physical presence of the victim. In juvenile court it is primarily the judge's role to articulate this appeal to the young person.)

A third strength of a communicative approach lies in its treatment of the accused as an active participant in the criminal proceedings. He is not made the mere object of interventions; decisions about his welfare are not taken over his head; he is valued and respected as a person with legal rights. But that is not done merely by reading him his rights, or having his interests defended by a lawyer. Of course, these things must be guaranteed, but a distinctive feature of a communicative approach is that the offender is to be asked to *present himself* in the best possible light. He is invited to explain in his own words how he views the moral significance of what he has done, and its meaning for those around him; and how he thinks he can make amends for the moral damage done by his action to the rule of law in general, but especially and in concrete terms to those around him. The interests of the community make their appearance in the proceedings through, as it were, this appeal to the offender to engage in moral reflection.

These three features are crucial to a communicative approach to the criminal process. The moral dialogue essentially involves an appeal to the offender to recognise the consequences of his wrongdoing. These consequences include, of course, the pain that the offender has caused to the victim by his action, but also the pain caused to his family and other loved ones, and the damage to himself as a moral person, to his self-perception and to his image of his future. This key focus of the moral dialogue, on the pain caused by the wrongdoing, is rooted in an ethics of care. (By 'an ethics of care' I mean not only the kind of feminist ethical position that is often so labelled, eg Gilligan, 1982 and Noddings, 1984, but also the kind of philosophical-anthropological analysis offered by Frankfurt, 1988 and Cuypers, 1994, and recent attempts to bring these positions together such as Baier, 1994.) What characterises an ethics of care is, first, the centrality of notions like empathy, care, love, trust and concern. Secondly, it implies that such classic liberal notions as identity, autonomy, self-determination and self-fulfilment, whilst not merely secondary, must be interpreted in relational terms.

Summarised in a few words: who I am is a matter first of all of what and whom I care about, which implies that who I am and who I want to become are always connected with those who care for me. From this perspective, identity and autonomy are not characteristics of beings that are quite unattached and with no social strings; rather, they depend on special forms of attachment to others.

5.2. 'Crime Scenario'

In a communicative approach it is the task of the magistrate, in addressing the young offender, to ask what and whom he cares about, and to try to induce a reflection on his wrongdoing in the light of what and whom he cares about. A distinction can be made between reflection on actions and reflection on their agent. The first concerns the offence and its meaning for the community and the victim; the second concerns the image which the offender forms of himself in the light of his crime, and which he evaluates via the (imaginary) judgements of people who are important to him.

In response to a serious criminal offence, the offender, the victim and other members of the community who are involved ask themselves such questions as: what was in the offender's mind; how did things get to that stage; how did the offender come to act like that? The court must try and find answers to these questions. The court will, for instance, try to gain some impression of what is known in forensic diagnostics and social work as the 'crime scenario', the whole gamut of deliberations and actions that directly preceded the offence. In this way it is hoped to track down a pattern of actions and considerations that led to the offence. If, through a dialogue between the court and the accused (with or without the aid of expert reports), such a pattern is discovered, and if the deliberations of the offender which seem to offer at least a partial explanation for the offence are identified, then attempts can be made to anticipate similar situations in the future.

This concentration on the deliberations preceding the offence zooms in on two aspects. First, attention is focused on 'technical' questions such as how the offender planned the offence, when and how he crossed the legal and moral threshold and decided to do it, and what pros and cons he considered in coming to that decision. Second, focusing on and reconstructing his deliberations as he planned the offence should raise moral questions and should point in particular to the victim, above all to the victim's fear and pain. Especially with children and juveniles, the magistrate has an active educative role to play here, which must be performed with the utmost care. She must of course satisfy herself to some extent about the reasons that led the young person to act as he did (or in some cases the notable absence of reasons): but provided that the dialogic procedure is carried out with the necessary educative sensitivity and caution, it can also make a contribution to the young person's developing self-awareness, in particular his awareness of how he came to be responsible for a criminal act.

5.3. Self-Reflection

In addition to reflection on the offence and its consequences for the victim, a different species of reflection is also involved here—self-reflection, and in particular two processes that can be designated self-identification and self-evaluation. To take responsibility, or to understand and accept responsibility when I am held responsible, I must be able to identify with myself, and to reflect on and judge that self critically. Identifying myself involves identifying something that functions as a set point, a guide in my personal life, something that goes beyond the mere moment and seems to be long-lived. Self-identification refers, therefore, to what is important to us, to what we care about and feel attached to. It is not the momentary and first intention that is at the heart of our self-identification, but those things that seem to come back over a longer period of time, things that have become a habit in us and that are experienced as an 'inner need'. Personal identity is not a concept that is all about the will. A person would be without identity if there were no limits to his will. It is the things that are important to a person that demarcate his will and give substance to it. The things that matter to him put limits on his will and give it its distinctive individual character (see Cuypers, 1994: 118; Frankfurt, 1988).

This does not mean that identity and responsibility are unchanging facts, a simply given lot that the person has to bear. Whilst responsibility presupposes a self that one did not freely choose, it also implies that one reflects on that self, continuously subjecting it to critical review and evaluation. That process of self-evaluation deserves further consideration. It is often assumed that self-control and self-evaluation take place using strictly self-chosen norms and values. But people do not take the critical judgement of themselves from themselves. We cannot create our standards by which we can then judge ourselves. Self-evaluation should rather be seen as the imaginary processing of the judgements of significant others: self-evaluation is dominated by a longing for recognition from those who mean a lot to us. It is a process in which we first of all try to imagine how significant others would judge our identifications. Significant others may be people who are present in or absent from our lives, or even those that only exist in our thoughts. In judging who we are, we try to imagine who we are in the eyes of our parents, grandparents, lovers, friends, teachers and colleagues, those whom we would like to be our friends, and sometimes even those who may come to judge us later, our children and pupils. Self-evaluation means that we try to view our identity through the eyes of others. Because these others are people who mean a lot to us, to whose opinions we feel closely tied, self-evaluation means doubling our awareness of what we care about: we reflect from whom we care about on what we care about.

Many juvenile court judges hesitate to get the child to start reflecting on the meaning of his offence for the community and the victim during the court hearing itself. Remarkably enough though, they often make an appeal to the young person's self-identification as a matter of course, even if it is only by asking questions such as 'Don't you think what you did was cowardly?' and 'Do you still recognise yourself in that?' What I am arguing, therefore, is that the juvenile court judge should do this in a considered and systematic way as part of his educational role. When the young person appears before the juvenile court, he is being addressed because of the way his offending affects the community. However, given that his responsibility is, in principle, contra-factual, it is the judge's job to help him to fully realise the social and moral implications of what he has done. In this sense, the task of giving substance to moral education rests on the shoulders of the juvenile court judge. Not by conveying norms and values: moral education is not a lesson in what is and what is not decent behaviour. Rather, moral education should be regarded as asking critical questions that help the young person to correct his own behaviour, attitude and self-image. These are questions that the young person usually 'overlooks', 'forgets' or simply refuses to ask himself.

5.4. Moral Emotions

Encouraging self-reflection is about trying to induce thought processes through which we hope that the young person will be stimulated to realise what is really important to him, what he wants to try to become, to whom he is attached and how he wants to express this. It is about encouraging self-identification and self-evaluation. These thought processes must be set against the background of the moral condemnation of the offence as expressed by the court. The dialogue in the courtroom can be seen as a means of encouraging self-reflection by rejection of the type of person who identifies himself with the offence. Here we again come across the moral feelings involved in this dialogue. Shame is certainly involved, but not in any active way, as 'shaming', as for instance John Braithwaite would have it (Braithwaite, 1989; Braithwaite & Mugford, 1994). In the kind of dialogue envisaged here, shame should not be entirely absent, but should be present only in the background, as a reserve, as a firm taboo on any offender's identification with a person who accepts the offence as normal, morally acceptable or even worse. (Compare Duff's argument, in ch 6 of this volume, that the offender should not be allowed to argue that his conduct was justified.)

A communicative approach cannot accept active shaming, since this implies criticising the identity of the offender and undermining his self-esteem, which, as Taylor and Olthof argue in part 3 of this volume, may be counter-productive in that it may provoke aggression and precisely preclude understanding, empathy and regret. The moral dialogue does not aim at criticism of the person of the offender but at stimulating him to distance himself from and to condemn the offence. Braithwaite's contrast between 'stigmatic' and 're-integrative' shaming suggests that he actually has a similar goal in mind: that, as Taylor and Olthof argue, we should attempt to induce feelings of guilt in the offender. From the perspective of an ethics of care, however, we should be seeking to induce not primarily feelings of guilt , but empathy, regret and remorse. The dialogue with the young offender aims to help him to recognise the moral consequences of his wrongdoing, the pain caused to his victim, and to his loved ones, and in the end to himself as a moral person, that is as someone whose relationship with his loved ones is severely disturbed. I conclude, therefore, with Morris and Taylor in part 3 of this volume, that juvenile justice should aim at getting the juvenile offender to feel remorse for what has been done and to accept the need to make amends to be able to restore his position in the moral community.

6. CONCLUSION

Responding to the double paradox of juvenile justice, I have proposed the combination of a communicative approach, as an over-arching justification for criminal law interventions, with an educational approach to the young offender, accepting that he cannot yet be held fully responsible and still needs to learn something. The young offender has to learn what citizenship means, by being held responsible for his actions to the community as well as to his parents. That implies that he has to learn to take responsibility for the moral implications and for the full weight of what he has done, the pain inflicted on the victim, on his family and other loved ones, and on himself. This learning process has to be moulded in a moral dialogue, which inquires into what the adolescent cares about. The dialogue is meant to stimulate both his critical reflection on the wrongdoing and his critical reflection on his identity as someone who wants to be taken seriously as a fully responsible citizen in the near future. This implies that the dialogue must aim primarily to induce feelings of empathy, regret and remorse.

REFERENCES

Baier, A C (1994) *Moral Prejudices. Essays on Ethics* (Harvard University Press, Cambridge, Mass).

Bazemore G & Walgrave L (eds) (1999) *Restorative Juvenile Justice: Repairing the Harm by Youth Crime* (Criminal Justice Press, Monsey).

Braithwaite, J (1989) *Crime, Shame and Reintegration* (Cambridge University Press, Cambridge).

Braithwaite, J & Mugford, S (1994) 'Conditions of Successful Reintegration Ceremonies. Dealing with Juvenile Offenders' 34 *British Journal of Criminology* 139–71.

Buss, E (2000) 'The Role of Lawyers in Promoting Juveniles' Competence as Defendants' in T Grisso & R G Schwartz (eds) *Youth on Trial. Developmental Perspectives on Juvenile Justice* (University of Chicago Press, Chicago/London) 243–65.

Carlen, P (1976) *Magistrates' Justice* (Martin Robertson, London).

Cauffman, E & Steinberg, L (2000) 'Researching Adolescents' Judgement and Culpability' in T Grisso & R G Schwartz (eds) *Youth on Trial. A Developmental Perspective on Juvenile Justice* (University of Chicago Press, Chicago/London) 325–43.

Cuypers, S E (1994) *Persoonlijke Anugelegenheden. Schets van een Analytische Antropologie* (Van Gorcum/Leuven University Press, Assen/Leuven).

Duff, R A (1986) *Trials and Punishments* (Cambridge University Press, Cambridge).

—— (1996) 'Penal Communications: Recent Work in the Philosophy of Punishment' in M Tonry (ed) *Crime and Justice. A Review of Research*, vol 20 (Chicago University Press, Chicago) 1–97.

—— (1998) 'Desert and Penance' in A von Hirsch & A J Ashworth (eds) *Principled Sentencing*, 2nd edn (Hart Publishing, Oxford) 161–67.

—— (2001) *Punishment, Communication, and Community* (Oxford University Press, New York).

Eggermont, M (1994) *Stomme Streken. Jongeren over hun Beleving van Straf* (Samsom Tjeenk Willink, Alphen a/d Rijn).

Fairchild, E & Dammer, H R (2001) *Comparative Criminal Justice Systems* (Wadsworth, Belmont).

Feinberg, J (1970) 'The Expressive Function of Punishment' in his *Doing and Deserving. Essays in the Theory of Responsibility* (Princeton University Press, Princeton) 95–118.

Frankfurt, H (1988) *The Importance of What We Care About* (Cambridge University Press, Cambridge).

Gilligan, C J (1982) *In a Different Voice* (Harvard University Press, Cambridge, Mass).

Goldman, A H (1979) 'The Paradox of Punishment' 9 *Philosophy & Public Affairs* 42–58; reprinted in: A J Simmons *et al* (eds) *Punishment. A Philosophy & Public Affairs Reader* (Princeton University Press, Princeton, 1995) 30–46.

Grisso, T (2000) 'What We Know about Youth's Capacities as Trial Defendants' in T Grisso & R G Schwartz (eds) *Youth on Trial. A Developmental Perspective on Juvenile Justice* (University of Chicago Press, Chicago/London) 139–71.

Hampton, J (1984), 'The Moral Education Theory of Punishment' 13 *Philosophy & Public Affairs* 208–38; reprinted in A J Simmons *et al* (eds) *Punishment. A Philosophy & Public Affairs Reader* (Princeton University Press, Princeton, 1995) 112–42.

Hart, H L A (1968) *Punishment and Responsibility. Essays in the Philosophy of Law* (Clarendon Press, Oxford).

Hoefnagels, G P (1970) *Rituelen ter Terechtzitting* (Kluwer, Deventer).

Hokwerda, Y M (2000) *Jeugdstrafzittingen, Een Leerzame Ervaring?* Unpublished undergraduate thesis, Utrecht.

Hudson, J, Morris, A, Maxwell, G & Galaway, B (1996) *Family Group Conferences. Perspectives on Policy and Practice* (Federation Press, Wellington).

Komter, M L (1998) *Dilemmas in the Courtroom. A Study of Trials of Violent Crime in the Netherlands* (Lawrence Erlbaum, Mahwah, New Jersey/London).

Levering, B (1991) 'Zelfverantwoordelijke Zelfbepaling Kan Echt Niet Meer' in F Heyting *et al* (eds) *Individuatie en Socialisatie in Tijden van Modernisering* (SISWO, Amsterdam) 169–77.

Marková, I (1982) *Paradigms, Thought and Language* (Wiley, Chichester).

Masten, A & Coatsworth, J (1998) 'The Development of Competence in Favorable and Unfavorable Environments', 53 *American Psychologist* 205–20.

Mollenhauer, K (1986) *Vergeten Samenhang. Over Cultuur en Opvoeding* (Boom, Amsterdam).

Morris, H (1981) 'A Paternalistic Theory of Punishment' 18 *American Philosophical Quarterly* 263–71.

Noddings, N (1984) *Caring: A Feminine Approach to Ethics and Moral Education* (University of California Press, Berkeley).

Scott, E , Reppucci, N & Woolard, J (1995) 'Evaluating Adolescent Decisionmaking in Legal Contexts' 19 *Law and Human Behavior* 221–44.

Spiecker, B (1982) 'De Pedagogische Relatie' in B Spiecker, B Levering & A J Beekman (eds) *Theoretische Pedagogiek* (Boom, Meppel/Amsterdam) 97–114.

Steinberg, L & Cauffman, E (1996) 'Maturity of Judgment in Adolescence: Psychosocial Factors in Adolescent Decision-making 20 *Law and Human Behavior*, 249–72.

Trépanier, J (1999) 'Juvenile Courts after 100 Years: Past and Present Orientations' 3 *European Journal on Criminal Policy andResearch* 299–301.

Van Rossum, W (1998) *Verschijnen voor de Rechter. Hoe het Hoort en het Ritueel van Turkse Verdachten in de Rechtszaal* (Duizend en Een, Amsterdam).

Walgrave, L (2000) *Met het Oog op Herstel. Bakens voor een Constructief Jeugdanctierecht* (Leuven University Press, Leuven).

Weijers, I (1999) 'The Double Paradox of Juvenile Justice' 3 *European Journal on Criminal Policy and Research* 329–51.

—— (2000) *Schuld en Schaamte. Een Pedagogisch Perspectief op het Jeugdstrafrecht* (Bohn Stafleu Van Loghum, Houten).

Weijers, I & Hokwerda, Y M (2002) 'Patterns and Possibilities for Educational Communication in Juvenile Court: United Kingdom and The Netherlands' in F Dünkel & K Drenkhahn (eds) *Youth Violence: New Patterns and Local Responses* (Ernst-Moritz-Arndt-Universität, Greifswald).

Woolard, J L, Reppucci, N D & Redding, R E (1996) 'Theoretical and Methodological Issues in Studying Children's Capacities in Legal Contexts' 20 *Law and Human Behavior* 219–28.

Zimring, F E (2000) 'Penal Proportionality for the Young Offender: Notes on Immaturity, Capacity, and Diminished Responsibility' in T Grisso & R G Schwartz (eds) *Youth on Trial. A Developmental Perspective on Juvenile Justice* (University of Chicago Press, Chicago/London) 271–89.

Part III

Shame, Guilt and Remorse

8

Shame, Guilt and Remorse: Experiences from Family Group Conferences in New Zealand

ALLISON MORRIS

1. INTRODUCTION

I SPENT THE FIRST 20 years of my academic career carrying out research and writing about what I would now describe as conventional youth justice systems: in particular, children's hearings in Scotland and juvenile (now youth) courts in England. In these systems, young offenders and their families contribute little in comparison with the various professionals involved in the process, and others (panel members or magistrates) make the decisions about how the offending should be dealt with. Victims are excluded from these decisions and really play no role at all in the proceedings (unless the young person denies the offence). The young person's guilt is simply acknowledged or assumed through an admission and stigmatic shaming is not uncommon. This admission is also taken as an indication of remorse. Nothing more is required.

I now have 10 years experience of carrying out research and writing about youth justice in New Zealand. Central to this youth justice system is the family group conference in which young offenders, their victims and their respective communities of care[1] come together to decide how best to deal with the offending. Family group conferences are premised on a very different value system from conventional youth justice systems.[2] They encourage offenders not only to accept responsibility for their offences—this requires more than an admission—but also to express their remorse for their offending by making amends to victims for the harm done. It does not require offenders to feel shame or to be shamed.

---

[1] 'Community of care' means the collection of people with shared concerns about the offender, the victim, the offence and its consequences, and with the ability to contribute towards a solution to the problem which the crime presents or represents. These people can support and negotiate with victims and offenders about appropriate outcomes through restorative processes and are arguably in a better place than judges and other professionals to identify what might prevent future crime.

[2] Family group conferences are commonly used now as an example of restorative justice (NACRO, 1997; Dignan, 1999; Morris and Maxwell, 2000) and so the comments made in this chapter about family group conferences can be extended to restorative justice more generally.

This view of the role of shame, guilt and remorse in family group conferences is not uncontested. John Braithwaite's (1989) theory of reintegrative
shaming has been influential in providing a rationale for some types of conferences.[3] He also specifically described family group conferencing in New
Zealand as endorsing traditional Maori conflict resolution processes which, he
suggested, placed 'great importance on ceremonies to communicate the shame
of wrongdoing' (1993: 37). He went on to claim that the introduction of family group conferences in New Zealand in 1989 had the effect of 'bringing
shame back into the justice process'. Guy Masters (1998: 128) similarly writes
that family group conferences 'shame by the very nature of their process' and
that it is 'almost inevitable' that they will lead to the shaming of offenders.[4]
Gerry Johnstone (1999: 3) similarly suggests that 'one of the main emotions
which restorative justice seeks to develop in offenders is a feeling of shame
about their misdeeds' and that 'the idea of shaming offenders is central to the
practice of the restorative conference.' In this paper, I examine further the role
and relevance of shame, guilt and remorse in family group conferences in New
Zealand.

First, however, I set out briefly the key differences between conventional
criminal justice (both adversarial and inquisitorial) and restorative justice as
this underpins much of the discussion which follows (s 2). Second, I describe
what Braithwaite meant by reintegrative shaming as I think it is widely misunderstood (s 3). In s 4, I point to some of the difficulties which can arise in putting
'reintegrative shaming' into practical effect. In s 5, I explore some of the criticisms which have been made of reintegrative shaming. In s 6, I discuss the role
of shame, guilt and remorse in family group conferences in New Zealand.
Finally, in the conclusion, I urge some caution in basing policy and practice on
reintegrative shaming before further research unpicks its key ingredients.

I have chosen not to define shame, guilt or remorse in this chapter because I
did not find the definitions I came across particularly helpful or enlightening (see
s 3.1 below). We all have an intuitive sense of what these concepts mean and I
invite you to rely on that. I do not know for sure that we, as teachers and
researchers from different academic disciplines, have a shared or common
understanding. And, even if we do, I do not know for sure that offenders share
that understanding. Nonetheless, I think we can proceed to explore the relevance of these issues for conferencing.

---

[3] It formed the basis for the systems of conferencing developed by the police in Wagga Wagga
(Moore, 1993), in Canberra (Sherman *et al*, 1998), in Thames Valley (Young and Goold, 1999) and
in the REAL JUSTICE movement in the United States (McCold and Wachtel, 1998). It should be
stressed here, however, that the theory of reintegrative shaming was not constructed as a theory of
juvenile justice, but as a theory to explain how we should respond to predatory crime and, in particular, to the crimes of the powerful.

[4] He also quotes Retzinger and Scheff's (1996) depiction of a family group conference as 'an automatic shaming machine', without acknowledging that they were, in fact, referring to badly managed
conferences.

2. CONTRASTING CRIMINAL JUSTICE AND RESTORATIVE JUSTICE PROCESSES

In this section I clarify the differences between conventional criminal justice processes and restorative justice processes (see also Morris and Young, 2000).

2.1. Criminal Justice Processes

Courts in most jurisdictions are quite formal places—deliberately so. This formality is designed to give authority to the process, to maintain the dignity of the law and to signify the seriousness of the event. The rituals, procedures and language seem designed to be emotionally cool: there is no legitimate place for strong emotions. On the other hand, research consistently shows that many defendants, victims and families find these processes distressing (Carlen, 1976; Ericson and Baranek, 1982; Maxwell *et al*, 1994; O'Connor and Sweetapple, 1988; Morris and Giller, 1977; Morris and Young, 1987). For them, a court appearance *is* an emotional experience, but this remains unacknowledged, even an inconvenience. An adjournment for a tearful witness to recover his or her composure, for example, is mainly viewed as wasting the judge's time rather than as bringing home to the offender the consequences of his or her actions.

Even defendants who plead guilty are not necessarily expressing the emotion of guilt—that is to say, they do not necessarily *feel* guilt (or shame if we accept Braithwaite's view that theses two emotions are entwined). What they have done is accept the jurisdiction of the court to sentence them. In conventional courts, the judge is very much in charge and s/he is responsible for making all the decisions.

Thus courts are not environments in which offenders are likely to participate freely and say easily what they really think and feel. While for lawyers, judges and court staff, juvenile courts tend to be more relaxed and informal than other criminal courts, they are not necessarily seen in this way by offenders (or by victims for that matter). In addition, lawyers tend to speak for offenders.

Remorse is also taken for granted when the offender pleads guilty. There is no test of its genuineness (though offenders are rewarded certainly in the English criminal justice system by a reduction in their sentence). There is no corresponding 'reward' for victims even when offenders appearing in the court experience genuine remorse for their behaviour, because these victims never get to know of the offenders' feelings. Indeed, recently in New Zealand, cases have been reported in the media where offenders offered to meet with their victims to express their remorse but were expressly discouraged from doing this by their lawyers (*The Dominion*, 12 May 2001).

2.2. Restorative Justice Processes

In contrast to conventional criminal justice processes, a critical value underlying restorative processes is the involvement of those most affected by offending—victims, offenders and their communities of care—in decisions. Ideally, these parties come together to search for ways to resolve the harm that has been done.

Thus offenders are expected to directly participate in the process, to speak about their offending and matters associated with it, to interact with the victim, to accept responsibility for their offending, to contribute to decisions about eventual outcomes, to express their remorse about what has occurred by apologising, and to make amends for what they have done.

Victims too have the opportunity to say to the offender how they feel about his or her actions and what the consequences of these actions have been for them, to get some understanding of what happened and why, to contribute to decisions about the outcome and, in meeting the offender and the offender's family face-to-face, to assess their attitude and the likelihood of the offence recurring.

All of these conversations should be respectful of all the participants, should be non-stigmatising and should not blame or shame either the offender, the victim or their communities of care (Zehr, 1990). In essence, the social values underlying restorative justice depend on connections—connections between offenders, victims and communities—rather than on exclusion.[5]

2.3. Inquisitorial justice—A Middle Ground?

A crucial question here has to be whether or not courts can be transformed to create the kind of environment that gives reality to restorative justice principles. Can, for example, complex language be simplified so that the parties can better understand and be involved in the proceedings? Can lawyers be encouraged to allow parties to speak for themselves? Can environments which have tradition-

---

[5] Masters and Smith (1998) suggest that restorative justice and family group conferences in New Zealand are similar to the 'ethic of care' outlined by Gilligan (1982) and developed by feminist writers on justice (see, for example, Heidensohn, 1986; Daly, 1989). Indeed, they quote one New Zealand youth justice co-ordinator (Stewart, 1993: 49) as saying 'today I have observed and taken part in justice administered with love'. It seems to me, however, that restorative justice goes much further than the 'ethic of care'. As articulated by Heidensohn and Daly, the 'ethic of care' is already part and parcel of conventional criminal justice systems through, for example, the use of community service and compensation. Restorative justice, on the other hand, attempts to transform conventional justice systems by inverting hierarchies and by giving participants the opportunity to decide matters for themselves. This could result in the use of conventional outcomes like imprisonment—reflecting, in Heidensohn's terms, Portia rather than Persephone—but such outcomes take on a different character in a restorative context when they have been truly agreed to by the parties.

ally worked in formal, structured and hierarchical ways be changed to truly involve the key parties to the offence? And can judges engage offenders in ways that lead to remorse?

I am very doubtful that these changes can be made. Even in New Zealand, where radical changes to youth court proceedings were introduced by statute in 1989, the youth courts changed little (Maxwell and Morris, 1993). It has been suggested that inquisitorial traditions offer more possibilities for restoration than adversarial approaches. I do not accept this. Jurisdictions based on inquisitorial rather than adversarial approaches are admittedly somewhat different. In France, for example, and in some other parts of continental Europe, when a case is referred to a judge, s/he is most likely to deal with the matter informally in his or her office (Hackler, 1991; Humphris, 1991). Because these meetings take place in the judge's office, the formal attributes of a court hearing are not present and the main focus of the judge is on the needs of the young person rather than imposing a penalty. The judge's role here is more akin to that of a social worker than to a conventional judicial role. It is only in more serious offences or where the young person continues to offend that the case is dealt with in court. There, at least in France, the judge, sitting with two lay 'judges', takes the lead in examining witnesses, including both the young person accused of the offence and any victims, and the lawyers representing the parties take a subsidiary role. However, the decision about how best to deal with the offending is the judge's. The involvement of young offenders and victims (and their families) in determining this is minimal. The judge, like the magistrates in England and panel members in Scotland, remains the central decision-maker.

3. BRAITHWAITE ON SHAME, GUILT, REMORSE AND REINTEGRATIVE SHAMING

In this section, I try to convey the gist of Braithwaite's views on shame, guilt, remorse and reintegrative shaming, although it is difficult to summarise a book and numerous articles in a paragraph or two. There seem to me to be four key areas.

3.1. The Entwining of Guilt and Shame

Braithwaite sees 'shame' and 'guilt' as intimately entwined. He says that 'guilt is only made possible by cultural processes of shaming', that 'to induce guilt and to induce shame are inextricably part of the same social process' and that 'the consciences that cause us guilt are . . . formed by shaming' (1989: 57). To try to unravel this, I ventured into the legal, philosophical, psychological and sociological literature on shame and guilt. For me, this was a confusing journey; I found the research complex and contradictory. Some of the psychological literature reviewed by Tjeert Olthof in his chapter in this book seems to support the view that the two emotions are entwined but other psychological research does not, and guilt and shame are not viewed as entwined by Gabriele Taylor in her chapter in this book. The resolution to this is that, in practice, it may not matter much. Braithwaite claims that, from the offender's perspective, 'guilt and shame may be indistinguishable' (1989: 57). However, for me, the key issue is slightly different. It is: should family group conferences (or, more broadly, restorative justice processes) be set up to specifically induce either guilt or shame in offenders. I return to this point in s 6 below.

3.2. Defining Shaming

Braithwaite defines shaming as

> all social processes of *expressing disapproval which have the intention or effect of invoking remorse* in the person being shamed and/or condemnation of others who become aware of the shaming' (1989: 100, my emphasis).

What is important for Braithwaite then is 'disapproval' and 'remorse' rather than what is conventionally or popularly thought of as shame or shaming. But choosing the words 'shame' or 'shaming' to describe the mechanisms used for invoking remorse is, for me, more than a semantic quibble because it, in effect, also entwines shame and remorse. I return to this point in s 6. Also, it is apparent from this quote that Braithwaite is concerned with both the disapprover's intention and its effect on the recipient (the offender). Entwining intent and effect is also, for me, problematic. I return to discuss this point in s 5.3.

3.3. Distinguishing 'Stigmatic Shaming' and 'Reintegrative Shaming'

The distinction Braithwaite makes between 'stigmatic shaming' and 'reintegrative shaming' is crucial. Braithwaite is firmly opposed to stigmatic shaming[6] and

---

[6] Historically, many of the rituals of the criminal and penal systems served to signify the separation and segregation of defendants: for example, the placing of defendants in public stocks or the wearing of distinctive clothing by prisoners. Some rituals continue to signify this: for example, the isolation of the offender in the courtroom vis a vis the other players. Without doubt, however, stigmatic shaming has had a troubling revival, particularly in the United States. Massaro (1991) cites as examples the convicted child molester who was required as a condition of his probation to place in a newspaper an advertisement proclaiming his status along with his photograph, and offenders who were required to wear signs which again alerted others to their status (see also Garvey, 1998; Karp, 1998). Lee (1998) provides another example of stigmatic shaming from England: police cautioning, at least in some areas. Stigmatic shaming was achieved by such strategies as manipulating the spatial arrangements in the room in which the caution was to occur so that the child would be in front of and close to the police officers while the parents were placed behind the child so that the child could not see them, or by dressing down the child and highlighting his or her status as an offender.

sees it as likely to be counter-productive.[7] Reintegrative shaming, on the other hand, is seen as likely to be effective in controlling crime (1989: 4). Reintegrative shaming means that the offence rather than the offender is condemned and the offender is reintegrated with rather than rejected by society. It is said (Makkai and Braithwaite, 1994, cited in Harris and Burton, 1998: 231) to be achieved through certain steps: disapproval of the offence while sustaining a relationship of respect for the offender and without labelling the offender as 'bad' or 'evil'; ceremonies to certify the offending followed by ceremonies to decertify it; and not allowing the offending to become a master status trait.[8] Thus the shaming must be followed by efforts to reintegrate the offender back into the community through 'words or gestures of forgiveness' (1989: 100). The problem here is the difficulty of putting this ideal of reintegrative shaming into practice and I discuss this further in s 4.

3.4. The Shame that Matters

Braithwaite suggests that the shame which matters most is not 'the shame of remote judge or police officer but the shame of the people they most care about' (1993: 37). The problem here again is the difficulty of putting this into practice. Many of the examples of conferencing which have relied most heavily on Braithwaite's theory have been managed through the police. I discuss the implications of this in s 4.

Braithwaite also sees communitarian societies as more able to deliver both 'more potent shaming . . . and shaming which is more reintegrative' (1989: 87). Communitarian societies are societies characterised by a 'densely enmeshed interdependency', 'mutual obligation and trust' and 'group loyalty' (1989: 86). The problem here is that it is not clear that such conditions can readily be replicated in twenty-first century Western societies. Braithwaite acknowledges this.

---

[7] The potential dangers of stigmatic shaming are well recognised in the psychological and socio-logical literature. Stigmatic shaming seems deliberately set to trigger a change in the offender's self-concept and in society's concept of the offender. Psychological studies (for example, Tangney *et al*, 1996) certainly confirm its success in this: they show that shame can have negative consequences for self-esteem. Miller (1996: 151) calls shame the 'bedrock of much psychopathology'. Labelling theorists (for example, Lemert, 1971) would similarly argue that labelling or stigmatising an offender increases the likelihood of subsequent deviant behaviour. They introduced terms like 'secondary deviance' and 'deviance amplification' to capture this. Vagg (1998: 250) suggests that shame may produce feelings of 'humiliation, rage and desire for revenge rather than feelings of guilt and remorse'. Massaro (1997) agrees and sees guilt as the reparative emotion and shame as triggering efforts to restore the damaged self which can include violence towards the shamers. It seems important, therefore, to get the type of shaming right!

[8] Braithwaite and Mugford (1994) elaborate 14 conditions for successful reintegrative shaming. These include 'uncoupling' the offence and the offender so that the offence can be viewed as 'bad' (and denounced) but not the offender, facilitators who identify with all participants as well as the public interest, the empowerment of victims, offenders and families through control of the process, the encouragement of empathy and generosity, rituals of inclusion and reintegration, avoidance of power imbalances, completion of agreed outcomes and further 'ceremonies' if reintegration fails.

But we also need to explore whether or not it is possible to replicate such conditions within local communities, or even within communities of care.

4. PUTTING REINTEGRATIVE SHAMING INTO PRACTICE

There are at least three versions of conferencing which are based on 'reintegrative shaming': diversionary conferencing in Canberra, the model of conferencing promoted by Real Justice in parts of the United States and elsewhere and restorative conferencing in the Thames Valley police authority.[9] Police officers have been quite involved in these forms of conferences as facilitators and, partly as a result of this, conferences may be held in police facilities. Sometimes, facilitators follow scripts aimed at eliciting certain key responses from offenders although there has been some debate about the appropriateness or usefulness of this. All three versions have been (or are continuing to be) evaluated (Sherman *et al*, 1998; McCold and Wachtel, 1998; Young and Goold, 1999) and a range of positive findings have emerged, especially in any comparisons between conferencing and courts.[10]

However, from the offenders' perspective, police stations are not necessarily neutral territory and police officers are not necessarily neutral facilitators.[11] Indeed, Walgrave and Aertsen (1996) question the value of shaming by official representatives of the community such as by police officers. There is some empirical support for this suggestion in the research on restorative conferencing in the Thames Valley police force. Restorative conferencing there is promoted as an alternative to old style cautioning by the police (which was more akin to stigmatic shaming). However, Young and Goold (1999) found a number of similarities between restorative conferencing and stigmatic shaming: in particular, the dominance of the police officers in the conferences and their apparent stress on deterring the child from future criminal behaviour. Thus Young and Goold argue that the shift from 'degrading cautioning ceremonies to reintegrating shaming sessions' is, as yet, 'incomplete' (1999: 137).[12]

Commenting more generally on police-led conferences, Young (2001) writes that shaming the offender as a person might occur if *participants* fail to maintain the crucial distinction between the doer and the deed demanded by Braithwaite's theory or if *offenders*, through having their behaviour shamed, come to feel that they are shameful people. However, Sherman and Strang

---

[9] The type of conferencing introduced by the police in Wagga Wagga (New South Wales) in the early 1990s also relied on Braithwaite's theory of reintegrative shaming but it is no longer followed there. Young (2001) comments that the design of the Wagga Wagga model certainly appeared to prompt the explicit shaming of behaviour.

[10] To date, the evaluation of conferencing by the Thames Valley police is less positive but this is ongoing action research and practice is likely to have changed since the interim evaluations.

[11] It is perhaps no accident that the police have been quick to endorse reintegrative shaming. Blagg (1997: 494), however, cites many recent examples in Australia of the police promoting shame as part of a programme of humiliation, not reintegration.

[12] In fairness, these data come from an early stage in the research; see n 10 above.

(1997: 2) reported that the Canberra police were generally successful in 'making offenders *feel* ashamed of what they have done without making them into shameful people' (emphasis in the original). But this equally means that the police were not *always* successful in this. This is the risk run when shame and shaming are put on the conferencing agenda.

Reintegrative shaming, as noted previously, demands that the offender—the person to be shamed—should respect the shamer or at least should acknowledge the legitimacy of the shamer's authority. There is some doubt that those young people most likely to be part of a conference have such attitudes towards the police. Generally, young people do feel quite positive towards the police: they think that the police do a 'good job' (Anderson *et al*, 1994; Aye Maung, 1995). However, positive support for the police seems to decline with age and it is likely that this is explained not only by an increase in young people's contact with the police as they grow older, but also by the nature of that contact. A surprisingly high proportion of young people—for example, just over half of those to whom Anderson *et al* (1994) spoke—report 'adversarial' contact with the police. Repeated contact with the police also had a significant negative effect on young people's perception of the police, especially if this was the only kind of contact which the young person had with them.[13]

Collectively, these research findings seem to support Walgrave and Aertsen's (1996) views about the inappropriateness of using the police in reintegrative shaming 'ceremonies', views with which, as noted earlier, Braithwaite agrees. Tjeert Olthof in his chapter in this book also points to the difficulties which exist in devising shame- and guilt-based youth justice procedures, stresses that the audience which attempts to induce shame must be 'salient' to the offender and warns of the potential 'hazards' of inducing guilt. He concludes that 'there are many ways in which things could go wrong' (below, 203).

5. CONCERNS ABOUT 'REINTEGRATIVE SHAMING'

I focus here on four concerns commonly raised about reintegrative shaming: its failure to address structural issues (s 5.1), its cultural specificity (s 5.2), whether the key variable is the 'shamer's' intent or the actual effects of the shame on the 'shamed' (s 5.3), and difficulties in measuring 'reintegrative shaming' (s 5.4).

5.1. Individualising Crime

White (1994: 195) sees reintegrative shaming as 'fundamentally flawed at the levels of conception and execution'. The essence of his critique is the failure of

---

[13] Loader (1996) also highlights the police's ambivalence to young people. This too must affect their ability to shame reintegratively.

reintegrative shaming to challenge the 'inequities and inequalities of our social institutions' (1994: 185). Reintegrative shaming, he argues, fails to acknowledge the structural causes of youth crime or to explain how and why only certain young people are identified as 'offenders' and subsequently processed through the youth justice system. It focuses instead on individual offenders and places responsibility for the 'choice' to offend squarely on them. However, no matter how remorseful or shamed an offender might be, and no matter how welcoming the offender's communities of care might be in his or her return to the fold, if the structural causes of that offending remain untouched then reoffending seems likely. Reintegration into communities of care is insufficient if offenders (and their communities of care) remain marginalised and socially excluded.

However, Braithwaite did discuss the ways in which patterns of shame are structured by patterns of domination, the low shame attached to corporate crime and the gendered nature of shame. Also, to be fair to Braithwaite, there is no youth justice system—irrespective of its philosophic base—which challenges the 'inequities and inequalities of our social institutions.' These have to be addressed through wider social, economic and educational policies. Some advocates of restorative justice believe that restorative justice has at least the *potential* to deliver more 'justice' than conventional criminal justice processes by addressing the offender's social exclusion and by strengthening marginalised communities. These remain, however, untested aspirations.

5.2. Culture and Shame

Massaro (1997: 672) argues that we do not know precisely how shame works: 'it is a highly context-, individual-, and culture-dependent emotion.' Thus the meaning of shame varies widely across cultures. In some cultures, shaming is seen as a powerful and efficient way of enforcing community norms. Japan is commonly cited as an example of this (see, for example, Braithwaite, 1989: 61–65; Massaro, 1991: 1906–10). The fear of shame and the resulting loss of status are seen as key factors in explaining the low crime rate in contemporary Japan. However, some Japanese have been critical of Braithwaite's depiction of Japan and dispute that shaming there is reintegrative (Tadashi Moriyama, personal communication).[14]

Braithwaite promotes shame and shaming as cultural universals. He claims that nowhere in his historical readings or travels has he found a culture in which shame is not seen as 'terribly important' (1997: 504). Blagg (1997), on the other hand, challenges the relevance of reintegrative shaming specifically for Aboriginals in

---

[14] Hong Kong also, according to Vagg, represents a culture with an 'explicit concern with shame' (1998: 260). He states that there is a high level of intolerance there for offending and offenders with the result that there are high expectations that they will show remorse and contrition. Indeed, these expectations are described as so high that many offenders are unable to avoid stigmatisation and subsequent exclusion.

Australia. He doubts that the many displaced Aboriginals in Australia live within the kind of community required for reintegrative shaming to 'work.' Aboriginals in Australia, he suggests, tend to have loose affiliations rather than tightly knit group membership. Braithwaite disputes these claims and writes that 'one does not have to spend long with Aboriginal people to see examples of disapproving of particular acts while treating those who commit them with great respect' (personal communication).

I cannot comment on this one way or the other, but I suppose the issue then becomes whether or not reintegrative shaming can be replicated within the dominant culture where many Aboriginals already have low status. Blagg (1997: 490) asks: 'how can [a reintegrative shaming ceremony] hope to be meaningful for those who have no public status to lose?' In a later paper, Blagg (1998) raises questions about how Aboriginals, whose pattern of experience has been harassment on the street by the police and discrimination in everyday life by the dominant culture, can realistically be expected to see the processes of shaming as resulting in reintegration within communities.

Howard Zehr (2000), in a recent conference paper, reaffirmed this concern. He quoted an Aboriginal colleague from North America who said that her community had been so distorted by shame that she could not envisage any positive use of the concept. Braithwaite, of course, recognises the way in which shame has contributed to the destruction of indigenous communities. The issue is the extent to which any shaming (or disapproval) in these communities can now become reintegrative, and there has to be some doubt about this given what was said above about their experience of policing (and their experience of the criminal justice system more generally). It would, of course, be a different matter if Aboriginals were supported by communities of care, and if any shaming (disapproval) required was carried out not by criminal justice or social work professionals but by those whom Aboriginals respect—which is what Braithwaite advocates.[15]

5.3. Intent or Effect?

Both reintegrative and stigmatic shaming require an audience; the difference with respect to reintegrative shaming is that the audience must include individuals whom the 'shamed' respects and values and who take steps to reintegrate the offender (see, for example, Massaro, 1991: 1902). Presumably, however, it is the individual being shamed and not the shamer who will determine whether or not the shaming is actually reintegrative: the shamer cannot determine the

[15] I suggest that we can extend Blagg's and Zehr's concerns about shaming in a reintegrative way those who already feel shamed to include all those who are socially excluded—many young people, the unemployed, the poor and so on—in short, many of those likely to come into the criminal justice or youth justice systems. They too need to be supported by communities of care and any shaming (disapproval) needs to be carried out by those they respect.

effect. Despite our good intentions, therefore, the shaming we intend to be reintegrative might be taken by the offender to be stigmatic. The benchmark for
actions must be their impact, not their intent.

I have already referred to the difficulties which have occurred in the Thames
Valley police force in their promotion of restorative conferencing. Earlier in that
same article, Young and Goold (1999: 136) also claimed that the conferences
which were judged to be successful by the police were those where the offender
had shown 'visible signs of remorse or shame'. Two obvious points arise from
this: first, remorse and shame are being used interchangeably; second, success is
being judged by 'visible signs' of either. These signs, however, are certainly not
the only indicators of remorse or shame and may not be the best. 'Visible signs'
are shaped by cultural expectations: for example, avoiding eye contact or
speaking in a low voice means different things in different cultures and, more
importantly, signs which indicate remorse or shame in one culture can be mis-
interpreted as a lack of remorse or a lack of shame in another (Eades, 1988, cited
in Blagg, 1997: 500). Further, even if such signs are noted, we have to ask
whether they were provoked by the particular situation the offender found himself or herself in or by the offender's view of his or her offending. Offenders may
show what we take to be visible signs of shame or remorse but their views on
their offending may remain unchanged.

5.4. Difficulties in Measuring 'Reintegrative Shaming'

There have been a number of attempts to measure 'reintegrative shaming.'[16]
The most systematic attempt to do so was in the Canberra experiment bearing
that name: RISE. Harris and Burton (1998) report on the observational measures used there: reintegration was measured by 'respect for the offender', 'the
offender is forgiven', 'offender apologises', and 'disapproval of the offender';
and shaming was measured by the 'disapproval of the act'. These items were
noted during the observation of conferences and court cases (the systematic
observation instrument). In addition, observers completed a 40 item question-
naire at the end of each conference or court case which asked observers to rate,
for example, the amount of support given to the offender, how sorry or remorseful s/he was and how much reintegrative shaming was expressed (the global ratings instrument).

---

[16] Zhang (1995), for example, operationalised 'shaming' by using a 22 item scale which measured
parents' perceptions of non-verbal shaming, verbal shaming, physical shaming and what he called
'communitarian' shaming (talking to other people about the child's behaviour). Some difficulties
were reported with this as a measure—for example, it did not tap into the parents' own shaming
behaviours (such as their embarrassment) and thus demonstrated the limitations of self reported
measures. 'Reintegration' was measured by a 15-item scale which primarily focused on the interdependency between the children and their parents. However, this relates to an ongoing relationship
and not to a specific response to a specific behaviour.

Each case was observed by two people and Harris and Burton (1998) show that the inter-observer reliability on most measures in the systematic observation instrument was quite high.[17] The agreement scores in the global ratings instrument seem mixed but were high for the question about 'how much reintegrative shaming was expressed'. Consequently, Harris and Burton (1998: 238) concluded that 'reintegrative shaming' could be 'observed reliably'.

This is not really the issue though. The important question is whether or not the measures used to indicate 'reintegrative shaming' actually measured it. I remain unconvinced and it seems circular to me to simply ask 'how much reintegrative shaming was expressed.' Even if two observers, trained in a particular way, agree about what they are looking for or at, it does not necessarily mean that reintegrative shaming took place either from the offenders' or victims' perspective or, indeed, at all.

To some extent, of course, Harris and Burton (1998) acknowledge this is so in their reference to the use in the RISE project of other methods also aimed at measuring 'reintegrative shaming' and so I will turn to those now. The researchers there constructed a series of questions for offenders aimed at measuring reintegrative shaming and stigmatic shaming (Sherman *et al*, 1998). Though, overall, they found that there was more reintegrative shaming in conferences than in courts and that there was more stigmatic shaming in courts than in conferences, there were, in fact, few significant differences between the court and conference samples on the 12 items used to measure reintegrative shaming[18] or on the six items used to measure stigmatic shaming (Strang *et al*, 1999).[19]

Interpreting what this means is not straightforward. First, it might mean that the claim that conferences are likely to reintegratively shame and that courts are likely to stigmatically shame is too simplistic: both conferences and courts can shame reintegratively and stigmatically. Second, it might mean that offenders do not respond differently to reintegrative or stigmatic shaming and that despite different intentions the shaming had the same effect. To repeat a point made in the previous section: the benchmark for actions must be their impact, not their intent. Third, it might mean that we are not yet able to tease out in our questions the subtleties of reintegrative and stigmatic shaming.

6. SHAME, GUILT AND REMORSE IN FAMILY GROUP CONFERENCES IN NEW ZEALAND

Family group conferences, introduced in New Zealand in 1989, directly involve those most affected by the offending—specifically the offender, the victim and

---

[17] The item 'disapproval of the offender' was an exception; here there was a low level of agreement.

[18] The only exception was the item 'people said I could put the offence behind me'.

[19] The exceptions were, for the juvenile personal property sample, 'treated as though I was a bad person', for the juvenile property (security) sample 'treated as though I was a criminal' and, for the youth violence sample, 'people will not let me forget what I did'.

their families—in determining appropriate responses to it. Family group conferences in New Zealand do not follow a set script and the format they take is very much in the hands of the participants who are also consulted about the venue for and timing of the meeting. Participants are guided by a facilitator (the youth justice co-ordinator) but sometimes this role is handed over too if it is culturally appropriate to do so. The aim of the conference is to involve the key participants (offenders, victims and their communities of care) in decisions about how best to deal with the offending, to hold offenders responsible for their actions and to make amends to the victims. The most usual outcomes are apologies and community work and, in the main, the tasks agreed to are completed. And so where do shame, guilt and remorse fit into all of this?

6.1. Guilt

'Guilt' is not a concept used in the New Zealand youth justice system. Even in the youth courts, young offenders are not asked whether they plead 'guilty' or 'not guilty'. Rather the approach there is to ask whether the charges are 'denied' or 'not denied.' In family group conferences, young people are then asked whether or not they admit the offence. Is this a semantic quibble? I think not. The young person can dispute some of the circumstances surrounding the alleged offence, but can nevertheless agree that the behaviour was criminal (wrong). The focus in the family group conference (and in the youth court) can then shift to the young offender's acceptance of responsibility for the harm done.[20] And this acceptance of responsibility may occur even when there is a technical defence to the charge.[21]

6.2. Involving Offenders

There is no research which has explored the role of family group conferences in New Zealand in inducing guilt in young offenders as a technique for rehabilitation or reintegration. However, involving young people in the decisions about how to deal with their offending is seen as a technique for holding them responsible for their offending. And about a third of young offenders in the research on conferencing by Maxwell and Morris (1993) said that they had felt involved in the process. If responses indicating that the offender felt 'partly' involved are added

---

[20] McElrea (1995) has proposed asking all adult defendants whether they admit or deny the charge. If they admit it, he favours referring the defendant to a conference and reserving courts for denials.

[21] Certainly, some of the youth advocates who took part in research by Morris *et al* (1997) said that they would not run a technical defence where it was not, in their view, in the young person's interests to do this.

to this, then we can conclude that nearly half felt involved in some way. They were able to say what they wanted to and to speak openly without pressure.

Of course, conversely, this means that almost a half felt that they had not been involved in the family group conferences and that decisions had been made about them, not with them.[22] Is this because they felt too 'shamed' to speak? I do not think so. From my observations, I would suggest that the young offender's voice can be subsumed within the family's and, importantly, that this is often quite acceptable to the young offender, especially if s/he is Maori or of Pacific Island descent.

In one case, for example, which I observed, the young Maori woman hardly uttered a word despite frequent attempts by the youth justice co-ordinator (the facilitator) to encourage her to speak. 'Don't worry', said Mum, 'she's used to us speaking for her.' There was no condemnation in this conference of the offences the girl had committed (in fact, with respect to the assault by her on a police officer the girl's actions were explained as her trying to protect herself from being choked by him) and many positive things were said by the parents about the girl. In an interview with the girl after the conference, she said she did not experience shame at the conference but felt she had made amends for her offending by making apologies and doing community work.

6.3. Emphasising the Effects of Crime

I have observed many family group conferences and these are frequently very emotional experiences; indeed, the expression of emotion is expected and accepted. One of the aims of family group conferences is to give offenders a sense of the consequences of their actions and an understanding of how victims feel. This is done not by a process which emphasises disapproval (shaming), but by a process which emphasises the effects of the crime on the victim.

For example, I observed a victim at a family group conference telling the offender who had trashed her house as part of a burglary what it felt like to vacuum from the floor the spilled ashes of her dead parent. And I observed another victim speaking of her sadness at the theft of tapes which included a farewell from a dying sister. I have no doubt that these stories 'touched' the young offenders concerned in ways that judges never can and, importantly, victims can see this and may feel better as a result.[23]

---

[22] It needs to be acknowledged here that even this relatively 'low' rate of involvement in conferences is still considerably higher than offenders' involvement in conventional courts.

[23] Research showed that many victims found their involvement in conferencing positive (Maxwell and Morris, 1993). About 60% of the victims interviewed described the family group conference they attended as helpful and rewarding and said that they felt better as a result of participating. About a quarter of the victims, however, said that they felt worse as a result of attending the family group conference. There were a variety of reasons for this. Important in the context of this paper is that some victims did not feel that the young person and/or his or her family were truly sorry. There are, of course, potential difficulties in victims correctly 'reading' offenders' feelings and this can be aggravated by

I would not wish to convey the impression that this always happens or that participants are always satisfied with the way the process was handled or with the agreements reached. But I have observed victims who initially expressed their hurt and anger move towards comforting the offender or the offender's family; and I have observed grief-stricken victims receive some comfort from seeing the offender's remorse and from hearing offenders express their sorrow and regret. I have also observed many examples of reintegration on reconciliation: hugs and handshakes between offenders and victims, invitation from victims to offenders and their families to join them for a meal, offers of jobs or accommodation by victims to offenders and so on.

6.4. Shame

It is likely that, on occasions, as a result of such experiences, these young offenders do feel shame. However, there is certainly nothing in the processes or practices of family group conferences in New Zealand that is explicitly geared towards inducing or eliciting shame in the offender and I have not observed this happening. If it happens, it comes from the conferencing process and is not deliberately 'constructed' by the youth justice co-ordinator (the facilitator). Moreover, as Young (2001) points out, sometimes shame is neither 'sought by participants [n]or warranted by the circumstances.'[24] This would be problematic if the whole essence or rationale of the conference was to elicit or induce shame. On the other hand, there is an expectation in New Zealand family group conferences that the offender will accept responsibility and show remorse by making amends.

Braithwaite (1993: 39–40) cites how one member of a family group conference which he observed in New Zealand communicated to a boy his contempt for the deed and, at the same time, his respect for the boy:

> Stealing cars. You've got no brain boy . . . But I've got respect for you . . . I've been to see you play football. I went because I care for you. You are a brilliant footballer . . . We're not giving up on you.

It is hard to know how much weight to give to this. Potentially, there is both stigmatic and reintegrative shaming here. But we don't know from this account how the boy felt, what any victim said, what the boy felt about that and whether

cross-cultural differences. For example, in one conference which I observed, the female (Asian) victim kept asking the young (Maori) offender to look at her. She could not. The youth justice co-ordinator (the facilitator) said to the victim that this did not mean that the girl was not sorry for what she had done and, in fact, the girl mumbled an apology. However, in a later interview, the victim said she did not believe that the girl was sorry for what she had done.

[24] Examples which Young (2001) cites are offences committed as part of a political protest, strict liability offences, and offences committed as a result of wretched social circumstances (such as stealing food when hungry, breaking into an empty house for shelter when homeless and so forth).

or not the boy re-offended. It is certainly not uncommon in family group conferences to find participants emphasising good things about the offender: he is doing really well at school or she is part of a champion football team. However, in my experience it is unusual in family group conferences in New Zealand to hear specific condemnation of the offending. It seems rather that everyone takes this for granted (although, of course, the very act of convening the conference to deal with the offending implicitly conveys condemnation of that offending).

6.5. Empathy and Remorse

What we really need to know is how young people feel about what they have experienced and whether or not that impacts on their likelihood to re-offend. Maxwell and Morris (1999) attempted to do this.

They examined the reconvictions of the young offenders who had participated in their earlier (1993) research and reinterviewed as many of these young offenders (and/or their parents) as possible.[25] Similar proportions of young offenders—over a quarter—were not reconvicted at all over this period and were persistently reconvicted.[26] A number of different types of statistical analysis were carried out to discover what distinguished those persistently reconvicted from those not reconvicted.[27]

Young offenders and their parents were specifically asked a number of questions about the family group conference they participated in[28] and what had happened in the intervening years.[29] A number of important findings emerged. First, not being made to feel a bad person or a bad parent (not feeling shamed) was significantly related to not being reconvicted; second, the young person feeling remorse[30] or the parents feeling that their son or daughter was sorry for

---

[25] They were able to track and re-interview 72% of the young offenders in the original sample.

[26] Reconviction is only a partial measure of reoffending. In order to test the validity of relying on the reconviction categories, Maxwell and Morris (1999) asked the young offenders whether or not they had committed any undetected offences and if, so, what kinds of offence they had committed. In this re-analysis, they excluded traffic and other minor infringements and personal marihuana use and, in the main, the original categorisation was confirmed. Two of those classified as 'non reconvicted' reported several undetected offences. We considered the possibility of reclassifying these two offenders. However, the interviewer suspected that one of those respondents was 'pulling his leg' when replying to the undetected offending questions and the other had also reported reconvictions of which there was no official record. Maxwell and Morris, therefore, decided that this information on self-report offending was not sufficient to alter the original conviction-based classification.

[27] These included canonical discriminant analyses and path analyses.

[28] These included whether or not the young offenders and their parents agreed with the decisions and felt involved in the process, whether or not remorse and shame were felt, and whether or not tasks were completed.

[29] These included information about the young person's subsequent education, training, jobs, relationships, mental health and feelings about the future.

[30] This construct was made up of the young person remembering the conference, completing the tasks agreed to, feeling sorry for what he or she had done and feeling that he or she had made good the damage done.

what they had done was significantly related to not being reconvicted; and, third, feeling good about oneself and that life had gone well was also significantly related to not being reconvicted. These young offenders had jobs and positive relationships with a partner.

There were also connections among these three variables. For example, among the most important variables in the first canonical variate to explain reconviction were 'feeling shamed at the conference' and 'not being remorseful'. On the second canonical variate, among the most important variables were not getting a job or training after the conference and not having close friends. Collectively, these findings do provide some support for Braithwaite's notion of reintegrative shaming: he stressed the importance of invoking remorse and rejected stigmatic shaming. However, the research does *not* show that disapproval (shaming) was necessarily the mechanism which invoked the remorse. Another way of interpreting these data is that *empathy* or understanding the effects of offending on victims was the trigger. If this interpretation is right, the practice and policy implications are very different from a continuing emphasis on shaming (disapproval).

Maxwell and Morris's (1999) research did not involve interviewing the victims involved in these cases. However, Daly (2001) in her research on conferencing in South Australia, found that offenders not showing remorse and offenders not taking responsibility for what they had done were the most frequently mentioned reasons for victims' negative judgements of offenders. Thus remorse and responsibility are important concepts not just for offenders but for victims too.

7. CONCLUSION

I have suggested in this chapter that we do not yet know enough about how shame, guilt or remorse are triggered, what shame, guilt or remorse feel like, what it means to be ashamed, guilty or remorseful, what the effects of shame, guilt or remorse are, what induces shame, guilt or remorse in individual cases and contexts, or what kind of shaming, guilt- or remorse-inducing activities are reintegrative. We need to know much more about all of these questions before advocating an emphasis on one moral emotion over another or even before advocating an emphasis on any. It seems entirely plausible that an offender might experience all or any of these emotions, and that they could influence his or her subsequent behaviour, irrespective of any actions by us. Equally, it seems entirely plausible that an offender might experience none of these emotions but nonetheless not re-offend.

I have also suggested that it is premature to use reintegrative shaming as a guide for developing policy and practice. Braithwaite himself (1999: 7) recently acknowledged that in some important ways his theory of reintegrative shaming is not right. For example, he cites Harris's research finding that shame and guilt are not separate dimensions and promotes, as a more fundamental distinction, guilt/shame and exposure/embarrassment. Maxwell and Morris (1999) did confirm the constructive potential of remorse and the destructive potential of stigmatic shaming. However, they were not able to say what *triggered* remorse. It is certainly *possible* that it is empathy which triggers remorse, and not shaming (disapproval). If this is so, it would mean that the emphasis in conferencing (or in other restorative justice processes) should be not on processes of shaming (disapproval) but on processes which focus on the consequences of offending for others (for families and communities as well as for victims).

This idea seems to correspond, on the one hand, with the emphasis on moral dialogue in chapter 7 of this book, where Ido Weijers stresses the importance of reflection on the consequences of wrongdoing. On the other hand, it seems to point in the same direction as the conclusion which Gabriele Taylor reaches in chapter 9 of this book. She first argues plausibly with respect to Braithwaite's theory of reintegrative shaming that '[g]uilt rather than shame is the reaction that fits the theory' (191). Thus shaming, in order to work, has to make the offender feel guilty. It is this, she writes, that involves recognition of the wrong done and the desire to make amends. But, in the end, she prefers remorse because, as she says, 'unlike guilt, and particularly unlike shame, it does not involve any specific self-directed perceptions which are potentially destructive' (192). This again points to the need for more research in this area and for further understanding of the emotional dimensions of restorative processes.

In the meantime, the use of the words 'shame' and 'shaming' in the development and refinement of reintegrative shaming is best avoided. They are too readily and easily misunderstood and it is not that difficult in practice to slip from the intent of 'reintegrative shaming' to the practice of stigmatic shaming or for intended reintegrative shaming to be perceived as stigmatic. Braithwaite himself (1989: 12) recognised that 'shaming is a dangerous game'. I sometimes wish that Braithwaite had called his theory 'reintegrative remorse.' I suspect, with hindsight, that he might prefer this too. However, even so, we would still disagree about the key mechanism for triggering remorse: disapproval or empathy? Research needs to explore this further too. This distinction is crucial for future policy and practice.

REFERENCES

Anderson, S, Kinsey, R, Loader, I & Smith, C (1994) *Cautionary Tales: Young People, Crime and Policing in Edinburgh* (Avebury, Aldershot).
Aye Maung, N (1995) *Young People, Victimisation and the Police: Summary Findings* Home Office Research Study No 140 (HMSO, London).
Blagg, H (1997) 'A Just Measure of Shame? Aboriginal Youth and Conferencing in Australia' 37 *British Journal of Criminology* 481–501.

Blagg, H (1998) 'Restorative Visions and Restorative Justice Practices: Conferencing, Ceremony and Reconciliation in Australia' 10(1) *Current Issues in Criminal Justice* 5–14.

Braithwaite, J (1989) *Crime, Shame and Reintegration* (Cambridge University Press, Cambridge).

—— (1993) 'What is to be Done about Criminal Justice?' in B Brown & F McElrea (eds) *The Youth Court in New Zealand: A New Model of Justice* (Legal Research Foundation, Auckland).

—— (1997) 'Conferencing and Plurality: Reply to Blagg' 37 *British Journal of Criminology* 502–06.

—— (1999) 'Shame and Crime: The Unfolding Debate' (Paper presented at the American Society of Criminology).

Braithwaite, J & Mugford, S (1994) 'Conditions of Successful Reintegration Ceremonies: Dealing with Juvenile Offenders' 34 *British Journal of Criminology* 139–71.

Carlen, P (1976) *Magistrates' Justice* (Martin Robertson, London).

Daly, K (1989) 'Criminal Ideologies and Practices in Different Voices: Some Feminist Questions about Justice' 17 *International Journal of the Sociology of Law* 1–18.

—— (2001) 'Conferencing in Australia and New Zealand: Variations, Research Findings and Prospects' in A Morris & G Maxwell (eds) *Restorative Justice for Juveniles: Conferencing, Mediation and Circles* (Hart Publishing, Oxford).

Dignan, J (1999) 'The Crime and Disorder Act and the Prospects for Restorative Justice' *Criminal Law Review* 48–60.

Eades, D (1988) 'They Speak an Aboriginal Language, or Do They?' in I Keene (ed) *Being Black: Aboriginal Cultures in Settled Australia* (Aboriginal Studies Press, Canberra).

Ericson, R & Baranek, P (1982) *The Orderings of Justice: A Study of Accused Persons as Dependants in the Criminal Process* (University of Toronto Press, Toronto).

Garvey, S (1998) 'Can Shaming Punishments Educate?' 65 *University of Chicago Law Review* 733–94.

Gilligan, C (1982) *In a Different Voice: Psychological Theory and Women's Development* (Harvard University Press, Cambridge, Mass).

Hackler, J (1991) 'Confusing the Drama with the Reality in the French Juvenile Court' in J Hackler (ed) *Official Responses to Problem Juveniles: Some International Reflections* (The Onati International Institute for the Sociology of Law, Onati).

Harris, N & Burton, J (1998) 'Testing the Reliability of Observational Measures of Reintegrative Shaming at Community Accountability Conferences and at Court' 31 *Australian and New Zealand Journal of Criminology* 230–41.

Heidensohn, F (1986) 'Models of Justice: Portia or Persephone? Some Thoughts on Equality, Fairness and Gender' 14 *International Journal of the Sociology of Law* 287–98.

Humphris, N (1991) 'Educational Aspects of French Cabinet Justice' in J Hackler (ed) *Official Responses to Problem Juveniles: Some International Reflections* (The Onati International Institute for the Sociology of Law, Onati).

Johnstone, G (1999) 'Restorative Justice: The Emotional Challenge' (Paper presented to the Howard League Annual Conference on *Citizenship and Crime*, Oxford)

Karp, D (1998) 'The Judicial and Judicious Use of Shame Penalties' 44 *Crime and Delinquency* 277–94.

Lee, M (1998) *Youth, Crime and Police Work* (Macmillan, Houndsmill).

Lemert, E (1971) *Instead of Court: Diversion in Juvenile Justice* (US Government Printing Office, Washington)

Loader, I (1996) *Youth, Policing and Democracy* (Macmillan, Houndsmill).

Makkai, T & Braithwaite, J (1994) 'Reintegrative Shaming and Compliance with Regulatory Standards' 32 *Criminology* 361–85.

Massaro, T (1991) 'Shame, Culture and American Criminal Law' 89 *Michigan Law Review* 1880–944.

—— (1997) 'The Meanings of Shame' 3 *Psychology, Public Policy and Law* 645–704.

Masters, G (1998) 'The Importance of Shame to Restorative Justice' in L Walgrave (ed) *Restorative Justice for Juveniles: Potentialities, Risks and Problems* (Leuven University Press, Leuven).

Masters, G & Smith, D (1998) 'Portia and Persephone Revisited: Thinking about Feeling in Criminal Justice' 2 *Theoretical Criminology* 5–27.

Maxwell, G M & Morris, A (1993) *Families, Victims and Culture: Youth Justice in New Zealand* (Social Policy Agency and Institute of Criminology, Victoria University of Wellington, Wellington).

—— and —— (1999) *Reducing Reoffending* (Institute of Criminology, Victoria University of Wellington, Wellington).

Maxwell, G M, Morris, A & Robertson, J (1994) *First Line of Defence: The Work of the Duty Solicitor Scheme* (Legal Services Board, Wellington).

McCold, P & Wachtel, B (1998) *Restorative Policing Experiment* (Community Service Foundation, Pipersville).

McElrea, F (1995) 'Accountability in the Community' in F McElrea (ed) *Re-thinking Criminal Justice*, vol 1 (Legal Research Foundation, Auckland).

Miller, S (1996) *Shame in Context* (Analytic Press, Hillsdale).

Moore, D (1993) 'Shame, Forgiveness and Juvenile Justice' 12 *Criminal Justice Ethics* 3–24.

Morris, A & Giller, H (1977) 'The Juvenile Court—The Clients' Perspective' *Criminal Law Review* 198–205.

Morris, A & Maxwell, G (2000) 'The Practice of Family Group Conferences in New Zealand: Assessing the Place, Potential and Pitfalls of Restorative Justice' in A Crawford and J Goodey (eds) *Integrating a Victim Perspective within Criminal Justice* (Ashgate, Aldershot).

Morris, A, Maxwell, G & Shepherd, P (1997) *Being a Youth Advocate: An Analysis of Their Role and Responsibilities* (Institute of Criminology, Wellington).

Morris, A & Young, W (1987) *Juvenile Justice in New Zealand: Policy and Practice* (Institute of Criminology, Wellington).

—— and —— (2000) 'Reforming Criminal Justice: The Potential of Restorative Justice' in H Strang and J Braithwaite (eds) *Restorative Justice: Philosophy to Practice* (Ashgate, Aldershot).

NACRO (1997) *A New Three Rs for Young Offenders* (NACRO, London).

O'Connor, I & Sweetapple, P (1988) *Children in Justice* (Longman, Cheshire).

Retzinger, S & Scheff, T (1996) 'Strategy for Community Conferences: Emotions and Social Bonds', in B Galaway and J Hudson (eds) *Restorative Justice: International Perspectives* (Kugler Publications, Amsterdam).

Sherman, L & Strang, H (1997) *The Right Kind of Shame for Crime Prevention* (RISE Working Paper, Canberra).

Sherman, L, Strang, H, Barnes, G, Braithwaite, J, Inkpen, N, & Teh, M (1998) *Experiments in Restorative Policing: A Progress Report to the National Police Research Unit on the Canberra Reintegrative Shaming Experiment* (Australian National University, Canberra).

Stewart, T (1993) 'The Youth Justice Coordinator's Role: A Personal Perspective on the New Legislation in Action' in B Brown and F McElrea (eds) *The Youth Court in New Zealand: A New Model of Justice* (Legal Research Foundation, Auckland).

Strang, H, Barnes, G, Braithwaite, J & Sherman, L (1999) *Experiments in Restorative Policing: A Progress Report on the Canberra, Reintegrative Shaming Experiment (RISE)*, www.aic.gov.au.rjustice/rise/progress/1999.html.

Tangney, J, Wagner, P, Hill-Barlow, D, Marshall, D & Gramzow, R (1996) 'Relation of Shame and Guilt to Constructive Versus Destructive Responses to Anger across the Lifespan' 70 *Journal of Personality and Social Psychology* 797–809.

Vagg, J (1998) 'Delinquency and Shame: Data from Hong Kong' 38 *British Journal of Criminology* 247–53.

Walgrave, L & Aertsen, A (1996) 'Reintegrative Shaming and Restorative Justice' 4 *European Journal on Criminal Policy and Research* 67–85.

White, R (1994) 'Shame and Reintegration Strategies: Individuals, State Power and Social Interests' in C Alder and J Wundersitz (eds) *Family Group Conferencing and Juvenile Justice* (Australian Institute of Criminology, Canberra).

Young, R (2001) 'Just Cops Doing "Shameful" Business? Police-led Restorative Justice and the Lessons of Research' in A Morris and G Maxwell (eds) *Restorative Justice for Juveniles: Conferencing, Mediation and Circles* (Hart Publishing, Oxford).

Young, R & Goold, B (1999) 'Restorative Police Cautioning in Aylesbury—From Degrading to Reintegrative Shaming Ceremonies?' *Criminal Law Review* 126–38.

Zehr, H (1990) *Changing Lenses* (Herald Press, Scottdale).

——(2000) 'Journey to Belonging', Paper presented at the International Conference on *Just Peace? Peace-making and Peace-building for the New Millenium* (Massey University, Albany, New Zealand).

Zhang, X (1995) 'Measuring Shame in an Ethnic Context' 35 *British Journal of Criminology* 248–62.

9

Guilt, Shame and Shaming

GABRIELE TAYLOR

1. INTRODUCTION

JUVENILE JUSTICE, I shall assume, should be restorative justice, that is, it should have as a principal aim the reintegration of the young offender into society. A focus is therefore the juvenile herself or himself and her or his status, and the question naturally arises as to what sort of attitude it is necessary or any-way desirable to try to induce in the young offender if she is to be an acceptable member of society. It seems fairly obvious that she will at any rate be expected to feel sorry for what she did, and this entails that she must be brought to see that what she did was wrong, and that she must accept responsibility for having done that wrong. Ideally this realisation should not just concern her past action but should stretch into the future: she should begin to think in terms of respon-sibility and right and wrong on other occasions as well, so that the chances of her re-offending would be much reduced. The problem remains of how this desirable state of affairs is to be brought about.

The juvenile offender, on this account, needs to be morally educated, needs to be made to understand and appreciate basic social values. To bring this about, it has recently been argued, we cannot do better than rely on the method of shaming, where shaming is conceived of

> as a tool to allure and inveigle the citizen to attend to the moral claims of the criminal law, to coax and caress compliance, to reason and remonstrate with him over the harmfulness of his conduct (Braithwaite 1989: 9).

To understand this alleged beneficial effect the notion of shaming will of course have to be examined and analysed, as indeed Braithwaite does himself, most importantly by drawing the distinction between 'stigmatic' and 'reintegrative shaming'. I shall return to this distinction, but will begin by an investigation of the state this procedure is meant to bring about in the offender.

The label suggests the requirement that the person concerned be brought to recognise her relevant behaviour as shameful and consequently now feel shame at having acted as she did. If so, an understanding of the benefit or otherwise of shaming her will depend on an understanding of the nature of shame and its effect on the person experiencing it. But as well as shame other, related, emotions are referred to by Braithwaite, and by Duff, Weijers and Morris in this volume, viz. guilt and remorse: it is therefore appropriate to try and discover how these are to be distinguished from shame, and whether perhaps, from the point of view of reintegration, it would be more fruitful for the offender to experience either one of these latter emotions rather than shame itself. To achieve some clarity in this area would surely assist at least to some extent those who are to apply the procedure which it is hoped will change the offender's attitude. What follows will therefore be a discussion comparing these emotions with each other, and this in turn requires an answer to the questions: what does each emotion consist in, what identifies it as being shame, say, rather than guilt or remorse?

2. IDENTIFYING EMOTIONS

In general, to try to identify a particular emotion and distinguish it from others is to look for certain conceptual restraints. So for instance a person feeling regret about having acted in a certain way will think the action mistaken or at any rate in some way unfortunate. If she lacks these thoughts, if she does not even dimly perceive something untoward about it, then her claim to be feeling regret would remain unintelligible to others as well as to herself. To make her emotional state more fully intelligible she will have to point out the features of her action because of which, in her view, it was in some way unfortunate. Or again, if, say, she experiences fear at the approach of the large dog then she will think that he is likely to cause her harm. Lacking thoughts of this kind, her feelings about the dog cannot be described as 'fear'. Such beliefs, thoughts or imaginings are the 'internal object' or 'intentional content' of the emotion. They are 'internal' objects in that they are constitutive of the emotion: they make, or contribute towards making, the emotion the particular emotion it is.

There will, in many cases, also be an 'external object' of an emotional state, which will be causally responsible for bringing about the state but not be constitutive of it (for a detailed discussion of this distinction, see Greenspan, 1988). The external object is the focus of the emotion which can be identified independently of the emotional state itself. In the simple example of fear, the external object may be a curiously shaped bit of wood mistaken for a dog, or the dog himself, possibly merely a harmless puppy. It is the wood or dog perceived in a specific way which is the fearful object. It is therefore the person's perceptions of and thoughts about the situation which are crucially relevant to the identification of her emotional state. Such perceptions have different degrees of complexity and may be more or less articulate, so that it may not always be possible, even for the person herself, to establish what it is she is feeling. It may, on the other hand, be possible for another person to point out that her own identification is mistaken since her thoughts about the situation are inappropriate to the particular emotion specified. It is also possible for that other person to show that the emotion is misplaced because the situation is misperceived: the dog is in fact quite harmless and has in any case lost all his teeth.

The implication of this account of the nature of emotions is that neither reference to painful or pleasurable feelings nor reference to physiological manifestations like blushing or the sinking of the stomach is by itself enough to adequately identify and distinguish them. Their identification hinges on the cognitive elements of the complex emotional experience. The experience is complex not only because it involves these cognitive elements as well as feelings and often physiological changes, but also because of the range of variations that are possible in the case of each emotion. Feelings of course may be weaker or stronger, they may or may not prompt action and influence future behaviour. The constitutive states of mind may be fully articulated beliefs or judgements, half-formulated or confused thoughts, imaginings or hypotheses. Since identification depends on the perceptions of the person experiencing the emotion it is determined by the nature of that individual's view of the world, which will be influenced by many different factors, such as social and cultural background, genes, upbringing and previous experiences.

The range of focus is therefore vast and may be quite eccentric, so that it may be difficult or impossible to decide whether the person in question is simply mistaken in her identification or is, rather curiously, indeed experiencing the emotion claimed. A person claiming to be proud of the fish in the ocean, for instance, may either be totally mistaken in her identification of the emotion as 'pride' since the fish neither belong to nor were created by her; or she may be right in thinking that her feeling is pride, believing, rather madly, that she has god-like qualities and had a hand in their creation.[1] Most importantly in the present context, the internal object itself will be complex in that it will consist of a number of perceptions which will occur in different degrees of clarity and dominance. In the case of closely related emotions like guilt, shame and remorse, the description of identifying thoughts is therefore difficult to pin down. Their boundaries may not always be clear since it may be that the difference on occasion is merely one of emphasis, of concentration of thought in one direction rather than another. But in spite of problems such as these, it should still be possible to find identificatory perceptions which apply to a wide range of standard cases.

Shame, guilt and remorse are alike in that their constitutive perceptions involve assessments of the situation which are broadly 'moral': in each case the agent thinks that she has done something (or, in some cases, that something has happened to her) which is wrong in some respect. In trying to distinguish between these emotions it is therefore necessary to try to isolate the appropriate type of wrong perceived, and to consider the specific implications of these perceptions. I shall begin with guilt (s 3), and proceed to remorse (s 4) and shame (s 5), before returning in s 6 to the idea of shaming.

---

[1] This is a case suggested by Hume, 1978: 2.1.9.

Guilt is primarily a legal concept. A person is deemed to be guilty if she breaks a law, whether human or divine. In doing so she has isolated herself from the society governed by the relevant law and has put herself in a position where she can expect some form of punishment or, given repentance on her part, may hope to be forgiven. From the point of view of being guilty the important point is that the person concerned has broken a law, that she has acted against the authority, whatever that might be, that is empowered to impose this law. It is irrelevant whether the law itself is a good or a bad one, whether the agent agrees with it or does not. So guilt is crucially connected with an action or omission which constitutes a breach of some authoritative injunction because of which the agent is liable to be punished in some form or other. She is punished because on a specifiable occasion she has acted as she did. If she accepts her guilt she accepts the authority of the law she has broken, and accepts that some sort of reparation is due from her. Punishment implies that since it was *her* action that was in breach of the law she has to take responsibility for whatever change she has brought about in the world, and in accepting her guilt she accepts that responsibility.

Emotional guilt has features which are analogous to those just enumerated, but as is to be expected in the untidy area of the emotional life the story is here more complicated. Being found guilty, and even accepting guilt, does not imply that the agent concerned *feels* guilty. While agreeing that she is in breach of some authoritative injunction she may not agree that she has done anything wrong. In her view, perhaps, the injunction is trivial, the authority far from admirable. She may even agree that what she did was wrong and be prepared to make amends and still not feel guilt. The matter does not touch her, but to feel guilty she must be engaged. Paradigmatically, the person feeling guilty will think, perhaps only fleetingly, that she should not have acted as she did, or should have done something she has omitted to do. She has failed to comply with some injunction which she ought to have respected.

The relevant injunction may but need not present itself to her explicitly as a taboo she has violated, a categorical imperative she has failed to obey; less formally, it may just occur to her that she has done something wrong. But if she is to experience guilt then the thought must have some power, it must be an oppressive thought which makes her feel uncomfortable. The degree and duration of discomfort will depend on how authoritative she believes the relevant injunction to be, how powerful she experiences it as being. At this moment, at any rate, she is not at ease with herself: her wrong-doing has left its mark on her, her sense of self-security has been impaired, her equilibrium destroyed. It may of course be the case that she no longer thinks of the injunction as being valid; her guilt-feeling is perhaps only a response to some rule drummed into her in childhood and long since discarded. In that case her discomfort will be short-lived. Should it persist, either she is still confused about the issue or she will regard her feelings as irrational and not pay them much attention. In serious cases, however, the perception of her wrongdoing will make its impression: she is responsible for the deed, and this is felt as a burden for her to carry. As a consequence it is now also her responsibility to make amends where this is possible, and this is a nagging thought contributing to her discomfort.

Again, the mark of guilt may be perceived as more or less disfiguring, the burden as more or less heavy, and the desire to put things right will vary in strength accordingly. The more important and authoritative the injunction infringed is taken to be, the greater the discomfort, and hence the more needful that some reparation should be made, that the guilt should somehow be purged. Naturally, the more disfiguring the mark of guilt left in her, the harder it is to put herself to rights again, and doing so may indeed not be possible at all. At least in the perception of the agent there may be no way to free herself of her guilt. This is famously the case for Lady Macbeth, whose obsessive washing of her hands does not succeed in removing the stain of her guilt. She finds that she cannot live with this permanently stained self, and so eventually commits suicide. For her the disfigurement of herself caused by being party to a murder is more than she can bear.

Macbeth himself, although initially more hesitant than his wife was to commit the murder, deals differently and in a sense more positively with his guilt once the deed is done. There are, from Macbeth's point of view, a number of taboos applicable to the situation: Duncan is his king, his kinsman and his guest. He trusts Macbeth. For all these reasons Macbeth, the man of honour, must not harm him. Once he has killed Duncan he can clearly no longer think of himself as a man of unimpaired honour who respects the obligations of kinsman, subject and host. What he has done has undermined this particular self-image, it is wholly alien to that conception of himself. He is quite aware that the deed has left a terrible stain upon him: he could not say 'Amen', 'Amen' stuck in his throat. His mind is full of scorpions. If he is not to live in emotional turmoil forever after, he somehow has to make this stain disappear. There is no straightforward way of doing so—it clearly cannot be washed away. Consequently, it seems, it has to be accepted, and he must change himself and his self-image to make them match the changed situation. From this new point of view he has done no terrible wrong: on the contrary, only the weak and cowardly are bound by obligations to king and kinsman; the strong and properly ambitious can ignore them. And Macbeth is not weak and cowardly. In this perverted way he has managed to achieve a new integrity, he has accommodated himself to a deed which was totally alien to his former self.

Those who are guilty of breaking a law set themselves apart from other members of the society governed by that law. Analogously, those feeling guilty feel themselves estranged to a greater or lesser extent from that community whose views of right and wrong they share, and thereby feel themselves estranged from that self which was and wishes again to be a member of that community. This is so at any rate in serious cases of emotional guilt where the person concerned is aware of the (actual or potential) adverse judgement of a community she respects. In that case she will be prepared to do whatever is required to make amends so that she can be re-instated. Since the 'external object' of guilt covers a very wide range, the community with which the agent identifies will also vary greatly in its nature. It may be simply the society in which she lives and whose basic values as expressed in its laws she accepts. But she may also feel intense guilt over actions which concern a wholly personal morality, legislating how she should behave and perhaps even feel towards others or towards herself. It was very wrong, she thinks, not to visit the friend in hospital, wrong to spend her days in idle pursuits. In such cases it seems rather artificial to think of her as isolating herself from a community, but in staying away from her friend or watching television all morning she still feels set apart from some community whose values she admires and wishes to live up to.

The general point here is that, whatever the particular case, such assessments and evaluations have their source in the community in which she lives. Consequently, the awareness that she belongs to a particular community held together by shared values, mutual respect and possibly attachment (where the 'community' is the family, say) contributes crucially to her feelings of self-security and sense of identity (see also Weijers in ch 7). It is for this reason that when acting against an injunction which embodies values she believes are accepted by that community someone feeling guilt feels herself to be alienated from both, herself and her community. It is also for this reason that although indifferent to, or not fully appreciating or even disagreeing with the content of a specific injunction, a person may nonetheless feel guilty when disobeying it, and not be able to shrug off the guilt: loss of membership of and approval from the community appears to her more undermining and so harmful to herself than would acting against her own desires or judgements. What matters most to her is that she be accepted by those she respects or loves. This I take to be the case of a child, though such a view of the matter need not be restricted to the young.

4. REMORSE

The perceptions which are constitutive of emotional guilt concern the relevant action or omission and the damage thereby caused to others or possibly to the agent herself; but they also and importantly concern herself as the agent responsible for the action. She thinks that since what she did has set her apart, something is now due from her, she has to make amends if she is to feel herself re-instated. What, then, is the relation between guilt and remorse? Remorse, the *Oxford English Dictionary* tells us, is a feeling of compunction or deep regret for a sin or wrong committed. When feeling remorse the person concerned wishes above all that she could undo the deed.

Perhaps, then, those feeling guilt will also feel remorse, for their thought that they should somehow 'make up' for their wrong-doing may seem to imply that ideally the wrong should be undone, if that were possible. But while in many cases guilt and remorse may well be experienced together this need not be the case. Dickens, in *Martin Chuzzlewit*, gives us a convincing example of the experience of the one without the other (ch XLVII): Jonas has killed his blackmailer and is haunted by guilt, but he feels no remorse, for he is not sorry that he has done the deed, he does not wish it undone. It was necessary to get rid of the man and he has done so in the only way open to him, but of course in doing so he has committed a terrible crime which leaves its mark upon him. It is similarly also possible, at least theoretically, to experience remorse and no guilt, for reasons which I hope will emerge.

Guilt and remorse differ in both range and emphasis of focus. Guilt covers a wider range, it may but need not be felt about what is perceived as a sin or serious moral offence, but may, at least to a degree and for a time, be experienced as what is perceived to be a relatively minor failure to act as one ought to have done. Remorse, as the dictionary suggests, does seem to be restricted to serious cases. Both share the feature that the agent feels herself to be responsible for the wrong done, but here again in cases of guilt the application of responsibility has a wider range than it does in cases of remorse. A person may feel guilty about something which she knows she has not brought about herself, as for example a German youth today may feel guilt about the treatment of Jews during the Nazi era (see Morris, 1987). There can be vicarious guilt, based on the identification of the person concerned with a community other members of which have acted criminally. The youth did not himself in any way bring about the crime committed, but he takes at any rate some responsibility for it.

Remorse, I think, cannot be felt under such circumstances; in remorse the agent feels responsible only for what she actually did. This points to an important distinction between guilt and remorse: remorse is wholly tied to the relevant action, and it is the action on which the appropriate thoughts concentrate. The guilty, too, give thought to the action and its effects on others, but they are equally concerned with the alteration in themselves. The boundaries here are clearly fluid. My suggestion is that in paradigm cases of guilt and remorse the two are to be distinguished from one another by self-directed perceptions, prominent in guilt but not in remorse.

5. SHAME

Shame shares with guilt such self-directed, uneasy perceptions; the difference between guilt and shame lies in the nature of these perceptions. Guilt is generally experienced as a voice telling one what to do, shame as critical or at least observing eyes being upon one. Shame-reactions seem to require an observer, and those experiencing shame seem to think of themselves in relation to some audience to which they are exposed. This is emphasised in the case Sartre regards as being typical of shame: a man makes a vulgar gesture. He then realises that he is being observed. This realisation makes him look at what he is doing through the observer's eyes. Seeing his action from this new point of view he becomes aware that what he is doing is vulgar, and he feels shame (Sartre, 1969, III.1). Sartre's case is certainly a possible one, is perhaps one of a range of standard cases of shame, but it is only a very simple example. Sartre assumes there to be a real observer who disapproves of what he sees, and assumes that it is recognition of a hostile view which prompts the agent's reaction. But there is no need for any real observer to be disapproving, or for the agent to think that he is. The observer's attitude may be one of indifference, or even approbation. In such a case the person feeling shame may think that being seen at all is humiliating, or she will feel shame precisely because she thinks that being approved of by that particular observer is itself degrading, for it means that she has sunk to his level.

There is no need, then, for the agent's view to coincide with that which she ascribes to any actual observer of her actions. Moreover, there is no need at all for any real observer to be on the spot, nor even for there to be an imagined real one in the agent's mind. Yet on the occasion of feeling shame there is a shift in the agent's point of view: she can no longer unselfconsciously be absorbed in what she is doing, she has to distance herself from herself and see and judge herself as if she were a critical observer of her actions. The audience is internalised. In contrast to the authoritative voice in cases of guilt, the observing and critical eye does not limit itself to some particular action of the agent's, but it views the whole person. Unlike guilt, shame is not localised: the action in question is not the central focus of her perception; it is merely the occasion which prompts her to take a new, less favourable view of herself. The metaphors of a stained or burdened self are not appropriate here as they were in the case of guilt. The person feeling shame feels degraded, she sinks in her own esteem, she perceives herself as not being the person she believed, assumed or hoped she was or anyway should be. To the man in Sartre's example it comes as a shock that he is capable of vulgar actions, is perhaps altogether a vulgar fellow.

The notion of an audience or observer has a role to play in emotional shame which is analogous to that of the authoritative injunction in cases of guilt, but the two emotions are focused differently. This crucial difference between them implies consequential ones. Since in shame it is not merely a particular action which is in question there is, in the agent's eyes, nothing she can do to make up for it, nothing for which either punishment or forgiveness is in place, for how could she make amends for what she is? Nor is there any point in her wishing a particular action undone, for while that action may have been shameful it merely served to show her what she is, and undoing it would not essentially alter her nature. So there is here no occasion for feeling remorse. Nor are there feelings of having alienated herself from the self she really is, for the trouble precisely is that what she did was not alien to her, but on the contrary showed her up as the lowly person she is. If this is so then there is no way in which she can re-establish herself and be again one of that community she respects and admires. She cannot hope to be forgiven, for forgiveness here has no proper object. She can only try to hide, to be no longer seen by observant and critical eyes, and so to be protected from them.

There is another consideration, distinct from but connected to shame's concern with the whole person, given which punishment and repayment are not appropriate to shame as they were to guilt. Shame is not related to responsibility as guilt was seen to be. We are normally held responsible for our actions in a way in which we tend not to be held responsible for what we are, and punishment for what we are seems both unfair and useless. The experience of guilt is always accompanied by feelings of responsibility, even where the guilt is vicarious, or where it is about some state which was in no sense brought about by us (being a member of a rich family, for example). Even if we could not have helped that state, and know that we could not have helped it, we take some responsibility for it, and feel that some reparation is due, such as making a point of contributing to charity. Failure to do so will increase the burden of guilt. This is not so if we feel shame in relation to states that we have not brought about ourselves: the person concerned feels degraded no matter how this has come about and whether or not she accepts responsibility for whatever it is that occasions the feeling. It is how she thinks she is now seen and is forced to see herself that is of importance. If she could feel herself responsible for that, perhaps she would also think that it might be in her power to lift herself again and not have the feelings of helplessness and hopelessness which are so prominent on the occasion of feeling shame.

While differing in their relation to responsibility, however, guilt and shame are alike in that both may be experienced vicariously: shame, like guilt, may be felt at the behaviour of another, if there is some identification with that other. It is *my* father, brother, friend or countryman who is behaving so atrociously and thereby involves me in his shame. In this respect both shame and guilt differ from remorse. While the German youth of today may feel guilt or shame at what was done during the Nazi-time, it would be very strange if he claimed to be feeling remorse.

There may be a further reason why punishment and forgiveness play a role in cases of guilt whereas they do not in those of shame: it may simply be that we feel guilt when we think of the harm we have caused another, and shame when we perceive that we have harmed ourselves by not living up to some standard or other we have set for ourselves. Hence the ascription of responsibility and all that entails matters much more in cases of guilt than in those of shame. This is not entirely correct: guilt may be felt about actions which have little or no effect on others, and shame may of course be occasioned by bad behaviour towards others. But there is some truth in the suggestion. This is so, perhaps, because authoritative injunctions tend to concern primarily behaviour towards others, and so guilt-feelings are most naturally aroused in this context. If so, then it may be that in 'healthy' cases of guilt the agent's thoughts concentrate more on the harm done to another than on herself as the agent who brought the harm about.

The more it is thoughts of the latter kind that occupy her consciousness the more neurotic tends to be her guilt, for her preoccupation will be to try to rid herself of the stain rather than to try to repair the damage as best she can. It is different in cases of shame. The standards invoked may well concern one's behaviour and attitude towards others, but since failure to comply is merely the occasion for seeing oneself in a less favourable light, thoughts here will in any case be primarily about oneself.

Feelings of shame, like feelings of guilt, will of course vary in strength and duration, and the uneasiness experienced will have a greater or lesser impact on the agent's view of herself. On second thoughts the depressing view she took of herself when experiencing shame may be revisable, the behaviour that occasioned shame merely a slip without much significance, the event seen as so undermining in fact not all that important. Again like guilt, shame may be excessive, deficient or totally misguided when seen from a relatively objective viewpoint. Both emotions may be seen as responses to the agent's perception of a threat to her integrity, though the specific perceptions are different (see Taylor 1985: v. 5).

Feelings of shame are about the agent's short-comings with respect to formulating or living up to her standards and ideals—to that which, in her view, makes her a worthwhile person leading a worthwhile life. When feeling shame she thinks, possibly only briefly, that her evaluations are superficial and shoddy, or that she fails to realise them in her life. Hence her loss of self-worth, her feelings of depression about herself and the life she leads. Those feeling guilt, on the other hand, will see an alien self emerging, a self capable of acting against authoritative injunctions. In many cases, of course, the particular action or omission may not be thought by the agent to be a very serious violation, or the violation of a very weighty injunction. In such cases the emerging self does not have much substance and is not much of a threat. Nevertheless, there is at least the glimpse of a split between the 'good' and the 'bad' self, and guilt is the response to the recognition of the appearance of a worse self. An alien self whose doings conflict with the agent's evaluations is something to fear, and so fear and anxiety are connected with guilt as depression is with shame.

6. SHAMING

The point of the examination of emotional guilt and shame was to try to see what the procedure of shaming a young offender is meant to achieve, and whether it can be seen as a helpful means of moral education. The discussion so far has been of those who feel guilt, shame or remorse on some particular occasion, and of their differing perceptions on that occasion. It is clear that all these emotional experiences involve evaluations, that the agent feels herself committed—at least at this moment—to certain views as to what is right or wrong, good or bad, worthwhile or despicable. Now we are to look at the situation the other way round: the young offender is to come to accept a certain evaluation of the situation through the experience of a relevant emotion.

In theory at least the suggestion is promising. If the young person can be brought to feel this emotion, she will thereby also accept the required assessment of what she has done. Moreover, if, as the label seems to suggest, the process of shaming is aimed at encouraging certain sorts of feelings in the offender, then this, too, is a step in the right direction. It might be thought that the aim of arousing painful and uncomfortable feelings is not necessary for shaming to be successful, and perhaps that it would be healthier and so better to do without such feelings rather than indulge them. Rational recognition of the wrong and the resolve to do better in the future is surely all that is required. But although it may perhaps not be necessary for the young offender to feel specifically guilt, shame or remorse to be reintegrated into her community, it would be natural and possibly more satisfactory for her to do so.

This is so because recognition of wrong and resolve to do better entail making an assessment of the situation which appeals to a range of values, and commitment to such evaluations involves the emotions. The belief that such-and-such a course of action is the right one, or that another is to be avoided because generally harmful, would be a rather vacuous belief if it did not connect with feelings of various kinds: admiration or hope, contempt or anger, and so on. Evaluations generally require some emotional reactions, or we should not take them very seriously. It would be very odd, to say the least, to believe some course of action to be very harmful and yet have no feelings of, say, dislike of those who engage in it, or admiration for those who resist in spite of strong temptations. It is true that guilt or shame or remorse need not necessarily be among such emotional reactions, but they are not emotions which occur in isolation. Rather, they are interrelated with a whole complex of other emotions, such as approval or disapproval, admiration or contempt, so that it would be natural for an agent who occasionally has such feelings also to feel guilt (shame, remorse) at the recognition that what she said or did was wrong. Failure in emotional reaction may strike one as inhuman in certain circumstances, and may be taken as an indication that the agent is not properly committed to her evaluations, that her beliefs are not deeply rooted. Absence of feeling tends to indicate a lack of sincerity in her apparent acceptance of a moral rule or value (see Williams, 1973). The process of shaming, then, appears to have a positive and acceptable aim.

The term 'shaming' does, however, have rather negative implications. It suggests that some relevant authority will see to it that the offending agent will feel shame, that is, feel bad and depressed about herself, excluded from her community. This is indeed how it is understood within the framework of so-called 'shame-cultures'. It is characteristic of such cultures that esteem for an individual depends entirely on that person's conforming to the code which embodies that society's values. Failure to do so results in loss of honour, and shaming consists in making it clear to her that she has lost her honour, has therefore lost the esteem of members of the society, and has forfeited any right to regard herself as belonging to that society. She is an outcast and is made to feel herself an outcast.[2] If in a shame-culture shaming does what it sets out to do, then the agent will feel shame and so lose her self-worth. She is now in an undermining and disabling position, affecting adversely others as well as herself, since she will now not think that she has any worthwhile contributions to make. This case of being shamed depends on the agent being a member of an honour-group, her acceptance of the relevant code and consequent demands on herself. Of course, feelings of shame nowadays and in our culture are unlikely to occur under such specific circumstances. Nor, I take it, is this form of shaming an ideal type of social control.

John Braithwaite proposes a rather different form of shaming. It is not, as in the shame-culture, a stigmatising but is a 'reintegrative' shaming:

> Reintegrative shaming means that expressions of community disapproval, which may range from mild rebuke to degradation ceremonies, are followed by gestures of reacceptance into the community of law-abiding citizens. These gestures may vary from a simple smile expressing forgiveness and love to quite formal ceremonies to decertify the offender as deviant (Braithwaite, 1989: 55).

The general idea is that the offending citizen is to be treated as a responsible, rational agent who can be reasoned with, and who may thereby come to see the harmfulness of her action and hence the justification of social disapproval. If this is her resultant view then she will be prepared to repair the damage as best she can and again become an acceptable member of the community. Braithwaite, who is primarily concerned with crime-control and hence with law-breaking, puts forward a moral theory of punishment which contrasts, for instance, with the deterrence theory of traditional utilitarianism: as he points out, the emphasis is on the moral aspect of the law, and on the moral dimension of the criminal. By 'moral dimension' he refers to what he takes to be the crucial characteristics of human beings, viz that they are rational agents responsible for their actions and capable of free choice. Their dignity is a value to be cherished, and so they must be treated and also punished with dignity.

But shaming, if this is to induce emotional shame in the offender, is hard to reconcile with treating her with dignity, for it seems to aim at undermining her self-esteem. The intention of reintegrative shaming is of course not to cause such deep and lasting shame which would make her feel isolated from her community. That would run counter to the whole theory. Yet Braithwaite's reference to shaming at one end of the scale involving a degradation ceremony makes it difficult to see how the line between stigmatic and reintegrative shaming is to be drawn. Shaming is shaming, and even if the shame induced is meant to be only short-lived, to be followed by a restorative process, the damage might be done. Rather than being a preparation for reintegration, it may lead to feelings of

---

[2] A paradigm case of such a culture is taken to be the world of heroes in Homer's *Iliad*. See Dodds, 1951.

resentment on the part of the offender, which would obstruct rather than aid respect for the community into which she is to be re-accepted.

The point here is not that feeling shame is always a bad thing, and certainly not that the possession of a sense of shame is undesirable. Such possession implies commitment to standards already established. The point is rather that to try to get a young offender to accept certain standards by means of shaming is an uncertain and possibly dangerous undertaking. Restorative justice is hardly best served in this way, and it seems that in practice the restorative process is unlikely to involve the attempt to induce shame (see Morris's discussion in ch 8).

Braithwaite's account of what the process is to achieve implies that he does not really think in terms of shame: he wants the juvenile offender to think of herself, not as a degraded creature, but as having done something wrong which can be repaired. Guilt rather than shame is the reaction that fits the theory, for it is guilt and not shame which concerns itself with particular wrong-doings, and links with responsibility, punishment and forgiveness. Braithwaite's 'shaming', then, consists in making the agent feel guilty, which will involve the recognition that she has done wrong, acknowledge this insight publicly, make whatever amends may be required, and re-join the community. If so, his label for this process is misleading, and, given its usual implications, unfortunate.

But making a person feel guilty also has its drawbacks. Firstly, it may not succeed in changing her attitude and making her realise that what she did was wrong. As pointed out earlier, she may experience this emotion not because she acknowledges that she did wrong, but rather because she is aware that she is being disapproved of, and she is anxious, above all, not to lose the respect or love of those around her. While an offender's awareness of the community's disapproval is no doubt a vital aspect of achieving restorative justice, by itself it falls short of the ideal solution, that she should accept and be at ease with the values of her community, or that at least she should be made to think seriously about her values. Of course, such a reaction is better than nothing, and from the point of view of crime-control it may be sufficient: once aware of disapproval and anger towards her she may not re-offend. It is a rather immature reaction, but given the youth of the offender it is perhaps the best that can be achieved; it may at any rate be a step towards getting her to think seriously about her values.

Secondly, and more damagingly, there is the point made by Olthof (ch 10): that guilt may linger and not match the nature of the offence, and not lead to a resolution. This is so because a person experiencing guilt perceives not only that she has acted as she ought not to have done, but also that she, as the agent responsible for bringing about the wrong, has thereby stained herself. It is always possible that this latter perception makes a stronger and more lasting impression on her than the former, so that instead of focusing on the harm done to the community, she concentrates on the harm she thinks she has done herself, possibly exaggerating the extent of her guilt. This would tend to be disabling rather than helpful and restorative.

7. CONCLUSION

There is a better option. Some contributors to this volume (Duff and Morris in particular) have spoken of aiming at getting the juvenile offender to feel remorse; given the characterisation of the three emotions this one seems the most appropriate to try to induce. Like all emotions, remorse may of course be felt to excess and so unnecessarily indulged in, but unlike guilt, and particularly unlike shame, it does not involve any specific self-directed perceptions which are potentially destructive. Remorse is closely tied to the action itself, and to feel remorse the agent must recognise that what she did was wrong and accept the need to make amends. She should feel blamed but not crushed. To achieve this attitude she must be able to relate to those who judge her adversely, and respect them. If she can do so, then her re-acceptance into the community will tend to help her to gain self-confidence and self-esteem, to feel pride in being a respected member of a respect-worthy society. Perhaps the most difficult task for those engaged in the exercise of restorative justice is to guide the juvenile offender towards desirable occasions for feeling pride, that is, to direct a positive emotion into the right channels rather than insist on inducing negative ones.[3]

REFERENCES

Braithwaite, J (1989) *Crime, Shame and Reintegration* (Cambridge University Press, Cambridge).

Dodds, E R (1951) *The Greeks and the Irrational* (University of California Press, Berkeley).

Greenspan, P S (1988) *Emotions and Reasons* (Routledge, London).

Hume, D [1739] (1978) *A Treatise of Human Nature*, L A Selby-Bigge (ed) P H Nidditch (rev) (Clarendon Press, Oxford).

Morris, H (1987) 'Nonmoral guilt' in F Shoeman (ed) *Responsibility, Character, and the Emotions* (Cambridge University Press, Cambridge).

Sartre, J-P (1969) *Being and Nothingness* H Barnes (trans) (Routledge, London).

Taylor, G (1985) *Pride, Shame and Guilt, Emotions of Self-Assessment* (Oxford University Press, Oxford).

Williams, B (1973) 'Morality and the Emotions' in his *Problems of the Self* (Cambridge University Press, Cambridge).

---

[3] This is, I think, also suggested by Weijers in his discussion on self-identification and self-evaluation in ch 7.

10

Shame, Guilt, Antisocial Behaviour and Juvenile Justice: A Psychological Perspective

TJEERT OLTHOF

1. INTRODUCTION

ONE OF THE functions that can be ascribed to feelings of guilt and shame is that these emotions help prevent us from committing moral and social transgressions. Since both emotions are unpleasant, individuals can be expected to ensure that they do not experience them by avoiding situations that would elicit these emotions. Ideally, an individual's moral and emotional development results in a sufficiently strong tendency to feel guilty or ashamed after having transgressed that the prospect of experiencing these emotions is a considerable obstacle to committing the transgression in the first place. Braithwaite's (1989) reintegrative shaming procedure, which actually consists in an attempt to induce feelings of guilt in the offender, is by definition, applied to individuals for whom guilt and shame were not adequate to prevent them from committing the offence that brought them into the courtroom. Accordingly, when seen from a developmental psychology perspective, Braithwaite's procedure is an attempt to instil in the individual something that his moral and emotional development failed to instil, ie a tendency to feel guilty or ashamed that is sufficiently strong to keep him from transgressing. This developmental perspective has implications for the question of whether the procedure is likely to work and for identifying the factors that are likely to affect its chances of being successful.

The general aim of this chapter is to outline these implications. In doing so, I will draw on existing theoretical and empirical work as much as possible. However, at some points the account goes beyond received wisdom in that hypotheses are described that still await empirical testing. Carrying out such tests is one of the aims of the project *Shame, Guilt, and Antisocial Behaviour in Children and Adolescents* that is currently being carried out at our department (Olthof *et al*, 1999). Before discussing how feelings of shame and guilt are related to antisocial behaviour, I will first briefly describe my views on the nature of these two emotions.

2. SHAME AND GUILT

According to the account of shame and guilt that is currently most influential in psychology (Lewis, 1971; Tangney, 1995), feelings of guilt result from seeing one's behaviour as bad, whereas shame results from seeing one's entire self as being defective. Similarly, Lindsay-Hartz, De Rivera and Mascolo (1995) argued that shame implies that one realises that one is what one does not want to be. Shame implies an unwanted identity (Olthof, 1996).

It should be added to this account that both guilt and shame are interpersonal emotions. Both theoretical (Olthof, 1996; Spiecker, 1991; Taylor, 1985, 1996) and empirical (Olthof *et al*, 2000; Olthof *et al*, 2001) analyses suggest why guilt-feeling individuals consider their behaviour to be bad, ie because they perceive themselves as having been involved in causing a moral wrong, usually, but not exclusively, because they caused some kind of harm or disadvantage to some-one. Their feelings of guilt and the resulting behaviours can be seen as attempts to repair the damage caused to their relationship with the victim (Baumeister *et al*, 1994).

With regard to shame, both empirical and theoretical analyses have stressed the role of an audience. In open-ended interview studies it has been found that shame involves a heightened concern with how others might evaluate the self (eg Ferguson *et al*, 1991). Based on a similar study, Terwijn (1993) reported that intense feelings of shame can result from thinking that other people consider one to be strange, ridiculous, queer, etc without the individual himself necessarily agreeing that there is anything wrong with his behaviour or person. These findings support theoretical claims that shame-related appraisals encompass one's awareness of how one appears from the perspective of a real or imagined audience (Crozier, 1998; Gilbert, 1998; Harris, 1989; Taylor, 1985, 1996). Accordingly, the unwanted identity that is implied in feeling ashamed does not necessarily reflect people's own ideas about what they are, but rather their infer-ences about what they are when seen from the perspective of a particular audience.

What exactly is it that can be seen from such a perspective, at least as imag-ined by the ashamed individual? Crozier (1998) argued that shame-related appraisals, unlike embarrassment-related appraisals, concern the individual's thoughts about how the audience would evaluate core attributes of the self. Crozier's prime example of such a core attribute is the self's moral standing. This claim is problematic, however, because shame arises not only when the individual commits a moral wrong, but also when committing social blunders that are not morally significant (Ausubel, 1955; Terwijn, 1993; Ferguson *et al*, 1991; Taylor, 1996; Olthof *et al*, 2000; Olthof *et al*, 2001; Sabini *et al*, 2001). Accordingly, the self's moral standing is unlikely to be the only or even the prim-ary core attribute of the self that is involved in shame.

What could be the core attribute of the self that is at stake in such diverse situations as being clumsy; a slip of the tongue; displaying incompetence in areas where one claims (or is supposed to claim) competence; being a left-wing politician who is publicly shown to have made large profits on the real estate market; being a right-wing defender of family values who is publicly shown to indulge in extra-marital sexual relations; and being a schoolboy whose class-mates expect him to want the same brand of shoes as worn by everyone else, while at the same time inferring from his not having such shoes that he lacks the money to buy them or the guts to steal them? In line with suggestions made by Olthof *et al* (2000), I propose that these and other shame-eliciting incidents have in common that they cast doubt on how well the self fulfils its role as *the author* of its own behavioural or appearance-related manifestations to the out-side world. Such incidents—when looked at from a particular perspective—reveal, or apparently reveal, the self as being unable or unwilling to authorise one of its manifestations to the outside world as originating from the self. The self is therefore revealed to be inconsistent and therefore possibly also *inco-herent*. It is clear from the above examples that suspicions of incoherence can be based on behaviours that reveal a lack of control, but also from discrepan-cies between individuals' real or assumed value-related desires and their actual behaviour.

By feeling ashamed, the self signals a desire to distance itself from the mani-festation of the self that elicited the suspicion of incoherence in the first place. Shame can therefore be seen as an attempt to repair the damage that was caused to one's identity. Behaviourally, these signals take the form of attempts to avoid being seen, as in hiding behaviour, or, when hiding is impossible, to avoid seeing oneself that one is seen, as in eye aversion. When considered from an evo-lutionary perspective, these are submissive behaviours that signal one's pre-paredness to conform to the norms of the particular audience that does the seeing (Gilbert, 1998).

3. MEASURING INDIVIDUAL DIFFERENCES

In present-day psychological conceptions of emotion, emotions are seen as basic-ally adaptive in that they provide signals to the individual himself and to his envir-onment that something is going on that is relevant to the individual's concerns. They affect the way a situation is interpreted and they guide the individual's response to that situation. Ideally, the emotional system is in balance, so that the whole range of emotions is available to serve the individual. Differences between individuals in terms of their tendency to experience particular emotions result from imbalances in their emotional systems and when such imbalances are severe, they are considered to be pathological (Cole *et al*, 1994; Magai & McFadden, 1995; Stegge *et al*, 1998). In this approach a distinction is made between two types of pathology, ie surfeit pathology (too much of an emotion) which occurs when an individual's emotional system is biased towards persistently experiencing one particular emotion, and deficiency pathology (too little of an emotion) when the individual is biased towards not experiencing a particular emotion (Malatesta & Wilson, 1988).

Much of the psychological research on guilt and shame of the previous decade has been directed at identifying such individual differences in people's propensity to feel guilty and/or ashamed. Currently, there still is debate about whether such measures should focus on the intensity of shame and guilt experiences in potentially shame- or guilt-eliciting situations, or on the frequency of experiencing such emotions, or on how long such experiences last (Andrews, 1998; Ferguson & Eyre, 2000). Nevertheless, by using one or more of these aspects, researchers have succeeded in obtaining reliable measures of shame- and guilt-proneness that can be used with children (Ferguson & Stegge, 1995, 1998) and with adults (Harder, 1995; Tangney *et al*, 1989). The resulting measures were subsequently related to measures of psychological adjustment and maladjustment. Several meaningful patterns have emerged from this research. In the following section I discuss some of these findings, while focusing particularly on those antisocial traits and behaviours that might bring a youngster into the courtroom, and on the pro-social behaviours that are a desired outcome of any shame- and guilt-based juvenile justice procedure.

4. GUILT, SHAME, AND ANTISOCIAL BEHAVIOUR

In the literature, both guilt and shame are usually designated as moral emotions (eg Emde & Oppenheim, 1995; Spiecker, 1991). The analysis given above implies that guilt is indeed a moral emotion, in that it results from thinking that one has been involved in causing a moral wrong. Accordingly, someone who is prone to feel guilty can be expected to avoid violating moral rules and to try and repair any damage that results when a moral rule is nevertheless violated.

This positive view of guilt is essentially confirmed in much of the recent psychological research on guilt. From the work of Martin Hoffman, Roy Baumeister and June Price Tangney it has become clear that guilt can be an adaptive response when one has caused harm to someone else. This type of guilt is based on empathic understanding of the victim's plight (Hoffman, 1982, 1998) and is positively related to tolerance of frustration and to pro-social behaviours like providing aid and care and volunteering for charity work. At the same time it is negatively related to antisocial behaviours such as aggression, expression of racist attitudes and sexually coercive behaviour (see Williams, 1998 for an overview).

However, there is also a darker side to guilt. In psychological theory, guilt has long been associated with pathology and recent empirical evidence indicates that a distinction should be made between adaptive guilt of the kind that Hoffman, Baumeister and Tangney described, and at least one type of lingering or chronic guilt that is far from adaptive (Ferguson & Stegge, 1998; Bybee &

Quiles, 1998; Ferguson & Eyre, 2000). Whereas the intensity of adaptive guilt matches the particular act of wrong-doing to which it is a response and prompts efforts to repair the damage that has been caused, the intensity of this particular type of lingering guilt does not necessarily match the seriousness of the event and it does not lead to a resolution. It may bother the individual for years and is related both to internalising problems (Ferguson & Eyre, 2000) and to antisocial behaviour (Bybee & Quiles, 1998).

Unlike guilt, shame has not had such a favourable press in the recent upsurge of psychological research on self-conscious emotions. Shame was designated as an 'ugly' emotion (Tangney, 1991) and shame-proneness was shown to be related to all kinds of internalising and externalising problems, including anger and aggression (Tangney *et al*, 1992; Tangney *et al*, 1995; Tangney *et al*, 1996). This picture of shame is probably too bleak. Its function in promoting conformity to group norms enhances one's membership of a group and one's sense of belonging (Stegge & Ferguson, 2000). Moreover, shame's push towards coherence and consistency also increases one's suitability as an interactional partner. Nevertheless, shame can actually lead to antisocial behaviour in at least two ways.

First, it follows from the analysis above that shame is not an inherently moral emotion. To the extent that an individual cares about how he is seen from a morally normative perspective, the prospect of feeling ashamed vis-a-vis an audience taking such a perspective can be expected to inhibit antisocial behaviour. However, when the individual cares more about how he is seen from a perspective that stresses other values, shame with regard to an audience taking such a perspective can elicit antisocial behaviours as well.

The example of Macbeth, also discussed by Taylor (1996; this volume), nicely illustrates this point. When Macbeth admits to Lady Macbeth his moral reservations about the idea of killing King Duncan, she responds by pointing out that his reservations are quite inconsistent with his previously expressed desires. As she expresses it:

> Art thou afeard
> To be the same in thine own act and valour
> As thou art in desire? Wouldst thou have that
> Which thou esteem'st the ornament of life
> And live a coward in thine own esteem,
> Letting 'I dare not' wait upon 'I would'
> Like the poor cat i' the adage?
> (*Macbeth* I.vii)

Accordingly, Lady Macbeth induces Macbeth to feel ashamed because he is inconsistent. Her shame-inducing speech is successful in that Macbeth is appalled by the prospect of having to feel ashamed for the reasons his wife points out, and he subsequently goes on to murder King Duncan. He prefers the prospect of feeling guilty to the prospect of feeling ashamed.

The example of Macbeth not only illustrates that shame can overrule guilt and thereby motivate antisocial behaviour, but also that individuals live amidst several different social groups that are likely to differ in terms of the value-related desires that they expect individuals to have. To take a present-day and more mundane example, imagine a 14-year old boy who hesitates to join his comrades in a shop-lifting expedition. He knows that his parents expect him to be decent and honest and/or to avoid behaviours that would disappoint them. Accordingly, his eventual shop-lifting behaviour would seem inconsistent when seen from the perspective of his parents, which would make it a shameful experience. However, when imagining how his friends would react to his refusal to join them, he realises that they attribute to him a desire to share in the loot, or simply to participate in any activity of the group, and that they would therefore interpret a refusal to participate as being inconsistent, which would make such a refusal shameful.

In sum, whether the avoidance of shame leads to morally acceptable or to antisocial behaviour depends on the relative salience of the different perspectives that an individual can use to look at the self. When the most salient perspective promotes conformity to moral rules, shame inhibits antisocial behaviour; when this perspective promotes conformity to other values, shame can elicit antisocial behaviours as well.

There may be a second reason why shame in our culture is related to antisocial behaviour. The sociologist Thomas Scheff has argued repeatedly that present-day western culture tends to deny the existence of shame and that this tendency is a major source of interpersonal violence and aggression (Scheff, 1988, 1995). Why is shame denied? Scheff (1988) argued that this is because feeling ashamed is in itself shameful. In the light of the previously given analysis of shame, this claim makes sense. A culture that places great value on personal autonomy and independence cannot help but see the submissive posture that results from feeling ashamed as something that should be avoided at all costs. Or, to use the terminology of the above analysis, the submissive posture of an ashamed individual is inconsistent with a desire that our culture routinely attributes to individuals, ie to be autonomous and independent. This inconsistency elicits shame about feeling ashamed.

Why is the denial of shame related to violence and aggression? That there actually is a link between shame and rage has been demonstrated extensively in both the clinical and empirical literature (Lindsay-Hartz *et al*, 1995; Tangney *et al*, 1992). The previously given analysis suggests two reasons why shame, or more precisely, attempts to deny or undo shame, elicits aggression. First, because shame results from looking at the self from the perspective of a particular audience, the shameful individual is easily tempted to blame that audience for making him feel ashamed, which in turn elicits a desire to take revenge. Second, because the active stance that is involved in being aggressive is more consistent with present-day cultural ideals of personal autonomy and independence than the submissive posture involved in shame, aggression and violence can serve as a defence against the humiliating submissiveness that is implied in feeling ashamed.

5. GUILT AND SHAME IN JUVENILE JUSTICE

Reintegrative shaming capitalises on the offender's capacity to feel guilty and ashamed. It seems to me that such an approach could aim to accomplish at least two different things. A first aim might be to induce in the offender the adaptive type of guilt described above. This would encourage the offender to apologise and to try to repair the damage he had caused, which would help him to improve his relationship with the victim. If successful, such a procedure helps the victim, because it is satisfying for him to see that the offender is now also suffering from the consequences of his bad behaviour, ie by experiencing the painful feeling of guilt (Baumeister *et al*, 1994). It would also help the offender, because feelings of guilt that are acknowledged and accepted by the victim enable the offender to see the offence as something of the past that he has in a sense 'paid for' by feeling guilty and by apologising, and that is now resolved. A successful offender-victim interchange would be beneficial for society at large too, because having experienced intense feelings of guilt is likely to motivate the offender to avoid similarly guilt-arousing situations in the future.

A second aim of a shame-and-guilt-based juvenile justice procedure might be to provide the offender with an audience that should at least have the following characteristics. First, the audience should place great value on the offender's adherence to moral norms and it should expect him actually to adhere to such norms. Second, the audience should be more salient to the offender than other available audiences with different value systems. This would motivate the offender to evaluate the self from the perspective of this particular audience, which would make it shameful for him to fall back into his old habit of offending. Thus, the motivation to avoid shame would have a similar effect on his behaviour as the motivation to avoid guilt, ie making future offences less likely.

The account of shame and guilt given above not only specifies the aims that a shame-and-guilt-based juvenile justice procedure could have, it also implies that reaching these aims is not an easy matter. In the next two sections I discuss some of the difficulties that one might encounter.

6. HAZARDS OF INDUCING GUILT

The behavioural correlates of shame and guilt described earlier, as well as the theoretical analysis of both emotions, suggest that young offenders entering the juvenile justice system are likely to differ from the population as a whole in terms of their tendency to experience feelings of guilt and shame. The least that can be said is that the prospect of having to feel guilty and/or ashamed apparently did not keep these youngsters from committing an offence. One possible reason for this is that they are below average on an adaptive-guilt-proneness dimension, which might again be due to a relatively weak tendency to show empathic concern with another's plight (Hoffman, 1982, 1998; Zahn-Waxler & Robinson, 1995). Although there is some evidence that a lack of empathic concern and the resulting tendency to feel guilty has genetic underpinnings, these are also likely to be related to the individual's upbringing (Zahn-Waxler *et al*, 1992; Zahn-Waxler & Robinson, 1995). Specifically, Hoffman (1982) has theorised that a weak tendency to show empathic concern and to feel guilty is related to styles of parental discipline characterised by the use of physical power or love withdrawal. A strong tendency to feel empathic concern and adaptive guilt, in contrast, is related to being subjected to an inductive style of discipline. In such a style, a perpetrator's attention is directed to the negative emotions that a victim might experience as a result of his behaviour and it is explained why that behaviour was wrong. This is mainly accomplished by verbal means, although some physical intervention may be needed to get the child-perpetrator to attend to what is being said.

To the extent that juvenile justice procedures include confrontation with the victim and letting the offender become thoroughly aware of the suffering that he has caused in the victim, these procedures can be seen as attempts to induce adaptive guilt in the offender through the use of inductive discipline. Whether such attempts can be successful in individuals who are by genetic endowment and/or by their upbringing relatively unprepared for experiencing this type of guilt is an important empirical issue that, to my knowledge, remains to be investigated. What seems clear, however, is that things can go wrong in several ways.

First, the offender might resist the pressure to feel guilty or to express feelings of guilt. For example, where the offence consists of serious physical aggression against a victim, the offender might consider his behaviour as a justified response to something the victim had previously said or done. I have argued elsewhere that many instances of aggression are actually perceived by the aggressor as a justified response to some previous act of the victim (Olthof, 1990). Such perceptions are most prevalent at the very moment that the event takes place, but in the population as a whole perpetrators usually change their minds with the passage of time, that is, when they have had a chance to consider the event from the perspective of the victim. An initial resistance to feeling guilty is therefore likely to wane over time (Ferguson *et al*, 1997), although this might, of course, be less true for the population of juvenile offenders.

Even when such a resistance is overcome and the perpetrator begins feeling guilty over an act that he considered justified when committing the act, there may be another obstacle to the expression of these feelings, ie, shame. Imagine a perpetrator who felt justified in causing harm to another person at the time of the offence, but who has to admit in court that there actually was no justification at all. Such a perpetrator could easily see his feelings of guilt as being inconsistent with his previous behaviour and therefore shameful. This in turn might lead him to resist the expression, even though perhaps not the experience, of guilt feelings. The potential shame-eliciting nature of being subjected to a guilt-induction procedure is illustrated in the following anecdote that I once heard from someone who had spent some time in hospital because of respiratory problems and who shared the room with several other men having similar problems:

> One day, a man in his early thirties was brought into the room. He had serious breathing-problems. He had been in hospital repeatedly with similar symptoms, that were at least partly caused by his smoking habits. After a few days he had recovered sufficiently for the lung specialist to start enquiring about his current smoking habits and about his compliance with the regime of medicine taking that he had recommended on an earlier occasion. It became clear that the patient's behaviour had been wanting in both respects. The specialist therefore made a serious attempt to induce feelings of guilt in his patient by pointing out angrily that he should blame himself for his current problems and that he was heading for even more serious health problems. This went on for a while without the patient giving much response, but as soon as the doctor had moved on to the next room, he rose from his bed and announced triumphantly to his room-mates: 'And now down to the shop for a packet of Caballero!'

The patient's expressed intention to replenish his stock of cigarettes was probably meant as a joke, but I do think the remark revealed something about his feelings. The doctor's speech probably did make the patient feel guilty, but to him the admission of such feelings in the presence of his room-mates would have been shameful. His joke was intended to make clear that he was not impressed by the doctor's admonitions, that he still was the same person as he was before, and that there was, therefore, no reason at all to feel ashamed.

Obviously, if something similar were to happen in the course of a shame-and-guilt-based juvenile justice procedure, ie, an offender refusing to express guilt or expressing guilt in a way that the victim perceives as being insincere, this would add to the victim's suffering and it would constitute a new obstacle for the offender's reintegration. As a partial remedy, one might consider minimising the chance for shame to arise by letting the guilt-induction part of a shame-and-guilt-based procedure take place in the presence of an audience that is not larger than strictly necessary for the guilt-induction procedure to work.

A second hazard of inducing guilt in the context of a juvenile justice procedure comes into play when the offender actually does express feelings of guilt that are also perceived as sincere by all those involved, but when the victim subsequently refuses to respond positively to the offender's feelings. He might, for example, consider the harm caused to him as being so great that no amount of guilt and guilt-related behaviour—however intense and sincere—could be commensurate with the harm done to him. This possibility seems particularly real in cases where the offender and the victim were strangers to each other at the time of the offence. As stressed by Baumeister *et al* (1994), adaptive guilt occurs most readily within close relationships and it works best as a reconciliatory device within such relationships. This might be because in close relationships the victim also has an interest in the relationship being repaired. Victims who had no prior relationship with the offender are likely to be less interested in any reconciliation.

When a shame-and-guilt-based juvenile justice procedure fails because the victim refuses to react positively to the offender's guilt, this can be expected to leave its traces in the offender. Specifically, intense feelings of guilt that are not accepted by the person to whom they are directed are likely to constitute one of the sources of the unresolved and lingering type of guilt that research has shown to be related to all kinds of psychopathological symptoms, including antisocial behaviour.

Third, even a guilt induction procedure that is successful, in that the victim accepts the offender's sincere feelings of guilt, is not altogether without costs (Baumeister, 1998). Even though the offender feels guilty, he might also feel some degree of resentment against those who caused him to feel guilty, which might find expression at some later date. This seems especially likely when the offender feels that the victim also bears a share of the responsibility for the offence—for example because he behaved provocatively—and that the victim should therefore also feel some guilt. Such costs can perhaps be minimised by ensuring that any grievances that the offender might have against the victim, and any corresponding feelings of guilt suffered by the victim, receive proper attention in the procedure.

7. PROBLEMS IN CAPITALISING ON SHAME

In the context of juvenile justice, one condition for capitalising on shame, ie the presence of an audience that places great value on the offender's adherence to moral norms, is by definition satisfied. Weijers (ch 7 in this volume) stresses the role of the juvenile justice system in providing a moral reference point for offending youngsters. Accordingly, the justice officials could serve as an audience that encourages the offender to look at the self from a moral perspective. This is likely to elicit shame in the offender, which might subsequently serve as a deterrent against committing any further offences. The problem is, however, that a second condition should also be satisfied for shame to be elicited, ie, that the audience is relevant to the offender. That is, shame will only have lasting effects when the offender cares about—and continues to care about—his identity when seen from the perspective of that particular audience. Offending youngsters without much respect for authorities may care very little about their identity as seen by these authorities.

This problem can, of course, be solved by assigning an important role to the offender's family or friends, or, in general, to an audience that is relevant to him. However, in that case, one needs to make sure that the audience actually does assign sufficient value to the offender's adherence to moral norms to make the offender feel ashamed when looking at the self from the perspective of that particular audience. Obviously, Lady Macbeth would not have made a suitable audience when attempting to reintegrate Macbeth.

The availability of a suitable audience may be especially problematic in cases like that of Macbeth and that of the 14-year-old boy who hesitates to join his friends in a shoplifting expedition, ie cases in which the relevant audience tends to see the offender's decision not to offend as an act of shameful cowardice. In such cases one will have to obtain the co-operation of a different audience that is even more relevant to the offender, or that at least has the potential to become more relevant in the course of the justice proceedings.

8. CONCLUDING REMARKS

When seen from a psychological perspective, the general upshot of the above account would seem to be that shame-and-guilt-based juvenile justice procedures could be feasible, but that much empirical research is needed to provide a solid empirical base for such procedures (see Harris, 1999 for a promising example of this type of research). A second conclusion is that there are many ways in which things could go wrong. To the extent that the potential problems described above may turn out to be real problems, it seems wise to try to pre-empt them. One could, for example, try to assess beforehand whether the offender is likely to show feelings of guilt on meeting the victim, whether the victim is likely to react positively to the offender's feelings of guilt, and whether the offender's supporters actually value his adherence to moral norms. Since making such assessments demands a considerable amount of psychological expertise, the large-scale use of shame-and-guilt-based juvenile justice procedures inevitably means to some extent that juvenile justice would be 'psychologised'.

Against this conclusion it could be argued that shame- and guilt-based justice procedures should not be seen as psychological techniques that can only be used safely by trained experts, but rather as attempts to arrange a moral meeting place in which moral agents talk to each other (Weijers, ch 7 in this volume). It seems to me that this view takes insufficient account of the fact that shame- and guilt-based justice procedures are not, or not only, free exchanges of moral viewpoints among equals. Apart from being a form of punishment (Duff, ch 6 in this volume), these procedures are also meant to promote change in the offender and to provide some kind of satisfaction to victims. As pointed out above, such attempts are not quite without risk to the psychological well-being of both victims and offenders. Duff (this volume) argues that the regular juvenile justice system should remain responsible for the use of shame- and guilt-based procedures to provide a safeguard against violations of the offender's legal rights. I believe that a proper use of existing psychological expertise on shame and guilt could provide some kind of a safeguard against unintentional threats to the psychological well-being of both victims and offenders. In my view, opponents of this kind of 'psychologising' of the juvenile justice system would do better not to consider using shame- and guilt-based procedures at all.

REFERENCES

Andrews, B (1998) 'Methodological and Definitional Issues in Shame Research' in P Gilbert and B Andrews (eds) *Shame: Interpersonal Behavior, Psychopathology, and Culture* (Oxford University Press, Oxford).

Ausubel, D (1955) 'Relationships between Shame and Guilt in the Socialization Process' 62 *Psychological Review* 378–90.

Baumeister, R F (1998) 'Inducing Guilt' in J Bybee (ed) *Guilt and Children* (Academic Press, San Diego CA).

Baumeister, R F, Stillwell, A M & Heatherton, T F (1994) 'Guilt: An Interpersonal Approach' 115 *Psychological Bulletin* 243–67.

Braithwaite, J (1989) *Crime, Shame and Reintegration* (Cambridge University Press, Cambridge).

Bybee, J & and Quiles, Z N (1998) 'Guilt and Mental Health' in J Bybee (ed) *Guilt and Children* (Academic Press, San Diego CA).

Cole, P M, Michel, M K & Teti, L O (1994) 'The Development of Emotion Regulation and Dysregulation: A Clinical Perspective' in N A Fox (ed.), *The Development of Emotion Regulation: Biological and Behavioral Considerations* (*Monographs of the Society for Research in Child Development* vol 59) 73–100, 250–83.

Crozier, W R (1998) 'Self-consciousness in Shame: The Role of the "Other"' 28 *Journal for the Theory of Social Behavior* 273–86.

Emde, R N & Oppenheim, D (1995) 'Shame, Guilt, and the Oedipal Drama: Developmental Considerations Concerning Morality and the Referencing of Critical Others' in K W Fischer & J P Tangney (eds) *Self-conscious Emotions: Shame, Guilt, Embarrassment and Pride* (Guilford Press, New York).

Ferguson, T J & Eyre, H (2000) 'Reconciling Interpersonal versus Appraisal Views of Guilt: Roles of Inductive Strategies and Projected Responsibility in Prolonging Guilty Feelings' (manuscript).

Ferguson, T J, Olthof, T & Stegge, H (1997) 'Temporal Dynamics of Guilt: Changes in the Role of Interpersonal and Intrapsychic Factors' 27 *European Journal of Social Psychology* 659–73.

Ferguson, T J & Stegge, H (1995) 'Emotional States and Traits in Children: The Case of Guilt and Shame' in K W Fischer & J P Tangney (eds) *Self-conscious Emotions: Shame, Guilt, Embarrassment and Pride* (Guilford Press, New York).

—— and ——(1998) 'Assessing Guilt in Children: A Rose by any Other Name Still Has Thorns' in J Bybee (ed.), *Guilt and Children* (Academic Press, San Diego CA).

Ferguson, T J, Stegge, H & Damhuis, I (1991) 'Children's Understanding of Guilt and Shame' 62 *Child Development* 827–39.

Gilbert, P (1998) 'What is Shame? Some Core Issues and Controversies' in P Gilbert & B Andrews (eds) *Shame: Interpersonal Behavior, Psychopathology, and Culture* (Oxford University Press, Oxford).

Harder, D (1995) 'Shame and Guilt Assessment, and Relationships of Shame- and Guilt-proneness to Psychopathology' in K Fischer & J P Tangney (eds) *Self-conscious Emotions: Shame, Guilt, Embarrassment and Pride* (Guilford Press, New York).

Harris, N (1999) *Shaming and Shame: An Empirical Analysis* (dissertation, The Australian National University).

Harris, P L (1989) *Children and Emotion: The Development of Psychological Understanding* (Basil Blackwell, Oxford).

Hoffman, M L (1982) 'Development of Prosocial Motivation: Empathy and Guilt' in N Eisenberg-Berg (ed) *Development of Prosocial Behavior* (Academic Press, New York).

—— (1998) 'Varieties of Empathy-based Guilt' in J Bybee (ed) *Guilt and Children* (Academic Press, San Diego CA).

Lewis, H B (1971) *Shame and Guilt in Neurosis* (International Universities Press, New York).

Lindsay-Hartz, J, De Rivera, J & Mascolo, M F (1995) 'Differentiating Guilt and Shame and their Effects on Motivation' in K W Fischer & J P Tangney (eds) *Self-conscious Emotions: Shame, Guilt, Embarrassment and Pride* (Guilford Press, New York).

Magai, C & McFadden, S H (1995) *The Role of Emotions in Social and Personality Development: History, Theory and Research* (Plenum, New York).

Malatesta, C Z & Wilson, A (1988) 'Emotion Cognition Interaction in Personality Development: A Discrete Emotions, Functionalist Analysis' 27 *British Journal of Social Psychology* 91–112.

Olthof, T (1990) *Blame, Anger, and Aggression in Children: A Social Cognitive Approach.* (Dissertation, Catholic University Nijmegen).

—— (1996) 'A Developmental Tasks Analysis of Guilt and Shame' in N H Frijda (ed) *Proceedings of the IXth Conference of the International Society for Research on Emotions* (ISRE, Toronto, Canada).

Olthof, T, Ferguson, T F, Bloemers, E, Deij, M & Stegge, H (2001) 'Illness-related Elicitors of Shame and Guilt in Children' (manuscript).

Olthof, T, Schouten, A, Kuipers, H, Stegge, H & Jennekens-Schinkel, A (2000) 'Shame and Guilt in Children: Differential Situational Antecedents and Experiential Correlates' 18 *British Journal of Developmental Psychology* 51–64.

Olthof, T, Stegge, H & Meerum Terwogt, M (1999) 'Shame, Guilt, and Antisocial Behavior in Children and Adolescents', Proposal for Research within the 'Breedtestrategie' A Developmental Approach of Problem-Children and Families (Dept of Developmental Psychology, Vrije Universiteit, Amsterdam).

Sabini, J, Garvey, B & Hall, A L (2001) 'Shame and Embarrassment Revisited' 27 *Personality and Social Psychology Bulletin* 104–17.

Scheff, T J (1988) 'Shame and Conformity: The Deference-Emotion System' 3 *American Sociological Review* 395–406.

—— (1995) 'Shame and Related Emotions: An Overview' 38 *American Behavioral Scientist* 1053–59.

Spiecker, B (1991) *Emoties en Morele Opvoeding* (Boom, Meppel).

Stegge, H & Ferguson, T J (2000) 'De Ontwikkeling van Schuld en Schaamte: Adaptieve en Problematische Aspecten' in J D Bosch, H A Bosma, R J van der Gaag, A J J M Ruijssenaars & A Vyt (eds) *Jaarboek Ontwikkelingspsychologie, Orthopedagogiek en Kinderpsychiatrie* 4 (Bohn Stafleu Van Loghum, Houten, The Netherlands).

Stegge, H, Meerum Terwogt, M & Bijstra, J O (1998) 'Emoties als Aangrijpingspunt voor de Diagnostiek van Psychische Stoornissen' in W Koops and W Slot (eds.), *Van Lastig tot Misdadig* (Bohn Stafleu van Loghum, Houten, The Netherlands).

Tangney, J P (1991) 'Moral Affect: The Good, the Bad, and the Ugly' 61 *Journal of Personality and Social Psychology* 598–607.

Tangney, J P (1995) 'Shame and Guilt in Interpersonal Relationships' in K W Fischer & J P Tangney (eds) *Self-conscious Emotions: Shame, Guilt, Embarrassment and Pride* (Guilford Press, New York).

Tangney, J P, Burggraf, S A & Wagner, P E (1995), 'Shame-proneness, Guilt-proneness, and Psychological Symptoms' in K W Fischer & J P Tangney (eds) *Self-conscious Emotions: Shame, Guilt, Embarrassment and Pride* (Guilford Press, New York).

Tangney, J P, Wagner, P E, Fletcher, C & Gramzow, R (1992) 'Shamed into Anger? The Relation of Shame and Guilt to Anger and Self-reported Aggression' 62 *Journal of Personality and Social Psychology* 669–75.

Tangney, J P, Wagner, P E, HillBarlow, B, Marschall, D E & Gramzow, R (1996) 'Relation of Shame and Guilt to Constructive versus Destructive Responses to Anger Across the Lifespan' 70 *Journal of Personality and Social Psychology* 797–809.

Tangney, J P, Wagner, P E & Gramzow, R (1989) *The Test of Self-conscious Affect* (George Mason University, Fairfax, VA).

Taylor, G (1985) *Pride, Shame, and Guilt: Emotions of Self-assessment.* (Oxford University Press, Oxford).

—— (1996) 'Guilt and Remorse' in R Harré and W G Parrot (eds) *The Emotions: Social, Cultural and Biological Dimensions* (Sage, London).

Terwijn, H (1993) *Een Emotietheoretische Benadering van Schaamte* (Unpublished Masters Thesis, University of Amsterdam).

Williams, C (1998) 'Guilt in the Classroom' in J Bybee (ed) *Guilt and Children* (Academic Press, San Diego CA).

Zahn-Waxler, C & Robinson, J (1995) 'Empathy and Guilt: Early Origins of Feelings of Responsibility' in K W Fischer & J P Tangney (eds) *Self-conscious Emotions: Shame, Guilt, Embarrassment and Pride* (Guilford Press, New York).

Zahn-Waxler, C, Robinson, J & Emde, R (1992) 'The Development of Empathy in Twins' 28 *Developmental Psychology* 1038–47.

Index

Please note that major references are in bold print while references to figures, diagrams and illustrations are in italic print. Footnotes are denoted by an 'n' after the page number.